Livable Cities?

Livable Cities?

*Urban Struggles
for Livelihood
and Sustainability*

EDITED BY Peter Evans

UNIVERSITY OF CALIFORNIA PRESS
Berkeley · Los Angeles · London

University of California Press
Berkeley and Los Angeles, California

University of California Press, Ltd.
London, England

© 2002 by
The Regents of the University of California

Library of Congress Cataloging-in-Publication Data

Livable cities? : urban struggles for livelihood and
sustainability / edited by Peter Evans.
    p.   cm.
  Includes bibliographical references and index.
  ISBN 0-520-23024-8 (cloth : alk. paper).—ISBN
0-520-23025-6 (pbk. : alk. paper)
   1. Metropolitan areas—Case studies.
2. Urbanization—Case studies.   I. Title: Urban
struggles for livelihood and sustainability.
II. Evans, Peter B.

HT330.L58   2002
307.76—dc21   2001027245

Manufactured in the United States of America
11 10 09 08 07 06 05 04 03 02
10 9 8 7 6 5 4 3 2 1

The paper used in this publication is both acid-free
and totally chlorine-free (TCF). It meets the
minimum requirements of ANSI/NISO Z39.48-
1992 (R 1997) (Permanence of Paper).∞

Contents

Tables and Figures

Preface

Sustainable Cities: Structure and Agency

Our blue planet is fast becoming a predominantly urban world. Probably around the time you are reading this book, we will be crossing the threshold of 50 percent of the world's population living in urban areas, up from 37 percent in 1970. Projections call for about two-thirds of the world's population to be living in cities by around 2025, including in areas, such as sub-Saharan Africa, that are still largely rural today—but whose urban population is growing by more than 5 percent per year.

Naturally, most urban growth is taking place in the so-called developing countries, where 85 percent of the people live. And the predominant form of urbanization is in fact the concentration of people in large-scale metropolitan areas that link with their surrounding hinterland over vast expanses of territory. Not only the southern China megalopolis between Hong Kong, Guangzhou, Shenzhen, and the Pearl River Delta; Jabotabek, around Jakarta; greater Mexico City; greater São Paulo; greater Calcutta; and Johannesburg-Soweto, but also New York–New Jersey, the Southern California metropolis, greater London, and so many other sprawling "edge cities" dotting the planet are concentrating wealth, information, and power—as well as poverty and environmental deterioration. The planet is at the same time becoming increasingly populated and increasingly concentrated in large-scale urban areas, which act as magnets for population and resources.

The forces behind this process of accelerated urbanization seem to be irreversible. The myth of futurologists of the information age, according to which our lives would take place in serene rural environments from where we would work and live in electronic cottages, is belied by the concentration of information and resources in only a few areas, globally networked thanks to telecommunications and computer-processing power. In fact, we live in a world of global networks that selectively connect localities throughout the planet, according to criteria of valuation and devaluation enforced by the social interests that are dominant in these networks. Further, cities are at the same time globally connected and locally disconnected. Society and the natural environment are processed according to these dynamics—often in conditions that threaten their sustainability.

Sustainable development is the code word for the most important social debate of our time. Is our model of development undoing our very existence or, for that matter, the maintenance of our planetary ecosystem? Under which conditions are economic growth, our consumptive patterns, and our ways of living reproducible over time without damaging the conditions of their reproduction? Is generational solidarity— that is, forwarding a livable planet to the grandchildren of our grandchildren—an achievable goal in the current context of social organization?

This fundamental debate is increasingly urban. For all the talk about the natural environment, it is the living conditions in cities (in fact, in large metropolitan regions) that determine the future of our livelihood. It is in large cities where we generate most of the CO_2 emissions that attack the ozone layer. It is our urban model of consumption and transportation that constitutes the main cause of the process of global warming and can irreversibly damage the conditions of livelihood. And it is the demand for natural resources from our megalopolitan complexes that uses the entire planet as the supplier of everything without restraint.

Furthermore, for all the wealth concentrated in cities, poverty is widespread, and the informal economy occupies the majority of the labor force in most cities in developing countries. The housing crisis, the collapse of transportation, the deterioration of public hygiene, and the contamination of air and water represent the dark side of the urbanization process.

In other words: in the midst of a most extraordinary technological revolution, we are experiencing the largest wave of urbanization in history, often in appalling conditions, and, generally speaking, with a high cost in terms of the quality of life, both socially and environmentally.

However, these are structural trends, not historical fatality. What happens in history and in society ultimately depends on human agency. And that is the theme of this timely and important book constructed by Peter Evans and his coauthors. On the basis of detailed case studies from various areas of the world, they examine how grassroots movements and urban politics transform—or do not—the conditions and outcomes of urbanization. How environmental projects are embodied in social actors, and how they prevail over self-destructive tendencies. Refusing to surrender to the dilemma between structural determination and free-floating utopias, the authors of this book engage in social research that examines the practice of urban and environmental movements in the urban context, the context where the real battle for sustainability is being fought. In so doing, they bring out the voices from the local communities at the forefront of the global debate. But they do so in the terms and with the tools of social science, transcending ideological proclamations in favor of a rigorous assessment of the emergent social projects.

The future of our world will not ultimately depend on technological innovation or on the global economy. It will be the outcome of what we, the people—the urban people—do about it, through our projects and through our conflicts. The missing link between environmental sustainability and social organization, in theory as in practice, is the relationship of urban communities to their environment. By observing this practice, and giving theoretical meaning to the observation, this book opens new paths of understanding on the social conditions of our collective survival.

Manuel Castells
Berkeley, December 2000

Acknowledgments

This book would never have come to be without the support of the Social Capital and Public Affairs Project of the American Academy of Arts and Sciences, directed by Robert Putnam and funded by the Carnegie, Ford, and Rockefeller Foundations. The Social Capital and Public Affairs Project, through its Working Group on Social Capital and Economic Development, provided both funding and the initial intellectual impetus for the project. We are also indebted to Fred Buttel, Sergio Margulis, Janice Perlman, Martha Schteingart, David Stark, Michael Watts, and Michael Woolcock, who provided invaluable comments and criticisms on individual papers and on our general ideas at the conference at which this volume was originally conceived. The success of this initial conference also depended on the tireless administrative and organizational efforts of Christina Getz. Extensive, insightful comments by Harvey Molotch and John Logan on an initial version of the manuscript stimulated substantial improvements in our formulations. Our collectivity also owes a large debt to Hwa-Jen Liu, who, in addition to her role as coauthor of chapter 3, also devoted herself unstintingly to the preparation of the final manuscript as a whole. Finally, without Naomi Schneider's faith in this project and the efficient energy with which she supported the transformation of the initial set of papers into a coherent, readable volume, this book never would have appeared.

Introduction

*Looking for Agents of Urban Livability
in a Globalized Political Economy*

PETER EVANS

The poor cities of the developing world are often vibrant hubs of global economic and cultural activity, but they are also ecologically unsustainable and, for ordinary citizens, increasingly unlivable. Three-fourths of those joining the world's population during the next century will live in Third World cities. Unless these cities are able to provide decent livelihoods for ordinary people and become ecologically sustainable, the future is bleak. The politics of livelihood and sustainability in these cities has become the archetypal challenge of twenty-first-century governance.

From Bangkok to Mexico City, levels of air and water pollution are rising. Getting to work takes longer and longer. Affordable housing is an endangered species and green space is shrinking. The large cities of the Third World are becoming "world cities," increasingly important nodes in the financial and productive networks of the global economy, but they are not providing livelihoods and healthy habitats for ordinary people. They are also degrading environmental resources inside and outside the urbanized area itself at a rate that cannot be maintained. Without new political strategies aimed at increasing livability, the future is bleak.

The coin of livability has two faces. Livelihood is one of them. Ecological sustainability is the other. Livelihood means jobs close enough to decent housing with wages commensurate with rents and access to the services that make for a healthful habitat. Livelihoods must also be sustainable. If the quest for jobs and housing is solved in ways that

progressively and irreparably degrade the environment of the city, then
the livelihood problem is not really being solved. Ecological degradation
buys livelihood at the expense of quality of life, with citizens forced to
trade green space and breathable air for wages. To be livable, a city must
put both sides of the coin together, providing livelihoods for its citizens,
ordinary as well as affluent, in ways that preserve the quality of the
environment.[1]

Sustainability is also contingent on the city's relation to its hinterland.
In the long run, cities must be judged not just in terms of the quality of
life provided to urban dwellers, but also in terms of the ecological relation between city and countryside (cf. Buttel 1998, 7). Just as livelihood should not be bought at the expense of quality of urban life, likewise cities must sustain themselves without imposing an unbearable
ecological footprint on surrounding territories. If they are to be sustainable, cities must not soak up resources, such as groundwater, at a rate
faster than they can be replenished or deposit the waste generated by
urban production in a way that fouls the rural hinterland. Finally, of
course, ecological sustainability implies intergenerational justice. Cities
that provide livelihood and quality of life through practices that rob
future generations of the same measure of well-being are not really livable. Real urban livability is the equivalent of "sustainable livelihood
security" in rural areas (Chambers 1987).

Making Third World cities more livable is a daunting practical problem. Arguably it is the premier challenge to any policy maker or analyst
interested in the well-being of the world's citizens. Facing this challenge
requires a clear set of ideas regarding the actors that shape cities, their
interests, and their ability to realize those interests. Questions of social
cleavage and collective action must be confronted anew. Urban elites
and impoverished slum dwellers share a common interest in livability,
but there is hardly overlap between the poor's dreams of urban homes
and elite imaginaries of the global city.

Questions of governance and prospects for new forms of politics are
even more crucial. Is there room for collective action on behalf of livability? If so, who might organize and channel it? Are local communities
still effective political actors? Are governments and political parties, the
traditional vehicles of collective projects, plausible candidates? Or must
trajectories of livability rely on less conventional institutional instruments, such as social movements or NGOs? Confronting the practical
problems of livability depends on having a theory of the urban political

economy that enables us to identify "agents of livability" and to assess the conditions under which they might be successful.

Theoretical Context

Confronting urban livability requires broaching fundamental debates on the dynamics of the contemporary global political economy. First, there is the question of markets. Neither side of the Manichaean thinking that pervades contemporary perspectives on markets is very useful to city dwellers. Triumphalist fantasies in which unfettered markets deliver generalized welfare do little for slum communities in search of potable water and clean, safe streets. Postmodern romanticism, in which virtuous peasants, as yet uncorrupted by Western culture, cut themselves off from global markets, makes even less sense in megacities. Markets have a contribution to make to livability, but their contribution is not automatic. Whether markets are part of the problem or part of the solution depends on the contested political processes through which social actors construct and transform them (cf. Fligstein 1996).

The question of markets connects directly to the question of agency. Economistic visions of global markets imply a vast and intricate mechanism whose complexity defies the ability of any human agent to produce more desirable alternative outcomes. Cultural visions of globalization in which a hegemonic capitalist culture removes even the possibility of conceiving alternative outcomes are even bleaker. Proponents of the two views have antithetical assessments of the extent to which market outcomes maximize human welfare, but they agree on the impossibility of alternatives. Confronting the problem of livability forces us to resurrect the question of alternative agency.

Analyzing livability also means transposing political ecology debates about sustainability and social justice from fields and forests to the streets, factories, and sewers of the built environment.[2] Invoking the goal of ecological sustainability has emerged as the most ideologically effective challenge to the "accumulationist" logic that privileges economic growth as the ultimate criterion of improved welfare. Nonetheless, theories that link arguments about the impact of humans on nature to debates about distribution and social justice are underdeveloped and still draw mainly on cases from the rural contexts that people are leaving. Looking at urban livability as a combination of livelihood and sustainability means applying political ecology to the sociopolitical arenas into which people are moving.

Theorizing that is explicitly about cities, such as Molotch and Logan's vision of "the city as a growth machine" or the variegated opus of Manuel Castells, must be considered along with general theoretical debates about political economy (or political ecology). Before moving on to these more specifically urban interlocutors, however, it makes sense to consider more closely how contemporary thinking on markets, agency, and political ecology intersects with arguments about urban livability.

Markets and Livability

In the technologized neoliberalism that emanates from sources such as *Wired* magazine, the increasing "openness" of global markets accelerates economic growth and stimulates new technology. The magic of technology and growth generate, in turn, solutions to problems of livelihood and ecological sustainability.[3] In this triumphalist structural analysis, all we need to do is make sure that the openness of a global market is not threatened by political reaction. The only politics necessary is an electorally determined system of succession that checks public interference in markets and provides the private elites who understand markets with access to policy decisions. Markets and technology will do the rest.

Most serious analysts are skeptical of the idea that the hegemonic twentieth-century formula for improved well-being—growth plus new technology—is an automatic remedy for problems of livelihood and sustainability. Third World cities facing an unending influx of would-be urbanites are unlikely to be able to grow themselves out of their environmental problems by becoming rich. For these cities, economic success has too often exacerbated urban environmental problems rather than solving them. Bangkok is the classic case of rapid growth going hand in hand with degradation (cf. Setchell 1995; Douglass, Ard-am, and Kim, this volume). Unfortunately, it is more typical than exceptional. This is not to say that economic growth is bad. Increasing productivity is an essential element in improving livelihoods; it also creates resources that can be used to provide the infrastructure and services essential to a livable urban environment. Nevertheless, for most developing cities the problem is connecting growth to livability.

The connection between the logic of the market and the logic of livability is anything but automatic. The markets that shape cities are first of all markets for land and, as Karl Polanyi (1957) forcefully reminded us half a century ago, land is a "fictitious commodity." When demand for "normal" commodities such as radios or CD players increases, economies of scale and technological change lower their prices, but trying to produce more land in a particular place becomes ever more costly.[4] When demand for land exceeds supply, speculative price increases are the likely result. A growing proportion of urban dwellers faces a discouraging disjunction between the salaries generated by city labor markets and the housing costs generated by the market for urban land. At the same time, "marketable" uses for land, such as housing for affluent individuals and commercial space for corporations, drive out nonmarketable uses, like parks and green space, making the city as a whole less livable.

The insufficiency of market-driven solutions also flows from the overwhelming importance of "externalities." Negative externalities generated by market transactions play a central role in shaping urban life. Using private automobiles as the primary means of urban transportation is the most blatant example of the prisoner's dilemmas inherent in individual market solutions. Not only does this private solution deprive all urban dwellers of the most classic public good—breathable air—but, as roads fill up and gridlock ensues, it also fails to reduce transport time even for those who are sufficiently privileged to own cars.

Pure market logic turns firms as well as individual consumers into polluters. In the absence of carefully enforced regulatory sanctions, the logic of "frontier economics" prevails (Colby 1991; Princen 1997). Pollution is free and preventing it costly. Environmental gains are an irrelevant by-product until some nonmarket force makes them relevant. Even if more environmentally friendly forms of production may ultimately be more profitable, systems of innovation driven only by a search for maximizing returns are unlikely to discover them. Only when markets are constructed in ways that internalize externalities and blend short-horizon private discount rates with long-term societal ones does the search for "green" production strategies become "rational" from the point of view of the unforgiving "bottom line."

All of that said, the fact remains that markets and the corporations which dominate them must play a fundamental role in urban solutions. Careful accounting of economic costs and benefits is a necessary part of evaluating future strategies for sustainability. A realistic appraisal of how cities can best take advantage of the economic opportunities that depend on global markets must be integral to any successful effort to generate livelihoods for their residents. The possibilities for "greening" the search for profit that have been set out in the literature on "ecological modernization" must be exploited to the full.[5] In the presence of even modestly effective environmental regulations, firms can be motivated to find profitable ways to reduce pollution. They may well develop solutions that are more efficient than those envisioned by the regulators. Some managers may well believe in the intrinsic value of the environment as individuals. If taking care of the environment can be made to seem compatible with their obligations to stockholders, such managers can be very effective environmentalists.

Rejecting markets out of hand works no better than blind faith in their efficacy. Markets must be taken seriously without being taken as "natural" or exogenous. Normally, the coalitions of private and public actors that construct markets have socially minimalist goals, the most important being preserving the property rights of the most powerful market. Replacing these "minimalist markets" with ones whose rules take livability into account is at the core of any quest for more livable cities. It is primarily a political task.

Agency in a Globalized Political Economy

A triumphalist "imaginary" in which minimalist markets are sufficient to maximize welfare and sustainability also ratifies a minimalist politics. Market triumphalists define democracy simply as electorally determined succession to political office. The increasing pervasiveness of elections complements the spread of "market openness." Together they constitute the "twin transitions" that supposedly maximize welfare and ensure sustainability. Unfortunately, this kind of minimalist democracy ends up ensuring that contribution-dependent politicians will allow maximum input from the same elites that dominate markets. Consequently, it is unlikely to create the capacity to reconstruct markets in ways that deal seriously with the undersupply of collective goods, the oversupply of negative externalities, or the social deprivations that flow from initial inequities in resource endowments.

For those convinced of the necessity of alternative forms of agency, politics is more complicated. Electorally determined succession is still a bedrock necessity, but democracy must go deeper. Mobilization strategies that give ordinary citizens the power to affect policy and make public officials responsive to their needs are also essential. Democratically controlled public institutions must have the capacity to respond to popular input and push firms out of a "frontier economics" mode into one more compatible with livability.

Traditionally, deciding on the legally enforceable parameters around which markets are constructed has been the prerogative of local and national governments. National governments have regulated minimum wages, hours of work, interest rates, and the supply of money. More recently they have restricted the rights of producers and consumers to damage the environment and have penalized polluters. The current neo-liberal global context challenges these traditional prerogatives.

Globalization has increased the ability of anonymous "market forces" to punish national governments that try to restrict possibilities for global profit. An emerging set of international rules and agreements increasingly limits not only the ability of states to restrict cross-border flows, but also the ways in which states can deal with enterprises operating inside their borders (Ruggie 1994). The growing power and intrusiveness of multilateral rules and organizations such as the WTO and the IMF is reinforced by aggressive U.S. efforts to enforce Anglo-American readings of international rules (Evans 1997a). These political and legal mechanisms preemptively remove the possibility of reshaping markets at the national level, even before "market forces" have passed judgment.

Curtailing the market-shaping prerogatives of national governments generates a climate in which nation-states are seen as lacking agency altogether, or as able to implement only those policies that ratify the demands of global markets. For some, the power of the nation-state has "just evaporated" (Strange 1995, 56).[6] While reports of such a demise are without doubt exaggerated, it is probably true that national governmental power has become a less potent instrument for generating alternative outcomes. Those stubborn enough to continue looking for ways to exercise agency on behalf of alternative projects—like livability—must expand their search to include other institutional levels.

In a neoliberal world, local and regional institutions become more interesting places to look for sources of alternative agency. Local governments have never had the same kind of market-constructing prerogatives that national governments enjoyed and have always been vulnerable to threats by investors to move to other cities or regions. Globalization may also have reduced the bargaining power of subnational political institutions in relation to capital, but the degree of agency enjoyed by local governments has changed less than in the case of national governments. Local governments' admittedly modest ability to shape markets still remains more intact.

Possibilities for combining local agency with complementary efforts at the global level have also become more interesting. Analysts such as Keck and Sikkink (1998a) have begun to pursue the possibility that the new ease of global communication might be used to increase the efficacy of globally legitimated social activists in their battles with intransigent local elites. The global arena provides a particularly rich set of political and ideological resources when sustainability is at stake (cf. Meyer et al. 1997). By building links with like-minded groups and individuals in other countries, local activists can gain access to complementary resources, both material and ideological (see also Evans 2000).

At the same time that the institutional complexity of alternative agency has increased, the banners under which support is mobilized have shifted. Environmental arguments have increasingly gained a place alongside traditional discourses of social justice.[7] Contemporary counterhegemonic discourse is as much about political ecology as about traditional political economy. Consequently, the analysis of urban livability must build on efforts to unite environmental and social justice arguments that have been developed in the analysis of rural struggles.

Adding an Environmental Dimension

Contemporary political ecology arose out of dissatisfaction with traditional conservationist versions of ecological arguments, which tended to ignore the dilemmas of people whose livelihood depended on the continued exploitation of natural resources.[8] It also arose out of an appreciation that environmental movements formed in opposition to the shortsighted exploitation of natural resources were often at their core livelihood movements aimed at preserving the "less developed" relations with nature that allowed groups marginal to the global economy to make a living (Friedmann and Rangan 1993).

Merging ecological and social justice arguments creates new imaginaries that help energize local struggles and draw in a more diverse set of allies. Traditional social justice struggles, in which workers fought with capitalists over wages or peasants fought with landlords over rents, left subordinate groups vulnerable to being portrayed as "selfish," as simply demanding a larger share of the pie, not just at the expense of their elite opponents but potentially at the expense of the citizenry as a whole (particularly in their diffuse role as "consumers"). Adding the ecological element gives the demands of subordinate groups a new claim to universality that can mobilize extralocal allies. For example, adding an ecological dimension transforms Amazon rubber tappers from exploited extractive workers trying to secure their livelihood in the face of encroaching capitalist agriculture into protectors of the "lungs of the earth." In this latter role, they become valuable allies for transnational environmental groups and through them can tap into the cultural capital and political access of the committed activists that these groups employ (cf. Keck 1995; Keck and Sikkink 1998a).

Studies of urban livability are the natural extension of existing work on environmental politics. While work on fields and forests has provided invaluable insights into the general dynamics of political ecology,[9] de facto neglect of urban environments is increasingly hard to defend. As David Harvey recently complained (1997, 25), "Why is it that we think of the built environment of cities as somehow or other not being part of *the* environment?"

At the same time, bringing an environmental perspective more forcefully into the foreground enriches existing approaches to urban political economy, complementing and extending traditional concerns with the tension between accumulation and distribution. The theoretical formulations of "liberation ecology" form a perfect complement to the long tradition of work on the tensions between the city as a place to live and the city as a locus for accumulation.

Agency and Accumulation in the Urban Political Economy

To complement the insights of the political ecology literature, analysis of livability needs to draw equally on the urban political economy tradition, which has focused primarily on advanced industrial cities. Some of the most influential work on American cities begins from the simple premise that "one issue consistently generates consensus among local elite groups and separates them from people who use the city principally as a place to live and work: the issue of growth" (Logan and Molotch 1987, 50).

The work of Harvey Molotch, John Logan, and their collaborators defines a now classic perspective on "the city as a growth machine."[10] The "growth machine" thesis is not simply economistic. It argues for a powerful Gramscian hegemony in which public officials, local media, and even labor union leaders are drawn into the coalition, working in surprisingly well coordinated unison on behalf of projects of accumulation. John Mollenkopf's 1983 historical analysis of the changing character of "progrowth coalitions" in U.S. urban politics extends the analysis by showing how much growth machines can vary. The progrowth coalition that prevailed from the 1930s through the 1970s at least supported important investments in urban infrastructure.[11] In the 1980s it was undercut by a more conservative coalition that promoted devastating disinvestment in the physical infrastructure on which city dwellers traditionally depended (1983, 255–56). For Mollenkopf this demonstrates that "we are not prisoners of history and social structure." Instead, political entrepreneurship and coalition building can have "a vast and demonstrable impact on the course of urban development" (1983, 299).

The premise that growth machines can vary in ways that have important implications for livability is also supported by Logan and Molotch's work. They argue that for certain privileged cities, the latitude of trajectories that can be derived from the growth machine model may even include elements that support sustainability. In the case of Santa Barbara, for example, the interests of local elites in tourism led them to oppose offshore drilling (for which economic benefits were nonlocal, while the costs were local), and the success of local referenda suggested that environmental concerns had become politically hegemonic (Molotch and Logan 1984, 487, 490).

In more recent work, Molotch contrasts Santa Barbara with the neighboring city of Ventura to show how small differences in the timing of extractive investments (oil) led to a more oppositional response in Santa Barbara (Molotch, Freudenberg, and Paulsen 1998). The resulting denser and more engaged associational life in turn helped shape a set of public policies that sustain an exceptional community culture, quality of life, and relationship to the natural environment. In this comparison, the inexorable operation of the growth machine fades into the background while the potential of distinctive trajectories shaped by the interaction of a multiplicity of urban actors moves into the foreground.

The opposite possibility, in which the contemporary U.S. growth machine moves in a thoroughly dystopian direction, is vividly portrayed in Mike Davis's 1998 vision of Los Angeles. In Davis's L.A., the reigning growth machine has no interest in public investment designed to enhance the well-being of ordinary city dwellers. The result is a nightmare for all but the most affluent. "With no hope for further public investment in the remediation of underlying social conditions, we are forced instead to make increasing public and private investments in physical security"

(1998, 364). Whatever fragile sense of security remains depends on a combination of "besieged, gun-toting homeowners" in working-class neighborhoods and "the private police forces of more affluent gated suburbs" (1998, 387). Finally, of course, the city is ringed by the only substantial physical infrastructure to which the new growth machine willingly devotes public funds—a burgeoning set of new prisons.

Davis, Mollenkopf, Molotch, and Logan give us a sense of the range of outcomes that varying political coalitions, all working in the same market-driven societal context, can produce over time and across cities. All of this work sees agency as depending on political entrepreneurship and coalitions while underlining the importance of microlevel cultural and social institutions in establishing particular (path-dependent) trajectories. The question is how useful a perspective based on the experience of developed cities might be in understanding the much wider range of circumstances that confronts urban dwellers in developing and transitional environments.

The work of Manuel Castells, whose focus ranges from the slum communities of Latin America to Asian world cities to social-democratic Europe, offers the most sweeping comparative urban perspective. At first it seems to be one that is much bleaker than the growth machine vision. In Castells's vision of the global city, first developed in *The Informational City* (1989) and brought to full fruition in his Information Age trilogy (1996, 1997, 1998), power resides in transnational networks from which ordinary urban dwellers are thoroughly excluded. Urban dwellers "interact with their daily physical environment" and with each other in the "space of places," constructing a "locale whose form, function and meaning are self-contained within the boundaries of physical contiguity" (1996, 423–25). The power to control and transform society is located in the "space of flows," in which information and resources are exchanged among nodes and hubs that are physically disjointed but unified in their participation in a shared global network. Local communities continue to be a source of identity (1997, 60–64), but not a source of economic or political power. Thus, for example, "Mexico City's *colonias populares* (originally squatter settlements) account for about two-thirds of the megapolitan population without playing any distinctive role in the functioning of Mexico City as an international business center" (1996, 380–81).

Others working on globalization and the urban political economy present a similar picture (for example, Friedmann 1986; Douglass 1998a, 1998b; Sassen 1991, 1997). Contemporary urban elites face a

new definition of economic "success." To succeed, a city must participate in transnational flows of capital and information and become a
suitable site for corporate command centers. While success in this global
competition does depend on providing elites with "quality of life," the
project of creating a world city is much more polarizing than the traditional growth machine project. The bifurcated economy of the world
cities, in which a very small number of elite financial and production-
services executives are catered to by a large but minimally rewarded
personal-service sector, is reflected in the built environment (Sassen
1988, 1991). Shining high-rise cores of corporate office space and luxury
apartments are combined with exclusive islands of gated residential af-
fluence on the one hand and growing proportions of infrastructure-
deprived, self-built slums on the other. As Castells puts it, "The global
city and the informational city are also the dual city" (Borja and Castells
1997, 44).

At first glance, the Castellian vision of the global city seems to allow
no room for agency on behalf of projects of livability, especially in Third
World contexts. Third World replications of Mike Davis's L.A., which
exaggerate even the appalling dystopian quality of the original, are easy
to imagine, but it is hard to find political and economic space for variations on Molotch's Santa Barbara. Looking more closely, however, the
network society is more plastic in its potential than it first appears.

Castells's 1997 collaboration with Jordi Borja, written as the Information Age trilogy was being completed, is dedicated to figuring out
"how to turn cities, their citizens and their governments into the actors
of this new history" (Borja and Castells 1997, 6). It provides a wealth
of ideas for the construction and enhancement of local capabilities.
Other analysts of world cities also recognize structural constraint without relinquishing the possibility of agency. Mike Douglass, for example,
having chronicled the perverse consequences of Asian cities' efforts to
secure favorable places in the hierarchy of world cities, still argues that
in Asia, with "the 'discovery of civil society' associated with the rise of
the urban middle class, organized labor, voluntary organizations and
heightened political action from all quarters of society . . . [t]he array of
possibilities for social mobilization and the enlargement of democratic
spaces to create alternative development paths is greater than much of
the received world system theories or mainstream economic theory allow" (1998a, 109).

The first-order logic of the global political economy is powerful and
compelling. It imposes a globalized version of an inexorable growth

machine that swallows agency and makes the potential for multiple trajectories disappear. Yet, just as probing more closely at the evolution of
American cities led Molotch to focus on a second-order logic of local
differences, a closer look at Third World cities suggests that multiple
trajectories are still possible.

Despite being subjected to a common global logic, Third World cities
continue to vary substantially in terms of livability. Singapore and Bangkok may both be aspirants for world city status but they are vastly
different cities in terms of the delivery of collective goods. Even within
the same national context there is significant variation. In Brazil, for
example, the cities of Pôrto Alegre, Curitiba, and Belo Horizonte have
all, in very different but equally imaginative ways, attacked the problem
of livability, while other Brazilian cities, facing the same global logic,
remain unable to deliver services or protect their remaining patches of
urban green space (cf. Figueiredo and Lamounier 1996). Globalization
has not extinguished the ability of local political logics to make a difference to the lives of city dwellers.

While it would be foolish to understate the degree to which urban
futures are constrained by the logic of the global political economy, it
is too soon to dismiss as utopian the possibility of trajectories leading
in the direction of greater livability. The possibility of "green growth
machines" or even "urban livability machines" cannot be ruled out, even
in the Third World.

Agents of Livability

Admitting the theoretical possibility of alternative agency is simple
enough. Constructing a clear picture of who might exercise such agency
and how is more complicated. Who are the potential political agents of
livability? Is "civil society" the answer? Can "ecologically modern"
firms be enlisted? Can NGOs or local communities provide the necessary
political impetus? Or do we have to turn to more traditional political
institutions, such as political parties? Are local governments and public
agencies part of the solution? The cast of characters and their roles are
by no means obvious.

The first candidate—civil society—became, as Douglass (1998a)
points out, a considerable source of political hope in the closing decade
of the century, not only in countries where civil society has recently
emerged from a truncated existence, as in Eastern Europe, but around
the world. When overthrowing the rule of a repressive, self-perpetuating

state elite is the principal item on the political agenda, then everyone except state elites shares a common interest, and it makes sense to talk about civil society as a coherent actor. Unfortunately, if the quest for livability is the primary goal, civil society loses its political coherence. The concept lumps together plutocrats and the poor. When social justice and distributional questions are at stake—as they are in the political struggles surrounding the quest for livelihood—denominating "civil society" as the relevant political actor glosses over the conflicting interests that separate private elites from ordinary citizens.

Firms are the next candidate. In the contemporary market-oriented world, they are unquestionably powerful agents, but the problem with them has already been made clear in the earlier discussion of markets. Whether firms can be transformed into agents of livability depends on whether the markets in which they operate can be reconstructed in a way that provides the necessary constraints and incentives. Only if we can identify other agents with the political capacity to reconstruct market rules in ways that make livability attractive to profit-oriented managers will firms become interesting as agents of livability.

Local communities, translocal intermediary organizations such as NGOs and political parties, and last but not least, the variegated collection of organizations that constitute the state are all more promising candidates. These three categories of actors have their problems as well, but in combination they provide a good beginning for constructing a vision of agents of urban livability.

Communities against the Growth Machine

Looking at communities focuses attention on the politics of collective action among households with connections to one another. Communities build identities based on geography, history, and shared adversity. Their members share life-chances. They are vulnerable to the degradation of the places to which they are attached. Talking about "communities" enables us to connect livelihood struggles of ordinary citizens to issues of sustainability while retaining the critical insight that these are not simply individual battles but always have an element of collective contestation.

Despite the attractiveness of communities as alternative agents, the idea that neighborhoods of dis-privileged urban households might become agents of livability is audacious. The romantic vision that "community" automatically entails homogeneity and unity of purpose is misleading even in traditional rural settings; urban communities contain an even more daunting spectrum of interests, identities, and political positions (cf. Watts 1999, 10–11). Communities also lack power. As long as they act by themselves, the capacity to reshape the larger urban environment is beyond them.

Castells's classic 1983 work of the political role of urban communities typifies the ambivalence with which urban analysts view poor communities. Starting from the premise that "grassroots mobilization has been a crucial factor in the shaping of the city, as well as the decisive element in urban innovation against prevailing social interests" (1983, 318), Castells still arrived at a pessimistic assessment of the ability of local communities to act as agents of structural social change. For Castells, the power of local movements is undercut because "[f]or any historical actor to handle satisfactorily the production and delivery of public goods and services, it has to be able to reorganize the relationship between production, consumption and circulation. And this task is beyond any local community in a technologically sophisticated economy that is increasingly organized on a world scale" (1983, 329).

If only autonomous action can reflect local interests, then communities are relegated to a limited role as agents, whether of livability or of any other project. Sticking to a view that communities can be important requires keeping open the possibility that linkages with nonlocal groups can reinforce the interests of local communities rather than undercutting them.

The political centrality of ordinary communities is absolutely clear when increased livability depends on the delivery of collective goods. Public transportation, water, and sewers are delivered to places. Without place-based collective action they will always be undersupplied. Elites can afford private alternatives to collective goods. Secluded air-conditioned residences are substitutes for public campaigns to stop pollution. Weekend resorts substitute for city parks. Poor communities lack such alternatives and must therefore fight for collective goods.

Poor communities are also most likely to be at the battlefront when it comes to "collective bads." As studies of "environmental racism" and "environmental (in)justice" have shown, poor communities bear the brunt of the most toxic forms of pollution (cf. Szasz 1994). Either their places are likely to become dumping grounds or the market is likely to push them into places that are already dumping grounds.[12]

The immediacy of poor communities' confrontation with environmental issues stands in contrast to diffuse and distant issues such as global warming or the depletion of the ozone layer. Buttel may be right when he argues that "for most citizens notions such as global environmental change or warming are largely irrelevant to their immediate concerns" (1998, 7), but for poor communities defending their local space, environmental issues could not be more immediate (cf. Castells 1997, 115, 127). This gives poor communities a natural engagement not just with livelihood issues but with sustainability issues as well.[13]

As Harvey points out, accretions of "militant particularism" often provide the foundation for general social mobilization (1997, 25). In trying to solve the environmental problems of their own local space, the poor can become agents of more universal interests. For example, poor communities pressing their demands for the extension of sewer systems into their neighborhoods are also reducing the likelihood of cholera for city dwellers as a whole (cf. Watson 1992, 1995). Successful struggles against toxic waste raise the cost of industrial pollution and push industry toward more sustainable production practices (cf. Szasz 1994). In both cases, particular community struggles simultaneously serve more universal goals.

Interests with universal implications are one thing; the capacity to realize them is another. The empowerment of poor communities is crucial (cf. Douglass 1998, 135; Friedmann 1992; Friedmann and Salguero 1988). Yet there is no reason to expect that poor urban communities will necessarily be endowed with the kinds of norms and networks, or "social capital," that enable collective action.[14] For a set of households to construct a sense of shared identity and common purpose sufficient to enable them to act collectively, it takes uncommon imagination and heroic effort. Even if the members of a community do manage to act collectively, improving their own livability is likely to require support from the political structures that surround them, and their leverage vis-à-vis the rest of the political structure is unlikely to be sufficient to allow them to change the way the city deals with problems of livelihood and sustainability.

Fortunately, the ability of communities to affect outcomes cannot be dismissed. There are too many recorded cases of surprising successes. To take just one, Susan Eckstein chronicles the case of a slum community of one hundred thousand people in central Mexico City that managed to put internal solidarity and external linkages together in a way that secured new housing and left "much of the vibrant informal social and economic life of the community intact" (1990a, 285).

It is important to remember, however, that specifying the conditions under which ordinary communities can realize their potential as political actors is a central challenge, both theoretically and empirically, in any analysis of livability. Moreover, although it is true that there is a natural affinity between community interests and livability, a romantic view in which communities are automatically seen as stewards of the environment, or in which community quests for livelihood are automatically considered consistent with the interests of the city as a whole, is untenable. Communities do have a natural interest in preserving the environment insofar as it impinges on their daily lives, and the livelihood interests of one community are likely to have a great deal in common with those of other communities of similar economic status. Nevertheless, communities are, by their very nature, parochial and therefore imperfect agents for the realization of the goals of the city as a whole.[15]

Even in dealing with their own neighborhoods, communities may find that solving livelihood issues within the constraints imposed by the broader political economy pushes them to ignore issues of sustainability. Reinforcing Indira Gandhi's warning that "poverty is the greatest polluter," Castells argues that "throughout the world, poverty has been shown, again and again, to be a cause of environmental degradation" (1997, 132). Given a choice between creating a public health hazard by occupying areas where their sewage will flow onto public land or being pushed out to locations where they will have no chance of finding work, poor communities are likely to feel that they have no choice but to fight for the right to pollute.

Fundamental to determining whether communities act to further universal goals or whether their parochial needs put them in conflict with the interests of the city as a whole are the questions of "scaling up" (Fox 1996) or "linkages" (Woolcock 1997). When a community's livelihood interests run afoul of sustainability goals, surmounting the contradiction will almost certainly depend on the involvement of institutions or organizations with broader vision and greater expertise than communities themselves can muster. Dealing with the problem of "scaling up" requires going beyond a community-focused analysis and dealing with other kinds of actors.

Translocal Intermediaries — NGOs and Political Parties

Even the most well organized communities often lack the political clout to protect their own local interests, to say nothing of being able to advance more universalistic sustainability goals. For communities to be effective political actors, they must be able to find allies, either in the form of other, similarly situated communities or in the form of organizations with extralocal scope. In Woolcock's terminology (1997, 15), "integration" (internal solidarity) must be complemented by "linkages" (ties to larger-scale organizations). They must be able to "scale up."

NGOs, broadly defined, are the most promising source of the translocal organizational and ideological resources necessary for scaling up.[16] While they are likely to have strong affinities for place-based struggles for livability, NGOs are as likely to be actors in the "space of flows" as in the "space of places," which gives them resources and leverage that communities lack. Especially when mobilization involves questions of environmental sustainability, NGOs are likely to be part of international networks that transcend local politics (Keck and Sikkink 1998a). The scope of their networks allows NGOs to play a role in articulating the shared interests of different communities, projecting them onto a larger political stage and constructing alliances among socially disparate groups.

The potential role of translocal actors becomes even more important in cases when livelihood and sustainability are in contradiction. Communities in these circumstances need either new ideas that will enable them to find a way to reconcile their needs with ecological imperatives, or access to wider political leverage that can loosen the constraints imposed by the political economy in which they are forced to operate. Reforestation can help make favelas built on hillsides less ecologically devastating, but the favela communities themselves are unlikely to have either the expertise to undertake such a project or access to the inputs that would be necessary to execute it (cf. Mega-Cities Project 1996, 12–15).

Scaling up may also involve more traditional articulating organizations, such as political parties. Despite the new salience of NGOs as actors in Third World settings, political parties cannot be ignored. Students of urban social movements have, with good reason, been suspicious of the relation between parties and communities.[17] Politicians are certainly prone to self-interested, "thin rationality" agendas aimed at preserving their own power and privileges. Even so, sympathetic party organizers can also become vehicles of broader agendas, and parties remain one of the few organizational forms available to aggregate interests. The success of the Partido dos Trabalhadores (Workers' Party) in stimulating the participation of local neighborhoods in shaping urban development in the Brazilian city of Pôrto Alegre is an excellent case in point (Abers 1996, 1997; Santos 1997; Baiocchi 2000). Even when party organizations per se are not resources, community leaders may find that party ties provide protection against repression from local elites by enabling them to invoke allies at higher levels. As long as improving neighborhood environments and livelihoods depends on reshaping rules and regulations or on securing some share of public resources, the networks and relationships that are articulated through parties will remain a likely ingredient in successful community revindications.

Any organization whose scope escapes the confines of the community itself may divert a community's energy to the outside organization's self-aggrandizing agenda, which neither solves problems of livelihood nor contributes to sustainability. This is true for both NGOs and political parties, but it doesn't change the fact that without translocal allies, communities cannot realize even their immediate goals, to say nothing of reconciling those goals with ecological sustainability. Communities need allies even if allies have potentially problematic agendas of their own. Among these potential allies the most problematic, but also the most interesting, is the state.

The Contradictory Multiple Roles of the State

Problems of livability are collective; they cannot be resolved by some "natural" aggregation of astute individual actions. They are problems of making rules, reconstructing markets, providing public goods, and constraining the production of "public bads." In short, they are problems whose solution requires action from public authorities and agencies. The current dearth of public institutions with the capacity and motivation to effectively engage problems of livability is one of the prime reasons for urban degradation.

There is no denying that state apparatuses at the national level have been part of the problem as often as they have been part of the solution. By definition, "predatory" states extract resources from society without providing collective goods in return and are thereby enemies of livability (Evans 1995). Even "developmental states," which can be plausibly argued to have played a crucial role in accelerating economic growth, are unreliable allies in the struggle for livability. Precisely the social ties and capacities that enable developmental states to contribute to the process of accumulation are likely to isolate state managers from poor communities and their livelihood problems. Growth machine theorists make exactly the same argument about city administrations. The connections and orientations that make city administrations successful in promoting growth bias them against projects of livability, which are almost of necessity redistributive.

Putting the obvious necessity of an active state role in any plausible project of livability together with the "accumulationist" bias of states leads to pessimism about moving Third World cities onto trajectories that lead to greater livability. Escaping such pessimism requires moving beyond a view of states as generic and monolithic. Reifying "the state" as a monolithic entity is just as dangerous as reifying "civil society." Much more than NGOs, social movements, or even political parties, states are complicated, contradictory creatures. The authoritative coordination that is fundamental to the generic nature of the state imposes some uniformities, but the panoply of agencies making up the public institutions of governance remain heterogeneous in their orientations and often pursue contradictory goals. Conflict and contradiction vie with cohesion and coherence within and among agencies. Public authorities are split into local and supralocal jurisdictions. Authority is parceled out among municipal, state, and national governments in complex and overlapping ways. Within any jurisdiction, and often cutting across them, agencies are divided by sector and function and have competing responsibilities and interests. The role of the state thus is really a variety of roles, often played out in contradictory ways.

From a traditional administrative perspective, the fragmented character of the state is an impediment to solving problems of livability. Ideal strategies for dealing with livelihood and environment should have the same integrated and interwoven character that ecological systems do. Fragmented states are unlikely to be able to construct and implement such strategies. Yet the fact that states are not monolithic is also an advantage. It means that communities, and the social movements and NGOs that work with them, do not necessarily have to "capture the state" in order to elicit favorable responses from public institutions. Creating alliances with the specifically relevant parts of the state may be sufficient.

Even if the state apparatus as a whole is likely to pursue agendas responsive to the self-defined interests and demands of actors with exceptional market power, alliances of communities and NGOs can still hijack public organizational capacity. Those responsible for particular jurisdictions are likely to care about the livelihoods of their constituents (especially when legitimacy requires electoral validation). Particular agencies, having been assigned responsibility for environmental or livelihood issues, have a collective vested interest in pursuing these issues. They may lack the capacity to resolve them, but they are still potential allies from the point of view of communities. Mobilized communities can have an impact in certain arenas of deliberation and decision making within given agencies, even if the state as a whole is focused on other agendas.

Creating instances of "state-society synergy," in which engaged public agencies and mobilized communities enhance one another's capacity to deliver collective goods, is not easy, but it does happen.[18] Some of the best examples involve the delivery of collective goods to poor urban communities. Elinor Ostrom (1997) uses the example of "condominial sewers." An imaginative group of engineers working in Brazilian public sanitation agencies realized that they had neither the fiscal resources nor the labor power necessary to deliver sewers to poor neighborhoods. By providing materials and, more important, technical and organizational support, but relying on the communities themselves to do the work, they were able to "coproduce" a crucial collective good that could not otherwise have been delivered.

In order for this kind of state-community interaction to take place there must be robust, competent state agencies oriented toward delivering collective goods. At the same time, communities must be able to engage these agencies collectively and politically, not just as individualized clients. Engagement does not preclude conflict. In many cases, conflict can be an important stimulus to synergy. The key is a combination of "complementarity" and "embeddedness." State actors and communities must both recognize that each has resources and capacities that the other lacks, which when combined can be complementary. When this combination occurs with "embeddedness" in the form of networks of ties that cross the "great public-private divide" and provide concrete, positive social ties between actors representing the state and activists working in communities, the resulting synergy can deliver an otherwise impossible set of collective goods.

Even if most public authorities function as cogs in growth machines, local as well as global ones, the interaction of states and communities can still take on a surprising variety of forms. Seeking out possibilities of state-society synergy from among this variety, exploiting them, and, ideally, identifying ways to replicate them are essential parts of any strategy of livability. Such public-private ties should be seen as part of an "ecology of actors" that may, as a collectivity, be able to push the city in the direction of greater livability.

Agents of Livability as an Ecology of Actors

Focusing on one particular type of agent or actor is misleading, analytically and practically. There is no one ideal type of social agent if urban livability is the goal. There is no heroic proletariat, encapsulating in its bosom a blueprint for a better society and compelled to do whatever is necessary to turn that blueprint into reality.[19] Individually, each of the potential agents of livability is flawed.

Neither the public authority of the state, nor the organizational networks and ideology of NGOs, nor the political energy and determination of communities themselves provides assurance of moving Third World cities onto more livable trajectories. Ordinary communities often lack the social capital and organizational capacity to pursue the livelihood goals that emerge unambiguously from their immediate lived experience. Even more seriously, their livelihood strategies are constrained by the political and economic matrix in which they are immersed in ways that often make them enemies of sustainability. States are as likely to become handmaidens to strategies of accumulation that degrade and threaten livelihood as they are to deliver the rules and collective goods that provide livable solutions. The NGOs and other intermediary organizations are only as effective as the communities and public agencies with which they work, and sometimes they introduce extraneous, self-interested agendas of their own.

As long as these disappointingly imperfect actors—communities, NGOs, and local public agencies—operate at cross-purposes, the quest for livability is certainly doomed. Even if each type of actor operates in splendid isolation without undercutting the others, the prospects of success are small. Only when they operate synergistically, each reinforcing the others' strengths and compensating for the others' foibles, is success likely. The question, then, is how strategies and agendas can be constructed so that the disparate strengths and capacities of public institutions, NGOs, and organized communities will complement and reinforce one another. Agents of livability need to be conceptualized as an interconnected, interdependent set of complementary actors—an "ecology of agents."

The ability of an interconnected and interdependent set of political agents to move Third World cities toward trajectories of greater livability could go well beyond the sum of what could be accomplished if the political potential of the individual actors were aggregated in a simple, additive way. Thinking in terms of an ecology of agents is the best way of rescuing ourselves from the paralyzing conviction that the contemporary global economy leaves no room for agency in service of livelihood and sustainability.

The concept of an ecology of agents extends the notion of state-society synergy and the idea of linkages as used by social capital theorists like Woolcock (1997). Nonetheless, the term should not be over-interpreted. The existence of an ecology of agents does not imply that, in some kind of Panglossian functionalist way, interconnection and interdependence are in themselves sufficient to enhance livability. Growth machines are also ecologies of agents. The connotation of a system that is inherently homeostatic, self-balancing, or in some sort of natural equilibrium also needs to be disavowed. "Ecology" should be taken in the minimalist sense as connoting an assemblage of actors whose prospects and capabilities cannot be assessed without taking into account the aims, strategies, and capabilities of the rest of the actors with whom they share a common arena. Focusing on sets of actors is useful not because interconnections are the solution in themselves but because it allows us to distinguish patterns of interconnection that enhance livability from patterns of interaction that undercut it. An understanding of urban livability must begin with the analysis of the variations among different ecologies of agents in different urban settings, always looking for possibilities of synergy but always sensitive to the possibilities of negative-sum interactions.

A Panoply of Urban Political Ecologies

If understanding variations in the way ecologies of local political actors work is the best way to build a vision of urban livability, then the six studies that follow constitute an ideal foundation. They all start with recognition of the powerful ways in which the logic of accumulation (local and global) circumscribes possibilities of livability in the cities they describe. At the same time, they explore possibilities for alternative agency. In each exploration, poor communities are closely examined not as isolated actors but in relation to NGOs, social movements, and local government agencies. An array of positive potential roles for the state, as well as an equal collection of negative ones, is scrutinized. In each case, the ecological dimension of urban political struggles is highlighted. In short, these studies provide exactly the kind of foundation that is necessary in order to move inductively toward a better general understanding of the dynamics of livability.

The cases are also apt because they are set against the background of the "twin transitions" to market-orientation and electoral succession: all the countries considered have moved in the direction of increased electoral competitiveness and increased reliance on markets during the periods examined. They give us a chance to assess how much difference these transitions make to the pursuit of livability across a range of settings.

The collective theoretical contribution of these studies is further magnified by the broad panorama of transitional and developing urban areas they reflect. They chronicle the experiences of eight major urban areas in three very different regions of the world. The first three studies are drawn from East and Southeast Asia, where rapid economic growth has propelled urbanization and threatened sustainability. A comparison of Seoul and Bangkok, cases around Hanoi and Ho Chi Minh City, and a study of Taipei provide a vivid picture of the variety of challenges that face agents of livability in Asia. From there the focus shifts to the environmental problems of the transition in Eastern Europe, as exemplified by the relations between Budapest and its surrounding hinterland. Two studies of Latin America's biggest megacities—São Paulo and Mexico City—complete the panorama.

Each of the studies is distinctive not only in the specificities of its setting but also in its focus within the setting. Some authors focus on industrial pollution, others on the inadequacies of basic urban infrastructure; some focus on the dilemmas of specific poor communities, others on a range of neighborhoods. Each author also uses his or her own distinctive conceptual approach to highlight the analytical lessons of the case examined.

Mike Douglass and his collaborators use the contrasting experiences of two slum communities—Wolgoksa-dong in Seoul and Wat Chonglom in Bangkok—to show how the ability of communities to contribute to livability depends on both microfoundations at the level of households and external linkages to intermediary organizations and the state. Comparing communities in the settings of Korea and Thailand is an especially valuable exercise, because it shows how the problems of achieving state-society synergy depend on the basic stance of the states involved.

Until democratization provided it with some political breathing space in the late 1980s, Seoul's Wolgoksa-dong had to struggle for its survival in the face of a hostile, repressive state: the Korean state, while more effective than the Thai state in providing infrastructure and even amenities to slum communities, at the same time suffocated the possibilities for local community organization. Wat Chonglom got almost nothing from the Bangkok administration until well after it had demonstrated its ability to transform its own habitat, yet it became a local model of livability. Despite admiring Wat Chonglom's success, however, Douglass, Ard-am, and Kim warn sharply against the conclusion that benign neglect of poor communities will lead to livability. Not only were external linkages key to Wat Chonglom's accomplishments, but this community also had internal resources that most other poor communities lack. Starting with the unusual level of households with stable, complex internal divisions of labor and going on to discuss the stability and longevity of the residents making up the community, Douglass and his colleagues outline the exceptional endowments of social capital that put Wat Chonglom at an advantage vis-à-vis other, equally poor communities. The comparison makes clear how important it is to look at the interaction of actors at different levels, rather than simply at the communities themselves.

In their study of Taipei, Hsin-Huang Michael Hsiao and Hwa-Jen Liu broaden the focus from poor communities to a range of communities in different circumstances with different and sometimes conflicting interests. Hsiao and Liu's study reminds us that communities should not be romanticized. They point out that in Taipei, the struggle of middle-class communities to improve their quality of life has sometimes been at the expense of poor and marginalized communities. Nonetheless, the activism of middle-class communities is essential in making sure that state policy does not reflect the narrow antilivability of growth machine goals promoted by the alliance of the dominant political party (the KMT), industrialists, and real estate developers. As in Korea, democratization has helped. Community leverage toward sustainability goals is provided by the emergence of local governments (in this case run by the opposition Democratic Progressive Party, or DPP) that perceive their ability to survive in the face of political dominance by the KMT to be dependent on the support of local communities mobilized around livability issues. This time it is the interaction of community activism and party competition that produces progress toward greater livability.

Like Taiwan, Korea, and Thailand, Vietnam has experienced rapid growth, but in the political context of a simultaneous transition from state socialism to a market-oriented economy. In this final Asian case, Dara O'Rourke's analysis of community battles against industrial pollution in Vietnam illuminates a different variation on the environmental politics of growth in Asia, one in which electoral politics plays a minimal role but local traditions of mobilization and protest are powerful. O'Rourke's model of "community-driven regulation" develops the idea of state-society synergy in a particularly useful way. Despite the unique character of this case, his model is potentially applicable to a broad range of other national settings.

O'Rourke carefully dissects the characteristics that allow communities to become more effective agents of livability. Yet he is clear that community success also depends on the ability to enlist allies within the state apparatus and that this ability may in turn depend on having other extralocal allies, such as sympathetic media or even international NGOs. Engaging the state on the side of livability depends on the mobilization of affected communities, but community success depends on finding parts of the state apparatus endowed with the capacity (and willingness) to stand with the communities themselves on the side of sustainability.

As in Vietnam, contemporary environmental politics in Hungary are shaped by the transition to a market-oriented economy, but Zsuzsa Gille's paper on the politics of toxic wastes shows us a very different picture of industrial pollution in this transition. It also adds a new dimension to the issue of sustainability. Gille's case exemplifies the danger that a city may secure its sustainability at the expense of its rural neighbors. Concretely, Gille describes the plight of the small town of Garé, which was relegated to "wasteland" status by the Budapest Chemical Works when this industrial giant (with the complicity of state planners) made Garé the recipient of the toxic wastes that were inherent in the firm's internationally successful economic strategy. Without in any way absolving the socialist state apparatus of its ecological failures, Gille makes it clear that while the oppressive, imposing socialist state was to blame for creating Garé's problems, the irresponsibly absent postsocialist state robbed the community of the institutional support it needed to resolve its problems.

Shifting the scene to Latin America's largest urban agglomeration—São Paulo, Brazil—Margaret Keck offers a cautionary yet curiously optimistic tale of the inability of this modern industrial metropolis to protect its water supply. She shows how the state's preoccupation with industrial growth distorted the foundations on which water policy was built. The state is clearly part of the problem, but this is no romantic fable in which the day is saved by the heroism of poor communities. Bereft of more sustainable ways of solving their livelihood needs, poor communities end up moving into the protected area surrounding the city's reservoirs and threatening the water quality of the city as a whole. At the same time, progressive technocrats within the government construct alternative visions. Affected middle-class communities use these visions in their own campaigns to protect the city's reservoirs. A more sustainable set of water policies is yet to be achieved, but what is striking is the resilience of the networks of activists, in and out of government, working to preserve the city's watershed and protect its water supply. At the end of Keck's story, the creation of "basin committees" signals a new opportunity to increase community participation and move water policy away from its "accumulationist" origins in the direction of greater sustainability.

Keith Pezzoli's analysis of Latin America's other megacity—Mexico City—focuses on the struggle of a particular set of communities to resolve the same contradictions between livelihood and sustainability that confront poor communities in São Paulo. Aided by the imagination of local NGOs, the collection of *colonias populares* known as Los Belvederes came up with a vision that reconciled their "illegal" settlements in the Ajusco ecological reserve with sustainability goals. The concept of the "ecologically productive settlement" *(colonia ecológica productiva)* proved to be an unattainable goal in practice, but the success of the campaign in defending Los Belvederes' claims to its land provides a dramatic demonstration of the powerful legitimacy that can be generated when communities can link their particular livelihood struggles to the more universal goal of ecological sustainability.

Pezzoli's discussion of the mobilization of Bosques del Pedregal (one of the communities that took the lead within Los Belvederes) illustrates the kinds of social capital that underlie collective action at the community level; at the same time, it makes clear how much community success depends on the ability to engage the capabilities of relevant state agencies. The overall political trends in which these community struggles are encapsulated echo the Asian cases. Just as the opposition party in Taipei provided communities with a new source of external leverage, likewise the opposition PRD's efforts to dislodge the PRI in Mexico City have opened new political space for the activists of Los Belvederes.

The extent to which common lessons emerge from this extraordinary diversity of cases is startling. Common themes and parallel conclusions reverberate across cities and across regions to paint a complicated but compelling picture of how ecologies of agents work. Taken together, these studies point toward the possibility of constructing a general framework for understanding a politics of livelihood and sustainability that works both in Asia and in Latin America and even makes sense in an industrialized but transitional society such as Hungary.

None of these studies encourages the reader to think about removing the question mark from *Livable Cities?* in the title of our volume. Rather than advertisements for successful formulas, they are analytic contributions that illuminate the kind of institutional changes that would be necessary for livability to be effectively pursued. Even so, they convey a sense of hopeful possibility. Their position echoes that of Albert Hirschman. In a collection of essays entitled *A Bias toward Hope* (1971), Hirschman defends his "possibilism," saying:

> In making my proposals, I refuse, on the one hand, to be "realistic" and to limit myself to strictly incremental changes. At the same time, however, these proposals are not presented as being so revolutionary or so utopian that they have no chance whatever to be adopted in the absence of prior total political change. On the contrary, I feel an obligation to make them in concrete institutional detail, thereby deliberately creating the optical illusion that they could possibly be adopted tomorrow by men of good will (p. 29).

Readers who want to understand why degradation is a continuing threat to Third World cities will find these studies valuable. Readers who, like Hirschman, are possessed by the "passion for what is possible" should find them an especially useful source of insights.

Notes

I would especially like to thank all of the contributors to this volume. The ideas that are presented in this chapter are drawn to a substantial degree from our discussions and their visions of the literature. From the beginning of our work together, their comments and criticisms have shaped (and improved) my efforts to think about these issues.

1. Cohen (1996, 96), discussing the agenda for Habitat II, makes an analogous plea for consideration of the dual character of livability by arguing that "the HABITAT II process must bring together two definitions of the word 'habitat': 'habitat' as human settlement (the 1976 Vancouver [HABITAT I] definition) and 'habitat' as ecosystem (the 1992 Rio eco summit definition)."

2. For a review of political ecology perspectives on environment and social justice, see Peet and Watts 1996.

3. In a highlighted *Wired* cover story, Peter Schwartz and Peter Leyden (1997) proclaimed, "We're facing 25 years of prosperity, freedom, and a better environment for the whole world. . . . You got a problem with that?"

4. In contrast to the ideal typical manufacturing cost curve, in which unit costs fall with increasing quantities of output, the ways in which new land is

"produced"—such as using distant land instead of nearby land or transforming unusable land into usable (filling bays or leveling mountains)—all involve rising costs.

5. For an overview of the "ecological modernization perspective," see Mol 1995 and Mol and Sonnenfeld 2000. An extensive literature now documents the fascination of at least an important segment of the corporate community with "green" strategies. See, for example, Schmidheiny 1992 and Eden 1996. At the same time, the traditional "treadmill of capitalist production" view (Schnaiberg 1980; Schnaiberg and Gould 1994), which posits an "enduring conflict" between the search for profits and the quest for sustainability, continues to capture the logic of a substantial range of corporate behavior.

6. This position can also be taken as a useful rationale for allowing national-level politicians to escape responsibility for problems of distribution and well-being. When it comes to providing support for global commerce, the extent to which the state's agency has been preserved remains impressive (cf. Evans 1997a).

7. For a nice discussion of the "greening" of sociopolitical discourse, see Buttel 1992.

8. Some would argue that political ecology has not gone far enough in this direction. Thus, Peet and Watts (1996) have called for a "liberation ecology."

9. See Peluso 1992 for a particularly nice example.

10. See, for example, Molotch 1976; Molotch and Logan 1984; Logan and Molotch 1987; Logan, Whaley, and Crowder 1997.

11. Mollenkopf's "progrowth coalition" might be seen as a new world successor to the coalition that produced what Harvey calls "the 'gas and water socialism' of the late nineteenth and early twentieth centuries" (1997, 20).

12. As Logan and Molotch put it, "Those who are unable to buy amenities in the market lose most from the unavailability of such resources. More concretely, since the poor are most likely to live and work in close proximity to pollution sources, the poor are more affected by growth-induced environmental decay than the rich" (1987, 95; see also Harvey 1973).

13. See Friedmann and Rangan 1993 for a nice set of case studies expanding on this theme.

14. The increasing prominence of the term *social capital* in contemporary economic and social analysis reflects renewed interest in the contribution of interpersonal networks based on trust and reciprocity to positive economic and political outcomes. Such social ties are now seen as important assets, hence a kind of "capital." Putnam (2000) analyzes the role of social capital in the twentieth-century United States. Woolcock (1997) provides an excellent review of the concept of social capital and its role in development. For an earlier analysis of the returns from community collective action, see Hirschman (1984).

15. If the focus is broadened to include more affluent communities, the potential for conflict between the interests of particular communities increases correspondingly. Concentrating pollution in poorer communities may easily represent a solution from the point of view of middle-class "NIMBYs," and in more extreme cases the proximity of poor communities may itself be seen as a threat to "the quality of life" of more affluent residents.

16. The referent for the label *NGO* has become as general as the term *civil society*. Any organization that is not explicitly part of the state is referred to as an NGO. Strictly speaking, the term should be restricted to formal translocal organizations with some professional staff and fund-raising capabilities, as distinct from community-based organizations (CBOs) and social movement organizations (SMOs). The discussion here refers primarily to NGOs in the strict sense of the term, but to the extent that social movement organizations become less place based, more ideologically defined, and more organizationally sophisticated they may play a role similar to that of NGOs (cf. Tarrow 1994).

17. Castells, for example, argues that while urban social movements must be connected to society by political parties, the *"sine qua non* condition" of their success is that "they must be organizationally and ideologically autonomous of any political party"(1983, 322; see also Perlman 1976).

18. For some case studies exemplifying the possibilities of "state-society synergy," see Evans 1997b. For a complementary perspective, see Migdal, Kohli, and Shue 1994.

19. At the same time, it should be pointed out that potential agents of livability do not confront the same kind of implacable foes that Marxist theory compelled the heroic proletariat to face. Even the firms that constitute the corporate heart of the growth machine can be induced to participate in more livable trajectories of development, provided that the markets that shape their interests are constructed with livability in mind. Consequently, there is no inescapable logic that compels states to serve as auxiliaries to degrading exploitation.

:: 2 ::

Urban Poverty and the Environment

Social Capital and State-Community Synergy in Seoul and Bangkok

MIKE DOUGLASS, ORATHAI ARD-AM, AND IK KI KIM

Urbanization and the Environment in the Pacific Asia Region

Over the past three decades East and Southeast Asian countries have been experiencing massive shifts of population from rural to urban areas. From levels of less than 25 percent in the 1960s, most countries are expected to have the majority of their populations living in cities within the next two decades (UNESCAP [United Nations Economic and Social Commission for Asia and the Pacific] 1993; United Nations 1997). While the urban transition is seen as indispensable to the processes of industrialization, economic growth, and material-welfare increase, it has also brought severe environmental deterioration. As urbanization in the region continues at an accelerated pace, 30 percent of the world's increase in urban population over the next quarter of a century will occur in Pacific Asia (United Nations 1994; Douglass 1998b). Similarly, much of the increase in world pollution and environmental deterioration will be associated with the use and misuse of energy and resources appropriated by expanding cities in this region. Environmental stress is already so great that it has raised the question of whether the mega-urban regions now forming in this area of the world will be environmentally sustainable. In Asia at least, the record shows that economic growth does not by itself lead to demonstrably better capacities to manage the environment; "rich city" has not meant "environmentally sound, livable city." In almost all instances, environmental degradation has accelerated with economic growth.

In every city the impacts of environmental degradation fall most heavily on low-income households and their communities. Areas available to the poor—sites along riverbanks or steep hillsides, under bridges, adjacent to major highways, or next to factories—are also those where flooding, untreated waste, contaminated water supplies, and air and land pollution concentrate (Douglass and Lee 1996). Because of their often illegal status and lack of political power, poor households rarely receive significant government support to improve their communities. At the same time, with land prices rising faster than per capita income gains in core metropolitan regions, market forces present constant pressures to replace slum and squatter settlements with more commercially remunerative uses. Thus, manifold, seemingly unrelenting forces challenge the viability of low-income communities. Understanding the powerful nature of these forces makes all the more impressive the findings that most of the housing construction and community building in Asian cities are carried out by the poor through mutual assistance largely outside the market system.[1] Furthermore, despite the entrenched political and economic forces working against them, some poor communities have been successful in improving their environmental conditions.

This chapter contrasts the strategies used to improve environmental conditions in two low-income communities in two different urban contexts: the Wolgoksa-dong squatter community in Seoul, Korea, and the Wat Chonglom slum community in Bangkok, Thailand.[2] Comparison of the two communities will construct a picture of possible social and political routes that might lead poor urban communities toward greater livability. In each case, the analysis moves from the level of the household and gender relations, through the level of community organization and leadership, to the linkages and conflicts that each community has to translocal organizations and the state.

Because the two communities are situated in two very different macropolitical contexts—Korea and Thailand—comparing them provides a dramatic illustration of how differences at the macropolitical level shape the strategies open to individual communities. The two communities also have distinguishing characteristics even within their own national and urban contexts: the struggles of Wolgoksa-dong are relatively typical of the struggles of slum communities that have managed to survive over the years in Seoul, whereas Wat Chonglom is as unlike the typical Bangkok slum community as it is unlike Wolgoksa-dong. The differences between the two are thus not simply reflections of differing macroenvironments but also illustrations of the range of variation that is possible at the micro level. It is the combination of differences at the macro and micro levels that makes the comparison such a rich source of general ideas about how communities can achieve greater livability.

The discussion starts by setting out the characteristics of each of the communities and their respective macro sociopolitical environments, namely Seoul and Bangkok. It goes on to show how patterns of household organization, gender relations, social networks, community composition, and community leadership contribute to the construction of social capital and to collective action, which, through very different mechanisms, make each community more livable. Comparing the two communities is a way of highlighting the distinctive characteristics of each, but it is not intended to move toward a conclusion that one community is necessarily "better" or "more successful" than the other. The aim is rather to show how different strategies are possible and indeed necessary in different contexts.

The analysis then moves beyond the borders of the communities to look at the role of intermediary organizations, and then the contrasting patterns of community-state relations and their consequences are laid out. The chapter conclusion brings the macro and micro levels together, summarizes the characteristics of two "pathways to state-community synergy" illustrated by the two cases, and discusses the broader implications of the two cases.

Seoul, Bangkok, and the Wolgoksa-dong and Wat Chonglom Communities

Wolgoksa-dong and Wat Chonglom reflect the cities in which they are embedded in quite different ways. Wat Chonglom is the exception to the rule among Bangkok slums—a community that has succeeded in the kind of sociopolitical environment that has proved inauspicious for most poor communities. Wolgoksa-dong, on the other hand, relates to the political economy of Seoul in a way that is much more typical of Seoul slum communities that have managed to stay in existence after decades of slum clearance programs. Nonetheless, in important ways each community is a product of its larger environment. To understand each of them one must also understand the cities of which they are a part.

Seoul

By 1990 almost three-quarters of the Korean population lived in cities, with Seoul dominating the national urban system. By 1995 the greater Seoul metropolitan region accounted for almost 21 million inhabitants— 46 percent of the entire national population (Chai and Kim 1999). Seoul's hyperdevelopment has brought with it serious environmental costs. The air is heavily polluted with suspended particulate matter: sulfur dioxide from coal burning and nitrogen dioxide from automobile emissions. Respiratory diseases, including pulmonary emphysema, have reached significant levels, with air-pollution-related deaths of factory workers leading to public demonstrations in the 1990s (Kim 1994). Water pollution is also beyond acceptable standards. Neither the supply nor the quality of the city water system is reliable or trusted; buying bottled water has become common among the city's middle- and upper-income strata.

In Seoul (as in Taipei—see chapter 3), the polarization of economic and population growth has led to intense pressure by land developers and speculators to convert land occupied by squatter communities into commercial and middle-class residential uses. Although slum razing by the state and programs of forced resettlement eliminated most of the larger squatter settlements in Seoul by the late 1970s, many were able to sustain their existence. Some have been regularized through incremental land titling, but many households remain classified as squatters. According to the Seoul city government, the city had 105 squatter settlements in 1990. With a total population of approximately one hundred fifty thousand people, these settlements were said by some researchers to account for less than 1 percent of the city's population (Kim 1991). Others, however, claim that as late as the mid-1980s as much as 20 percent of the population of Seoul lived in slum or illegal settlement areas (Clifford 1998).[3] More recently, the government has provided such environmental infrastructure as drainage systems, common washing areas, and shared latrines to selected squatter settlements. These gains were not granted by a benign government acting alone, but were the outcome of highly confrontational state-community and state–civil society relations, not infrequently marked by pitched battles between citizens and police.

Wolgoksa-dong Squatter Community

One of the remaining squatter areas in Seoul is known as Wolgoksa-dong, a community of about thirteen thousand people situated on a steep hillside slope only seven miles from City Hall. With a density of almost sixty thousand people per square kilometer, or three times the average for Seoul, Wolgoksa-dong is very crowded. In fact, many of the small houses have more than one family living in them. Although the population has been decreasing and aging (along with the Korean population as a whole), most of the current residents say that they do not want to move. Three-quarters of those interviewed in a 1994 survey said they had been living there for at least five years; one-quarter had resided there for more than twenty years (Kim and Jun 1996).

By the early 1990s, following implementation of policies to regularize the community through land titling, about 43 percent of the houses were owned by one of their occupants, with the rest of the houses either rented or classified as illegal. Designated as a "living environment betterment area" by the government in 1989, Wolgoksa-dong has been provided with a community hall, space set aside for the aged, a child-care facility, a children's playground, a neighborhood park, and three public latrines. These facilities have improved the physical ambience of the community but have also fueled fear of eviction among households that are still classified as squatters.

Interviews in the community reveal a common concern with air quality, water pollution from overuse of synthetic detergents, and food wastes in the waterways (Kim and Jun 1994). Noise and foul odors were registered as serious problems by half of the households. Most residents blamed big business and government for deteriorating air quality but acknowledged some responsibility for water and land pollution. The continued use of *yantan* (coal briquettes) for heating and cooking was cited as the most serious source of air pollution directly affecting homes, with deaths from carbon monoxide poisoning occurring in winter months. Houses often have combinations of coal and kerosene heaters, which have resulted in a high incidence of bronchitis and other respiratory illnesses, headaches, anemia, and possibly heart disease.[4]

The poor quality of piped water supplied by the city is perceived by residents to be the source of serious health problems and ailments in the community. Virtually all houses have water connections, but poor maintenance of the system and the steep slopes of the community itself mean that delivery is undependable. Roads, while paved, remain too narrow for city emergency services to access, and inadequately maintained drainage systems result in the accumulation of human and other wastes in the neighborhood drains. Only about half of the households have municipal trash pickup at their residences; the remainder must either transport the waste to a pickup point themselves or pay others to do it. With less than one-third of the houses having their own toilets, most residents rely on communal latrines provided by the city.

In sum, the overall situation is one of modest government assistance and piecemeal recognition of squatters' rights in a context of continuing pressure for eviction and redevelopment. On the positive side, these people have been able to remain in the core of the urban region and have even gained some upgrading of their homes and neighborhoods. But the hold remains precarious for many. Thus, according to residents, the inability to know about or anticipate the timing of government community redevelopment projects, which generally mean relocation of the poor, prevents them from deciding to invest in their housing or community. Evictions continued even after the democratic reforms began in the late 1980s, but there is hope that the newly established system of elected local government will better engage these communities in policy and its implementation (Kim and Jun 1994; KNCFH [Korean NGOs and CBOs Forum for Habitat] 1996).

Bangkok

Bangkok has gained the reputation of having among the most rapidly degraded and severely deteriorated urban environments in the world (DANCED [Danish Cooperation of Environment and Development] 1996). Air pollution from particulates and lead, surface-water pollution due to microbiological contamination, and traffic congestion are among Bangkok's most serious urban environmental problems (Ard-am and Soonthorndhada 1997). Breathing air in the city is now considered to be "dangerous" by the National Environmental Board. Lead in automobile emissions results in blood-lead levels for children and adults that are among the world's highest (Douglass and Lee 1996). A study of infants during 1989–1990 found average lead levels of 18.5 micrograms per deciliter, nearly twice the level that the U.S. Centers for Disease Control and Prevention consider dangerous.[5] Measures of water quality show more than twice the maximum acceptable levels of pollution. Depletion of groundwater already exceeded replenishment by the mid-1980s, and water demand in the region is expected to double over the next two decades (Phantumvanit and Panayotou 1990). Only 2 percent of Bangkok's population is connected to the city's sewer network.

Available data suggests that the slum population has dramatically increased over the past three decades. In 1966 there were an estimated thirty-nine to fifty major slum areas in Bangkok. Figures for 1980 placed the number at about three hundred, and estimates for 1985 show about four hundred (Pornchokchai 1992). By 1991 Bangkok had more than fourteen hundred officially recognized slums (Yap 1992). Together they accounted for about 1.1 million people, or about 230,000 households, which equaled about 15 percent of the population of the Bangkok metropolitan area (Kaothien and Rachatatanun 1991).

The majority of slum communities consist of housing constructed over areas of constant flooding, which have no sewerage or public garbage services. Electricity and piped water have come to some slum settlements, but most remain without even minimal environmental infrastructure or services. Human waste flows into community drainage channels, resulting in strong odors and waterborne diseases that lead to diarrhea, infections, and other health problems, which are among the leading causes of infant mortality and adult illnesses.

Wat Chonglom Slum Community

One of the slums of Bangkok is Wat Chonglom, a medium-size community of about 180 households. It is in the vicinity of Thailand's largest slum complex, Klong Toey, which is in the southwestern area of the city around the Port Authority of Thailand, where historically many of the jobs for the poor were found and government land could be invaded without significant resistance by the state or private sector. In contrast to many of the other communities in the area, however, Wat Chonglom sits on privately owned land, and as a result of earlier struggles the residents now pay a low monthly rent to the landlord, who is reputed to be one of the largest landowners in Bangkok. The location of the community—almost directly under a noisy highway overpass in an area where houses and pathways must be built above ground, because the ground is often covered by stagnant water—has made it undesirable for private development. As with many slums, unattractiveness to land developers is a form of security.

Established in the mid-1970s, the community is composed of long-term residents and has few recent migrants. Its population is highly stable in household composition, turnover, and number. Most of the houses are owned by their residents. Its approximately nine hundred residents are engaged in a wide range of economic activities, but until a few years ago they all had one common experience: severely degraded environmental conditions. Lanes between houses and shops in the community were makeshift constructions of wooden planks that ran above the often flooded, usually smelly, trash-ridden land below. Houses were densely packed into the area, which had few common facilities. Although piped water and electrical lines had been installed after direct elections of parliamentarians representing the area began in the 1980s, the community still had the ambience of an unhealthy slum.

By the early 1990s these conditions had dramatically changed for the better. The turnaround began in the late 1980s, catalyzed by two Mahidol University faculty members who, via a small injection of outside resources, stimulated a major project of cleanup and physical improvements.[6] It was an immediate success not only in terms of improving the health and safety of residents, but also in generating new economic activities and income-earning opportunities in the community. With the ambience decidedly improved, small shops started springing up in the community. Beauty shops, video rental stores, food stalls, and mini–dry goods stores appeared in the fronts of homes along the community's new cement walkways. Many were owned and run by women.

The success of its first efforts led to a long string of other projects. Among the major ones were piped water connections to all houses and, in part of the community, the connection of a new drainage system with that of the city. In addition to these environment-related improvements, a two-story community hall was built complete with a children's daycare center; it simultaneously allowed for a number of community activities, such as education about the environment, and freed time for mothers to work and engage in other activities outside the house. The center has subsequently become an important spot for meetings.[7]

Loans were also made available to individual families to improve their houses. Over time, these loans became more prevalent, with the result that by 1991 almost fifty houses had been renovated, with many adding bright colors and decorations and innovatively including spaces for growing flowers. A revolving credit cooperative was also established, to pool money that would allow for large loans to be made available to its members.[8]

The process was not without problems. Conflict occurred within the community, some households would not cooperate, and the government initially declined to give any support. But together the residents were able to minimize and overcome these limitations, and they gained a shared awareness of their problems and their capacity to improve their situation cooperatively. The two Mahidol faculty members who worked with the community summarized the mood in Wat Chonglom after the project's many successes as follows:

> There is no doubt that the community has achieved a large degree of self-reliance and self-help. They no longer accept "charity," which they perceive as offensive and expensive. They however accept collaboration if the aid agency accepts their conditions, i.e., the people manage their "own project" in partnership with the agency. . . . Many individuals and families have, because of their responsibilities over the project, changed their attitudes and behaviors. This has a major impact on such social problems as alcoholism. There is no drug addiction—there is an intensive campaign against AIDS—and there is no prostitution. Such human needs as self-esteem, self-actualization, sense of belonging, pride, sense of responsibility and accountability are obviously being fulfilled (Ard-am and Soonthorndhada 1994, 18).

The residents are proud of their collaborative accomplishments. In 1989 their community was awarded the local district prize as the best community, and in the following year it was selected as best community in all of Bangkok.[9] The state had discovered that within the space of less than a few years Wat Chonglom had made itself into a decidedly livable community, and it began to embrace the same self-help efforts as an archetype for the rest of the city. The national planning body (NESDB) adopted Wat Chonglom's "model" of community empowerment and has tried to apply it in five other communities nearby.

In recognition of these profoundly positive transformations, the community chairman was called upon to talk to other slum communities about how to make similar miracles happen. But, as detailed below, the majority of other slum communities do not have the wherewithal to "learn" from Wat Chonglom. The constellation of factors coming together that led to improvements in Wat Chonglom has proven difficult to replicate in other Bangkok slums.

Building Social Capital from Within

How do we explain the defeats and victories of these two communities in their struggles for livability? What kinds of general concepts and propositions do their stories suggest? The idea of "social capital" (Putnam 1993, 1995; Brehm and Rahn 1997; Woolcock 1997) is useful in analyzing both communities. But in these communities at least, it is not the voluntary associations or affinity-group clubs, which have often been the focus of social capital theorists, that appear to be the most important building blocks for trust and consequent capacity for collective action. Instead, more basic social institutions—notably households and inter-household support networks together with community leadership—foster cooperative action and provide more enduring foundations for social capital.

Households

Research on the question of community capacity-building in Asian cities confirms that a basic starting point is the household, a key institution in all societies (*AJEM* 1994). The findings of the research show that success in managing environmental resources and problems at the household level depends upon the capacity to maintain a complex intrahousehold division of labor (Douglass 1998a). They also consistently show that the poorest households are those with only one adult or parent; these households lack the wherewithal to cover the many types of tasks needed to daily reproduce the material and social bases for household sustenance.

Failures to manage environmental conditions and resources are more related to household size, composition, and type than to an assumed household prioritization of income needs over habitat and environment management.[10] The Wat Chonglom community in Bangkok is composed mainly of nuclear families of four or five members, which has allowed for a division of labor and sharing of tasks not possible in the adjacent slum community, separated from it only by a tall wooden fence and composed of dormitorylike rooms rented out to male construction workers, who share the small, crowded rooms with fellow workers. In Wolgoksa-dong, family size and complexity are found to be positively related to such environmental tasks as separating trash in households, with households that have more complex divisions of labor being twice as likely to separate trash as those on the other end of the spectrum.

The empowerment of women is also crucial to both social capital formation and the pursuit of livability. Women tend to be more knowledgeable about and aware of environmental problems, as well as more committed to joining in cooperative efforts to resolve them. Where women have greater decision-making roles and access to outside sources of support, environmental management is greatly improved (cf. Wignaraja 1990; Momsen 1991).[11] In Wolgoksa-dong, households, mostly through women's initiatives, are making conscious efforts to manage and improve the environment. These initiatives include efforts to reduce the use of detergents, save water, minimize electricity use, reduce noise, and prevent the dumping of waste—including that from latrines—in the community.

Women in Wat Chonglom are also responsible for most household activities, including cleaning, boiling water, and collecting, sorting, and dumping garbage. Men take charge of garbage burning and household repairs. Children assist in almost all of these activities, though sons have a much smaller role than daughters (Ard-am and Soonthorndhada 1997, table 4). At the same time, only about 11 percent of the households surveyed claimed that a wife has equal decision-making powers with her husband in household matters.

In Wolgoksa-dong the majority of married women work outside the community to earn incomes. With limited time to spend in the community and limited interaction with neighbors, their environmental efforts are more focused on conserving resources used by their families in their homes. Although many women in Wat Chonglom also work for money, a large portion of this work is carried out in the home and in the community. That may partly explain why there seems to be more association among women over community management tasks in Wat Chonglom than in Wolgoksa-dong. Consistent with the fact that it is more likely in Thailand than Korea to find women in higher-level government positions, university teaching, and business management, women in Wat Chonglom are engaged as leaders in more community-based programs than in Wolgoksa-dong, and this is undoubtedly a key aspect of the vitality of community life in Wat Chonglom.

Interhousehold and Interpersonal Networks

Maintaining networks of reciprocal exchange outside the household is of critical importance to household efforts to manage their habitat and environment. Managing shared or common spaces, caring for children, constructing houses, and borrowing money are key activities carried out through reciprocal relations with neighbors and others within and outside the community. As voluntary activities that also include "clubs" for regularly meeting for leisure activities such as playing mah-jongg or karaoke singing, they are the stuff of social capital.

In Wolgoksa-dong, the intense crowding of families in housing without basic washing or toilet facilities necessitates cooperation in maintaining clean and functioning common latrines and other infrastructure. As in most societies, underlying both this type of cooperation and, equally important, the propensity to engage in community organizations and social movements is "neighborliness." Surveys conducted in the community by Ik Ki Kim found that those household groups who frequented other households for celebrations and other events were more likely to join in community environment cleanup groups and environmental associations (Kim and Jun 1996, 23).[12] The converse was also true: those with few visits to other households joined few environmental groups.

These findings support the general social capital thesis that everyday forms of association provide the basis for more extraordinary cooperative efforts in community development. As previously noted, however, for the Wolgoksa-dong community as a whole, the level of association appeared to be low. One principal reason for the inability to translate an apparently robust level of household interaction into community improvement efforts has been the suppression of such efforts by the government. In contrast to Wat Chonglom, which was able to channel its social capital directly into community-building projects among its residents, social capital formation in Wolgoksa-dong was transformed into community-state contests of power.

Similarly, although both the Seoul and the Bangkok communities share the common traits of being highly homogeneous in terms of religion and ethnicity, the piecemeal awarding by the Korean government of land ownership to some members of the community but not others has driven in a decisive wedge over basic decisions related to community improvement programs. With landowners becoming less interested in supporting the plight of those without land, Kim and Jun (1996) conclude that these divisions present problems in maintaining solidarity against squatter evictions and in joining together in community development efforts.

In Wat Chonglom social cleavages also exist, but to a lesser degree, and they do not revolve around landownership. Most residents claim to be Buddhist, and after twenty years of existence, the community now experiences little population turnover. In at least one major cluster of houses, all the residents are related to the original group of settlers, who migrated from the province of Pathum Thani. The success of the initial community improvement project also had the cumulative effect of overcoming differences and forging stronger forms of association among residents. Following those successes, the community decided to organize itself into clusters of four to five households, with an elected representative of each cluster being a member of the Central Committee that works with the chairman on community-wide programs.

Conflict among community organizers in Wat Chonglom came, ironically, with the reintroduction in the decade of the 1980s of elected governments and political parties, the latter of which are numerous and are organized around particular candidates rather than party platforms. Most of these conflicts, which peak with rampant vote buying during election campaigns, are reported to be minor, and they are certainly much less intense than, for example, those perpetuated by political parties based on caste and religion in the slums of India's cities (Sengupta 1994).

Having noted various forms of conflict in Wat Chonglom, Ard-am and Soonthorndhada concluded that overall, "relationships are quite harmonious for most of the time" (1997, 47). As suggested by Evans (1997b) and others (Woolcock 1997), a major reason for the harmony is the cumulatively expanding social capital made possible by the very successes in the community improvement projects. With the initial harmony in the community providing an underlying social fabric for the community to organize and launch projects, the sense of efficacy gained through the projects transformed this cooperative spirit into a self-expanding problem-solving dynamic.

Research in Wat Chonglom shows that in comparison with a community in the same area that had not made improvements, the share of households participating in direct environmental-management activities is higher, with as many as two-thirds of all households saying they had joined in most activities in Wat Chonglom (Ard-am 1998). In addition to the walkway construction and community cleanup drive, these activities included clearing drains, making repairs, collecting garbage, helping in the construction of community buildings, and participating in festivals and events such as funerals. The importance of this higher level of community cooperation cannot be underestimated, for it is at this level of institution building that many of the most common problems, particularly that of the "free riders," or nonparticipating households who benefit from the work of others, are minimized through combinations of heightened awareness and enthusiasm, as well as social pressure on nonconforming members.

Community Leadership

Community leadership is crucial in mediating conflicts and adjudicating disputes. In Wat Chonglom, resolving disagreements and reducing conflict depends in good measure on the quality of and respect earned by the elected community leader and the willingness of community members to use his office for conflict resolution. In Wat Chonglom, as in urban Thailand as a whole, leaders are selected from within and by the community. They receive no official government status or pay. Where leaders enjoy popular community support, they can be quite effective in independently working with community members to solve problems without overt government control. Unfortunately, such leadership does not easily emerge from communities, and most slums in Bangkok lack leaders with broad community support.[13] The ability of Wat Chonglom to overcome rivalries among potential leaders and choose a man with a high degree of trust and respect is surely one of its special advantages.[14]

With leadership in Wat Chonglom established around the community chairman, over a short space of time it evolved into a more broad-based structure that included the setting up of a number of committees, starting with the Community Committee (Central Committee) and followed by a number of subcommittees, including the Child Care and Community Center Committee, Savings Cooperative Committee, Community Educational Fund Committee, Community Cleaning Committee, and other ad hoc committees formed around specific projects or problems such as flood control. Each normally holds a monthly meeting. The entire community is represented in the Central Committee, which consists of elected and volunteer members, both men and women. Over time the number of female members has increased. About half of the members of the Savings Cooperative Committee are women.[15]

In urban Korea, including Wolgoksa-dong, community organization and leadership are dominated by government. Following Japanese colonial administrative arrangements, urban communities are organized into subunits of neighborhoods that are expected to meet on a monthly basis and report to government about community affairs. These subunits exist principally to relay information from government to citizens rather than from citizens to government. Therefore, more authentic community leaders and activists emerge from other quarters, such as Christian churches. Since the reforms in Korea beginning in 1987, which brought the promise of more inclusive governance, the emergence of internal leadership functions in Wolgoksa-dong has been supplanted by the creation of the government-run office to oversee community development. Reflecting the continuing top-down nature of community organization, fewer than 10 percent of the residents claim to be involved in them (Kim and Jun 1994). While such groups as "Our Village Development Promotion Committee," "Decent Living Committee," and "Environment and Women's Committee" exist, the results of their activities have been minimal (Kim and Jun 1994, 36).

In sum, the capacities to build and expand on social capital from within the two communities under discussion differ significantly at various levels of social organization and relationships. In general, the comparisons suggest that the Wat Chonglom community was much better positioned than Wolgoksa-dong—and the vast majority of other slum communities in Bangkok— to expand its social capital and use it in the pursuit of livability. Table 2.1 summarizes the characteristics of the two communities as they have appeared at each level. None of the levels in the table should be seen as autonomous or subject to improvement in isolation of the others; changes in these communities rely on complex interdependencies among the different levels. The strength of social networks within a community is, for example, intricately related to household structure, gender roles, and the existence of leadership functions.

Relations with Intermediary Organizations

Just as the effects of different levels of social organization within each of the two communities are interdependent, likewise the communities' internal dynamics depend on, but also shape, external linkages to intermediary organizations and the state. Nongovernment sources of outside support that mediate between the community and the larger state–corporate economy nexus of power (Friedmann 1992) have come to play crucial roles in community mobilization (Chan 1986). In Asia as elsewhere, intermediary organizations have played a key role in terms of advocating for the rights of the poor in, for example, squatter evictions.

The actual roles played by intermediary organizations are, however, diverse. Much depends, first, on whether the state allows autonomous nongovernment organizations (NGOs) and similar organizations to exist. Even where intermediaries have autonomy and appear in large numbers, as in Thailand, they can operate in a manner that disempowers communities (Lee 1992). That is, they can supplant community leadership with their own offices and authority rather than facilitate the

TABLE 2.1

CAPACITY FOR SOCIAL CAPITAL FORMATION:
WOLGOKSA-DONG AND WAT CHONGLOM

Level / Relation	Wolgoksa-dong	Wat Chonglom
Household	Many husbands and wives work outside the community; small families with out-migration of younger members suggest somewhat limited capacity to engage in community-building activities.	Many women earn incomes at or near the home. Nuclear families of four to five members prevail, with intergenerational households as well, suggesting a relatively high potential for mobilization for community programs.
Gender	Women have voice in household matters but are not well represented in higher levels of decision making outside the community.	Compared to many Asian countries, women have greater access to positions of decision-making authority at all levels, including government.
Social networks	Networks limited in practice to neighborhood level and community religious associations.	Networks active throughout the community at the neighborhood and community level, particularly after the success of the initial walkway-improvement project.
Community composition / stability	Community homogeneous and relatively stable; cleavages emerging between residents granted land tenure and residents still classified as squatters, with high sense of insecurity among squatters.	Community well established, homogeneous, and stable in population composition. Location on rented land with long-term agreement with landlord provides high perception of stability.
Community organization / leadership	Leadership emerges from community Christian church to mobilize against state's treatment of squatter settlement. Government substitutes for leadership from within the community.	Leadership structure resolved in the early 1990s, resulting in visible community leadership autonomous from the state. Now organized into several committees, with women taking many leadership positions.

SOURCE: Ard-am and Soonthorndhada 1997; Kim and Hee 1996; Lee 1993; Douglass and Zoghlin 1994; Douglass 1998a.

emergence and practice of community leadership. In Asia's cities there are still very few NGOs that both are empowering and have environmental management in slum communities on their agenda. Nonetheless, intermediary organizations can play an important catalytic role, and despite the differences between Seoul and Bangkok with regard to the role of NGOs, intermediary organizations have had an important effect on the dynamics of change in both Wolgoksa-dong and Wat Chonglom.

Intermediaries in Seoul and Wolgoksa-dong

In Korea at least up to the late 1980s, genuine grassroots citizen organizations had to take on certain characteristics: since government saw their agendas as threatening and labeled them communistic, they had to be secretive and remain underground, taking action principally through spontaneous confrontations of state policies and actions. These were, in Castells's terms, forms of resistance to domination rather than socially transformative projects (Castells 1997). The first mass-based environmental organization appeared only in the late 1980s, concurrent with the intensifying movement for democratic reforms. With the "Great Uprising" that ended the Chun regime in 1987, the scope for participation of the broader urban middle class was suddenly enlarged (Lee 1995). Democracy, social justice (in this case poverty related), and environmental intermediaries emerged in parallel but separate channels. Each had a similar growth pattern: suppression by the government and association with churches and universities in the 1970s and 1980s, followed by mass organizations appearing in the late 1980s with democratization. Democracy movements were wrapped around issues of civic and human rights; social justice and poverty groups tended to focus on housing rights and the support of squatters and renters facing eviction for urban land-development schemes.

Universities and churches were the centers for the emergence of a fledgling environmental movement as early as the 1960s (Kim and Jun 1994). In 1988 key environmental groups merged and substantially broadened the base of their movement under the Korea Anti-Pollution Movement Association (KAPMA). New freedoms gained through democracy movements allowed the press to quickly disseminate reports about environmental scandals, and the focus of the environmental movement shifted along with each new crisis.[16] Successes by organizations in one of these three areas of focus—democratic reform, social justice, and environmental improvement—tended to empower those in the other two, but although consolidation of intermediaries became a significant trend in the 1990s, the three have remained distinct.

Intermediary organizations also appeared to support squatter communities and followed a similar pattern of centering on churches. State suppression of such organizations was pervasive from the 1960s to the end of the 1980s. As the Korean NGOs and CBOs Forum for Habitat II put it at the Habitat II conference in 1996:

> The anti-communist stance has been employed as a weapon against opposing opinions and all forms of citizen action not directly instigated by the government. . . . This has engendered a sense among many government officials and ordinary citizens that opposition to government policy is a threat to the political and economic system. For example, an official of the Korean National Housing Authority claimed in 1988 that allowing renters a right to participate in decisions on urban redevelopment projects would be contrary to the capitalist system (KNCFH 1996, 22).

By the 1990s, housing rights and social justice groups had arisen from secular sources as well. With the direct election of local governments in 1995, a new era of intermediary organizations emerging from civil society seemed to have arrived.

In Wolgoksa-dong, as in other slum communities, religious organizations were key intermediary organizations. Of the several Christian churches in Wolgoksa-dong, the Dongwol Church emerged as the largest in terms of membership. Established in 1977 at the peak of the community's resistance to eviction, the church also began to provide community services, which included building a playground and day-care center and sponsoring night schools for youths. But in 1992 the government declared the church to have been constructed without proper building permits and slated it for demolition (Lee 1993). A community-wide petition was signed and presented to the district office, which eventually reversed its decision. The celebration party in the community gave rise to the formation of a Community Development Association, but as reported by Kim and Jun (1996), it has remained relatively dormant, with only a small number of active members.

Overall, advocacy by noncommunity intermediaries has had mixed success. While Dongwol Church did help to secure the existence of the community through citywide protest movements, for example, the fact remains that religious organizations are vulnerable to state controls, and because they are not community organizations per se, they are ultimately autonomous from any given community. Churches of different denominations are known to split along ideological lines in the community, with reported intense condemnation of one by the other. What's more, when the minister of Dongwol Church switched his efforts from community development to labor organizing in the early 1990s, he effectively brought an end both to the role of his church in supporting the Wolgoksa-dong community and to much of the community solidarity that it had generated.

The community has thus found itself continuously returned to state-controlled organizations. Not surprisingly, a survey of residents found most of them declaring that government rather than community residents should be responsible for improving the quality of community infrastructure and, to a lesser extent, housing. They also expressed the view that they had no means or power to make the government act favorably toward the community (Lee 1993).

Intermediaries in Bangkok and Wat Chonglom

The Bangkok experience again contrasts with that of Seoul. NGOs historically have existed in larger numbers in Thailand than in Korea, and they are very active in slums and on poverty issues (TEI [Thailand Environment Institute] 1995; Yok-shiu Lee 1998). Government agencies regularly include representatives of independent intermediary organizations in public meetings, though they are kept to an advisory role. However, as with Korea, environmental organizations generally operate at a citywide or national scale and do not work directly with slum settlements; those NGOs that do work directly with slums and on poverty issues do not generally have an environmental-management orientation.

The 1973–1976 democratic period is often pointed to as the time during which support by NGOs for slum communities first went beyond land rights and anti-eviction concerns to include rights to public services and community infrastructure (Boonyabancha et al. 1988). By 1986 at least fifty NGOs that focused on slum issues were formally registered with the government (Yok-shiu Lee 1998). They included social welfare, community development, and slum-dweller anti-eviction associations. Surveys in the early 1990s, however, show that fewer than three hundred out of fifteen hundred slum communities had worked with any of these NGOs (Kaothien 1994). Most NGO programs have been arranged for a few communities rather than on a citywide basis. Major programs have been initiated by political parties, which have been able to draw upon government financial resources. But because of their origins in rival parties, coordination among these programs is absent, as are linkages with community organizations (Yok-shiu Lee 1998). Thus, while many NGOs exist in Thailand, attention to slum problems remains sporadic and piecemeal. As in Korea, most attention continues to focus on housing tenure and protests against evictions rather than on community environmental upgrading.

In the case of Wat Chonglom, two Mahidol University faculty members were the catalysts for community mobilization. Perhaps in recognition of the state-community context in Thailand, the university-based organizers who worked with the people of Wat Chonglom explicitly formulated their approach as one of self-reliance and expected little or no involvement from the state. They arranged the possibility of a $50,000 interest-free loan from Citibank for community improvements, with the stipulation that, in addition to setting loan repayment schedules, the community organize itself and set its own priorities. All the other slum communities approached by the two faculty members found the idea of collectively taking on external obligations to be threatening and lacked confidence that they could actually make effective use of the money or repay it on schedule. Wat Chonglom was different.[17] After some reluctance, arising from suspicion of the outsiders' intentions and from problems among rival community leaders, the community made the decision to accept a loan, with the first project being a massive cleanup of the land under its walkways and the subsequent construction of safe cement lanes throughout the community. Households and hired labor joined in the project. Soon all the 624 meters of lanes in the community were paved. By hiring prison inmates, a community-wide cleanup of garbage and trash that had been accumulating for a decade or more was also carried out.

Several other NGOs that have been involved in the community in recent years, which include Sikka Asia Foundation, YMCA, Foster Parents, and Urban Community Development Foundation, bring their own focus and agenda to the community. None has had an environmental-management orientation, though some of the education programs include health-related information about environmental risks (Ard-am and Soonthorndhada 1997). The combined presence of so many intermediary organizations does, however, offer Wat Chonglom a much higher potential for the translation of community energies into community improvement programs than has been the case to date in Wolgoksa-dong.

One of the most promising initiatives involving intermediaries, communities, and the government in Thailand was the inauguration of the Urban Community Development Office (UCDO) in 1992. Established by the government with a $50 million fund, it is designed to be a "nongovernmental government agency" that, although government-sponsored and under the National Housing Authority (NHA), is "semi-autonomous" in its decision making (Yok-shiu Lee 1998, 1000). Its semiautonomy derives from the composition of its board of directors, which consists of representatives from government and citizen organizations, including community groups. Its staff includes former NGO workers, who occupy its highest levels of decision making.

UCDO and its activities have been well received as a platform for generating positive community-state synergies by many community development activists in Thailand, and if financial resources alone could guarantee the kind of success that Wat Chonglom achieved, this new initiative would result in a thousand Wat Chongloms. Unfortunately, as the previous section has shown, the ability of new resources to serve as a catalyst depends on a complex combination of social factors internal to the community. Empowering initiatives by intermediary organizations can help, but unless the infusion of new resources is coupled with the construction of internal social capital, a genuine transformation is unlikely.

Community-State Relations

A core theme of Evans's discourse on livable cities (see chapter 8) is that to transform social capital into a sustainable source of livability, the state must become an active partner with community organizations. Others have similarly argued that state-community partnerships are likely to be more fruitful than either state or community efforts alone, and that cooperation among households is insufficient to the task of empowering the poor (Friedmann 1992; Douglass 1998b; Hardoy and Satterthwaite 1989). Local governments are particularly crucial in this equation. Cairncross, Hardoy, and Satterthwaite (1990), for example, claim that a precondition for reversing the deterioration of the urban habitat and poverty is the establishment of elected city and municipal authorities. Similarly, Friedmann (1992, 79) argues that "new ground rules for state-community partnerships" will have to be drawn to include "new roles for the local state, the democratization of the local state, the representative organization of the local community, and the opening up of a new political terrain in the regional and local spaces."

Despite democratization, these positive possibilities for community-state relations are yet to be realized in most of Pacific Asia. Both national and local governments in Asia have remained elitist, tied to corporate and military interests, and they continue to deal with urban issues as technical rather than deeply political questions. Local governments remain exceptionally weak in terms of delegated authority, competence of staff, and autonomous sources of financing. Citizen and state are further alienated when the citizen in question lives in a slum or squatter settlement. When state and corporate interests combine to promote real estate development in Asia's hyperdeveloped big cities, governments target "illegal" squatter communities not for improvement but for demolition (see chapter 3).

Korea and Thailand represent very different patterns of community-state relations, but neither approaches the ideal of "state-community synergy." Democratization and having elected officials have brought a higher level of state support for low-income communities in both countries. Yet the state in Thailand remains aloof and ineffectual when it comes to the problems of the urban poor, and community-state relations in Korea continue to be haunted by the legacies of repressive government.

Community and State in Seoul and Wolgoksa-dong

After decades of severe repression of civil society under regimes drawn from regionally based factions of the military, the Korean state apparatus was put in the hands of an elected civilian government in a multiparty system for the first time less than a decade ago. Yet the legacy of repression lingers: Even following the "democratic" 1990s, scandals of enormous proportions continue to surface in the new century, and people remain suspicious of the workings of government, with a feeling that although democratic structures are in place, state-business collusion is still high and the once-presumed moral authority of the state is still in doubt. Citizens continue to show a readiness to take direct action in the streets when a new outrage appears.

Government policy toward squatters and slum communities in Korea reflected the general character of a state apparatus that expanded during a quarter century of military rule (1961–1987) to directly control Korea's space-economy and political process. It was also part of one of the most thorough sets of urban land-use controls in the world (Kim 1995). Unlike in Thailand, a vast techno-bureaucracy that served to legitimate state autonomy from business and other elites was created in Korea and given substantial authority to implement these policies.

In Seoul, local government followed central government policies in the pre-1987 period, but in more recent years, as revenues from such sources as automobile registration have increased its budget, it has become a significant source of infrastructure improvements on its own. Similarly, authentic partnerships between citizens and local government were not fostered under the system of centrally appointed mayors. That system changed in 1995, when local governments were elected for the first time in Korean history, bringing accountability of government to the local level. With this change still so new, however, it would be premature to judge local governments' potential for collaborating with, rather than planning for, low-income communities.

As democratic rights were expanded, the government made new investments in housing and urban services, which were crowned in 1989 by a massive state-sponsored program providing 2 million housing units to Seoul residents; construction was completed in the early 1990s (Douglass 1998a). The housing was built for Seoul's growing middle class, but as part of the new attention toward responding to urban concerns, significant numbers of squatters were given land titles. In 1983 the "Hapdong" (cooperative redevelopment) program was launched by the government to convert slums into modern apartment complexes, but only landowners were eligible to live in the new units. This and related policies resulted in the majority of renters and squatters being evicted, with only an estimated 10 to 20 percent of the original residents able to remain in redeveloped communities (Lee 1993). Remaining squatter settlements continued with their struggles, which were highly dependent upon wider social movements for political reform.

A new policy of "residential environmental improvements" was put forth in 1989, with the purpose of providing roads, water, and sewerage to communities that otherwise did not qualify for redevelopment (Lee 1993). This appeared to be a radical departure by the government. Relaxing regulations seemed to implicitly give rights of residence to squatters and allowed communities the use of public land. The policy of the early 1990s became one of resettlement of low-income households into public housing, but eligibility requirements continued to disqualify large numbers of potential candidate families. In 1996, Korean NGO delegates to Habitat II continued to protest forced evictions, saying, "Forced evictions are inhuman, a threat to life and mental stability. Despite the

change to a civilian government, cruel forced evictions continue"
(KNCFH 1996, 7).

As already indicated, the relationship of Wolgoksa-dong to the state
is typical of poor communities in Seoul. Just as they are victims of the
state's continued repressive relationship to poor communities, they are
also beneficiaries of the state apparatus's relative effectiveness at delivering services and infrastructure. They enjoy the community hall, child-
care facility, playground, park, and public latrines, but many of them
live in fear of eviction and are consequently reluctant to make investments of their own to promote livability.

Community and State in Thailand and Wat Chonglom

Thailand has not had the degree of state-citizen confrontation that has
historically prevailed in Korea. Ever since the 1973–1976 democracy
period, Thailand has enjoyed a wide array of civic freedoms, particularly
those of free speech and the right to form NGOs—including community-
level organizations—focused on a variety of concerns. Although the
state has often been the target of these organizations, many have existed
and carried on programs in a nonconfrontational manner independent
of government. This has allowed communities to organize and to link
with intermediary organizations on a much broader scale than was the
case in Korea before 1987. In that sense, the successes and failures of
communities to improve themselves in Bangkok are also expressions of
the contributions and limitations of social capital formation in civil society without strong community-state synergies.

The situation of local governments is slightly more complex and, to
some extent, less promising in Thailand than in Korea. In the specific
case of Wat Chonglom's improvement, the locally elected representatives
to the national government have delivered more to the community than
has the Bangkok Metropolitan Administration (BMA). Neither central
nor local government can be said to facilitate community development.
As concluded by Ard-am and Soonthorndhada (1997), the interaction
of communities and government in policy and planning at all levels,
particularly with regard to slum settlements and environmental management, is minimal. Government remains highly centralized, responsible agencies are understaffed, legal frameworks are not clear, and the
connection between poverty and the environment is not being made
among government bureaus.

By neither launching anti-slum drives nor providing significant assistance to slum dwellers, the state has remained aloof from a process of slum formation that involves more than a million of Bangkok's inhabitants. Although the Thai government established organizations such as the NHA to carry out major slum-improvement programs, these programs have actually reached very few households. In the same period that the Korean government was building millions of subsidized housing units in Seoul, only a few hundred low-cost walk-up apartments were built with government assistance in Bangkok. The overall evaluation of these programs in Thailand concluded that they were ineffective in reaching the poor (UNESCAP 1993).

In 1983 NHA switched from slum upgrading to the relocation of slum households to fringe areas. The change in policy was immediately translated into action. From a level of twenty-one slums in 1983, which was the peak of NHA's slum upgrading activities, only three slum communities, totaling 630 households, were receiving NHA assistance by 1991 (Yok-shiu Lee 1998). During the entire 1978–1991 period, while NHA was ineffectively trying to upgrade about 130 slums, NGOs are reported to have assisted almost 300 slum communities (Yap 1992). Given that government programs cover only a fraction of housing needs and the private housing sector avoids providing affordable housing for low-income households, slum dwellers are implicitly expected by the housing-delivery system to build and improve their own housing. Most are not able to do so, and in the context of a state that has not developed the apparatus to deal with the manifold problems of rapid urbanization, slums have proliferated.

Unrepentant corruption, factionalism within the military, and government inability to address serious urban management issues came to a head in 1992, when popular protest in Bangkok, with the quiet backing of the king, displaced military rule for the second time in post–World War II history. Civilian governments were elected and a multiparty system came to life. But the continued factionalization of the party system led to equally unsustained commitments to policies and their implementation. As a result, the state remains weak and inconsistent in its urban programs, and these characteristics carry on into state-community relations.

Yet there are benefits from having elected governments. In Wat Chonglom, the election process has brought electricity and other amenities to its households. City garbage collection has also improved in the area. As previously mentioned, however, the location of the community on private land prohibited the state, through its own regulations, from carrying out housing and other improvement schemes. For example, Wat Chonglom was denied its requests for assistance to install a water system for fire prevention and to build a drainage system, even when the community volunteered to share in the costs of construction.

A *Summary of Contrasting Community-State Relations*

The contrasting dynamics of state-community relations in Korea and Thailand have created different potential pathways for community improvement. Whereas the Seoul experience has been essentially one of citizens compelling the state to be more supportive over time and to take on community improvement programs, the Bangkok experience has been one in which communities have been freer to organize autonomously and initiate self-improvement but lack effective state support.

In both societies the 1990s witnessed the emergence of new relations between civil society and the state marked by a widening scope of democratization and decentralization of state power. While it is too soon to clearly anticipate the fuller implications of these changes—especially since they may be partially negated by the economic effects of the financial crises of the late 1990s—one outcome seems irreversible: no matter how dire the economy or how imperfect the democratic process, promising economic growth or recovery is no longer an acceptable apology for keeping citizens excluded from the processes of governance. What is much less clear is whether these new norms are sufficient to create the kind of state-community synergy necessary to actually move poor communities in the direction of greater livability.

Table 2.2 summarizes the dimensions of community-state relations in Seoul and Bangkok with particular reference to the situations of Wolgoksa-dong and Wat Chonglom.

Conclusions: Self-Reliant vs. Dependent Pathways to State-Community Synergy

In building on the concept of social capital, Evans (1997b) argues that not just civil society alone but rather mutually supportive state-society synergies underlie the capacity for economic development. He further proposes that when the state facilitates and builds upon a storehouse of social capital, it also increases its own capacities and power through inclusive forms of governance. In demonstrating that the state has its

TABLE 2.2
COMMUNITY-STATE RELATIONS
IN SEOUL AND BANGKOK

Relation	Seoul	Bangkok
Citizen-state	Pre-1987 reforms: strict limitations on freedom of speech and civic rights. Post-1987 reforms: democratization with civilian government and multiparty system.	Broad freedoms of speech and assembly since 1970s. Civilian control of government sporadic since 1940s, with key periods being 1973–1976 and since 1992; fragmented, personality-based political parties with limited parliamentary powers.
Community-state	Pre-1987 reforms: general policy of squatter community eradication; politics of direct confrontation prevail. Post-1987 reforms: community betterment agencies set up by state with little community participation. Tenant and squatter evictions continue.	Community leadership chosen from within slums; government agencies interact with community leaders and organizations on a limited basis but do not provide significant public resources for slum improvement.
Local government–state	Elected local government only since 1995; powers of local government limited.	Elected municipal governments with limited powers since 1980s. Provincial governors are appointed. State slum-community improvements enacted through local members of parliament and National Housing Authority.
Community-landlord (security of land occupancy)	Wolgoksa-dong squatter community history one of extreme insecurity. Government began to give land rights in 1980s, but skepticism about the future prevails among many, with deep schism in community between landowners, many now absentee, and renters.	Wat Chonglom sited on privately owned land with low rent negotiated with landlord. Poor potential for commercial development contributes to residents' perception of long-term security. No possibility of residents owning land in community currently exists, but most residents own their houses.

Continued on next page

TABLE 2.2 *(continued)*

Relation	Seoul	Bangkok
Intermediary organizations and the state	Pre-1987 reforms: unions organize in major male-dominated manufacturing sectors, but intermediary organizations are limited. Religious institutions and universities take on NGO roles. Post-1987 reforms: flowering of intermediary organizations, but NGOs focused on environment and democratic reform are weakly connected to poor communities.	Large numbers of autonomous NGOs, community-based organizations, and other intermediaries have emerged since 1970s. Few, however, have taken on issues of environmental-infrastructure or -management issues in slum communities. More than five NGOs are active in Wat Chonglom.
Community improvement programs– state	Pre-1987 reforms: government assistance to squatter communities limited but increasing. Post-1987 reforms: state programs continue, with residents generally expecting government to provide services and infrastructure.	Wat Chonglom not qualified for government assistance. Infrastructure awarded on ad hoc basis to slums through political patronage channels. Wat Chonglom's improvements initiated without government participation.

SOURCE: Ard-am and Soonthorndhada 1997; Kim and Hee 1996; Lee 1993; Douglass and Zogh-lin 1994; Douglass 1998a.

own incentives to empower civil society, he thus proposes the possibility of a virtuous state–civil society synergy that, through time, can generate a cumulatively reinforcing expansion of societal capacity to address and resolve shared problems.

Social capital and state–civil society synergy concepts are by themselves too blunt to readily anticipate solutions to specific social problems, and in many ways the question of how to create livable cities poses more daunting challenges to both concepts than did questions of economic growth. Not only has the deterioration of the urban habitat gone far beyond the range of simple remedies in most countries, but theories of social mobilization around issues of the urban environment are much less advanced than those of economic development or natural resource management (Hardoy, Mitlin, and Satterthwaite 1992).

The question of how to relate environmental sustainability to poverty alleviation, which is the specific focus here, greatly complicates inquiry into discussions of social capital and related state-community synergy. Social mobilization for citywide environmental improvements must be analyzed in the context of widening social cleavages manifested in the rise of the urban middle class, the proletarianization of low-income workers largely drawn from rural areas, and the creation of vast environmentally degraded subaltern communities with little political voice. Much of the nascent environmental movement in Asia's cities is a middle-class phenomenon that, in supporting slum clearances and pushing unwanted environmental infrastructure such as landfill sites to less politically powerful communities, is often antagonistic to the interests of the poor (see chapter 3).

There are also limitations in referring to the community as a single, undifferentiated social unit, since to do so would ignore conflict within communities and neglect consideration of the household, which is the most basic arena for social capital formation and the foundation for what Friedmann (1992) calls "the whole economy." Finally, both social capital and state-community synergy concepts have largely treated society in a nonspatial manner, thus leaving out the critical role of constructing urban space through investments in the built environment, which generate social capital through cooperative engagement and make communities livable. This kind of investment is exactly the opposite of the sort of "growth machine / world city" pattern of development that dominates the evolution of the built environment in most Asian cities. When social cleavages, internal community divisions, and the trajectory of the built environment are all taken into account, it is clear that positive state-society synergies leading to greater livability in low-income urban communities constitute only one possible historical trajectory.

Implicit in Evans's argument on livable cities (see chapter 8) is the idea that simultaneous movement along two key dimensions is required for genuine state-community synergy to occur and cumulatively advance. The first can be summarized as democratic processes, which include an elected, accountable government; guarantees of individual liberties; civic rights to organize and form communities of association outside of the state; transparent governmental decision-making processes; legally protected rights of appeal; and due process in such matters as evictions. The second is community access to public resources and support, including financial and material support for constructing houses, environmental infrastructure and basic amenities, and the linking of community needs, such as solid-waste collection, to citywide public systems of urban management.

Progress along one dimension without progress along the other cannot be said to be moving toward state-community synergy, or "state-community partnerships," as they are termed in international-aid circles. Having the political room to organize without state support allows for a community to move toward a self-reliant mode of development, which can include support from nongovernment organizations. In contrast, having state support but no voice in directing that support leads to a community improvement pathway dependent on state decision making and resources. Neither can be said to be a process characterized by state-community synergy.

The least desirable situation is one in which communities are without civil liberties and the state is explicitly antagonistic to the existence of the urban poor and their settlements. This is represented in the lower left quadrant (I) in Figure 2.1, labeled "Regressive." The as yet unrealized goal is a situation in which communities enjoy the political guarantees and openness necessary to organize and at the same time can count on effective material and administrative support from government, which, in principle, acts in the name of the people. This is represented in the upper right quadrant (IV), labeled "Community-State Synergy."

When the trajectories of Wolgoksa-dong and Wat Chonglom are superimposed on the quadrants of Figure 2.1, it is clear that while both communities seem to be moving toward a more synergistic relation with the state, their pathways in this direction are distinct.

In the first decade of its existence, Wolgoksa-dong found itself in the most adverse situation (I), with an extremely repressive, nondemocratic political system and a government that sought to eradicate rather than assist low-income (squatter) communities. Its survival as a community was a matter of direct confrontation rather than cooperation with the state. The trajectory of Korean reform in the 1980s moved Wolgoksa-dong from the most regressive realm into one of dependence on the state for improvements (III). Community organizations did not emerge as major sources of collective action, and government took the responsibility for providing basic amenities such as shared washing areas and latrines. In sum, community improvements were achieved through a combination of confrontation with and dependence on the state, rather than through collaborative state-community synergies.

For Bangkok, from the rapid growth of slums beginning in the 1960s

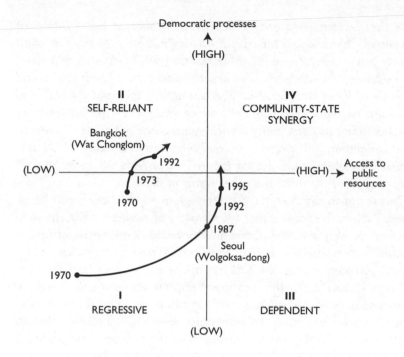

Figure 2.1.   Changing state-community relations in Wolgoksa-dong and Wat Chonglom.

I.   *Regressive:* politically repressive, anti-slum and -squatter policies prevail; extremely limited possibilities for community improvement.

II.   *Self-Reliant:* moderate to high civic rights but little or no access to state resources.

III.   *Dependent:* authoritarian/repressive state, but modest public resources are provided; little or no community-based planning.

IV.   *Community-State Synergy:* high level of citizen rights/democratic practices and high access by (low-income) communities to public support and resources.

on through the 1980s, the trajectory was toward greater self-reliance. Wat Chonglom, formed in the 1970s on privately owned land, was expected to manage its housing and community needs without government support. Thailand was a more open polity than Korea, and the government did not actively try to remove slum settlements on a large scale. However, government support for slum communities was minimal and generally ineffectual. Consequently, slums moved into a self-reliant mode (II) in which they had wide latitude to carry out their own projects without substantial government interference or effective assistance.

While it was successful beyond expectations in the special case of Wat Chonglom, attempts to follow the self-reliant model in other slum communities revealed the model's limitations. Most communities did not have the internal conditions—security of tenure, a composition of households that allowed for critical divisions of labor to support community investment, strong interhousehold networks, trusted and effective leadership—to undertake construction and management projects on the scale of those completed in Wat Chonglom. External support also could not be replicated: Citibank, which produced a public-relations video extolling its community involvement, chose not to offer loans to other communities. University activists who had devoted so much time to Wat Chonglom could not by themselves provide the same level of involvement for the thousand other slums in the city.

This is not to say that the Wat Chonglom experience should be ignored. Rather, the point is that for a variety of reasons, when the state is not proactively involved in community-based development efforts, it is difficult to translate a particular self-organized local success into a general program for an entire metropolitan region. As many theorists and activists involved in the question of poverty alleviation have argued, if improvement of low-income communities is to occur at the scale at which the problems exist, the state must be brought into the effort to create a strong and positive state-community collaborative planning process.

Looking toward the future, in the case of Bangkok a move into the state-community synergy realm (IV) would require a substantial enhancement of the state's capacity to respond to the manifold problems that are arising with the urban transition now peaking in Thailand. As a source of planning and urban management, the Thai state continues to be weak and has shown a limited ability to work with slum settlements. There have been improvements over the past decades in terms of electrification, flood control, and piped water, but environmental infrastructure and services remain very low for the nation at its level of per capita income (UNESCAP 1993). Local government remains exceptionally weak as well.

Significant advance has, however, been registered in the realm of democratization and citizen rights in Thailand, particularly since 1992. Increased political openness in the context of a state relatively unengaged in planning suggests that for Bangkok, the most likely trajectory for the near future is a continuation of modes of self-reliance in community development. If so, most communities will continue to exhibit serious deficits in capacities to mobilize households and resources to launch a Wat Chonglom–like process of self-reliant improvement. Extending the Bangkok metropolitan region's population growth rates of the recent past into the future under these conditions further suggests a continued expansion of its geography of poverty and environmental deterioration. With the metropolis also suffering from severe air, water, and land pollution and tremendous gaps in environmental infrastructure and services, such a future would move Bangkok even further from the ideal of a convivial, livable urban habitat.

Changes in the Seoul context might offer somewhat different future possibilities. Fundamental political reforms since the late 1980s, though still incomplete in practice, have substantially widened the potential for communities to organize and intermediary organizations to flourish. The national and Seoul city governments continue to have much higher capacities for and involvement in urban planning than do their Thai counterparts. Creating positive state-community synergies might therefore be more of a possibility in Seoul than in Bangkok. But the distance is still great in the case of squatter and other low-income communities.

In either case, Figure 2.1 presents at least two hopeful but uncertain trajectories for the urban poor. In their own ways, both Wat Chonglom and Wolgoksa-dong have shown, over the past decades, an admirable vitality and resilience in the face of highly adverse political and economic forces. There is every reason to believe that these communities, and others, will continue to exhibit the same vitality and resilience in the future.

Many of the key political elements for moving from self-reliant and dependent modes of action into an era of state-community synergy are now in place, but a number of macrolevel trends could work against the realization of hopeful trajectories. These include globalization, which has brought deep structural change and devastating financial crises to Asian economies, expanding urban class divisions and prompting new class struggles over the built environment. One thing is certain: the issues arising from the interplay of urban poverty and environmental degradation will continue to defy single-factor models and generic solutions.

Notes

1. In Jakarta, for example, more than 80 percent of the current housing stock was built by low-income households without either government assistance or the participation of private-sector housing developers (Douglass and Lee 1996).

2. Research on the communities in Bangkok and Seoul is part of a seven-city study in Asia on urban poverty and environmental management. The other cities are Bombay, India; Colombo, Sri Lanka; Bandung, Indonesia; Hong Kong; and Manila, Philippines. See *AJEM (Asian Journal of Environmental Management)* 1994 and Douglass 1997.

3. The difference in estimates is not simply a matter of government policies giving land titles to squatter residents in the latter half of the 1980s, but is more likely an artifact of criteria used and the lack of clear distinction between a "slum" and a "squatter" community. Thus, many areas that have been reclassified by government as not being squatter communities are actually mixes of households with and without land titles, and regardless of title status, many areas still have the characteristics of slums: substandard housing, limited infrastructure, inadequate public services, and poor environmental conditions. Many squatters also live in such small clusters of one to a few shacks that they are not counted at all.

4. The negative psychological effects of living in degraded slum areas were declared to be worse than the negative physical effects. For example, the inability to hang laundry out and have it remain clean while drying (because air pollution from nearby industrial areas discolors it) was seen as symptomatic of the powerlessness of the poor in alleviating the severe environmental problems in their communities. The source of this pollution is beyond their control, and yet they are relegated to living near it because of their social status and their low income.

5. Reducing ambient concentrations of key pollutants by 20 percent from current levels would reduce annual health-care expenditures in Bangkok by an estimated $400 million to $1.6 billion for illnesses related to particulates, and by $300 million to $1.5 billion for illnesses related to lead. Regarding traffic congestion, the study estimates that a 10 percent reduction in peak-hour trips, with its attendant reduction in air pollution, would provide health-related savings of about $400 million annually.

6. The initiators of the self-reliant, basic-needs approach at Wat Chonglom in 1988 were Orathai Ard-am (one of the coauthors of this chapter) and Roger Chical, both of the Institute for Population and Social Research at the Salaya campus of Mahidol University in Bangkok. Kusol Soonthorndhada subsequently joined Ard-Am to carry out community action and research activities, after the departure of Chical.

7. The center was built through combined financing from the community's first loan (arranged through Citibank by Ard-Am and Chical), the organization Foster Parents, the local member of parliament, and community funds. As of the mid-1990s, the day-care center provided about sixty children ages two to six with simple health care, meals, milk, education, and recreational facilities at a charge of five baht per day per child. The YMCA trained two young community members to manage the center (Ard-am and Chical 1993; Ard-am and Soonthorndhada 1994).

8. Every family that joins is a shareholder in the cooperative and is obliged to contribute from thirty to five hundred baht per month. Preference for loans is given to applicants seeking education or medical treatment or to satisfy short-term emergency money needs.

9. In addition, the community Cooperative Committee received an award from the National Housing Authority, which is the principal central government agency charged with slum improvement. Community leaders also received a prestigious award from the National Social Welfare Council.

10. Research in Bangkok (Ard-am and Soonthorndhada 1994; Douglass and Zoghlin 1994), Seoul (Kim and Jun 1996), and Bombay (Sengupta 1994) confirms that the degree to which environmental management tasks are routinely undertaken is significantly related to household composition and gender relations.

11. In Kanpur, India, women have formed neighborhood committees that, among other activities, locate sites for hand pumps (Sengupta 1994). In the squatter settlements of Diamond Hill and Sheung Yuen Ling Village, Hong Kong, women were found to be the principal organizers of many environment-related action groups (Chan, Chang, and Cheung 1994).

12. The proportion of those who participate in more than one environmental association is greatest among those who usually visit more than five households in the community.

13. Estimates for 1989 show that although requested by government and NGOs, less than 20 percent of Bangkok's slums had established their own community organizations (Rojpriwong 1992).

14. The leader elected in the early 1990s had been the chairperson for many periods because of his special character: he was calm, emotionally mature, and skilled at avoiding aggressive confrontations. He also exhibited a strong concern for the poorest segment of the community (Ard-am and Soonthorndhada 1997).

15. Ard-am and Soonthorndhada (1997) observe that members who usually are trusted and well-respected by the community are honest, devoted, active, modest, emotionally mature, Buddhist-oriented (or Dhamma-Dhammo), and enthusiastic. Better economic status than the others is also important, and many committee members in Wat Chonglom have finished secondary school.

16. National coverage of issues affecting everyday lives was crucial in bringing environmental issues to the forefront of politics in Korea. Content analysis of newspapers shows that from an average of fewer than five hundred environmental reports per year in the 1982–1986 period, the number doubled in 1987 to 873, and by 1992 it had risen tenfold to almost nine thousand annually (Lee 1992, 12). The *Chosun Ilbo* newspaper reported that in 1993 at least 175 groups were involved in environmental issues. In 1995 the consolidation of various environmental groups led to the foundation of the Korea Federation for Environmental Movement, which claimed twenty thousand members and twenty-one local chapters. Along with local elections, held for the first time that same year, environmental candidates won two mayoral elections. Environmental groups were also able to compel the national government to reorganize environmental planning bureaus and adopt an environmental impact assessment system. The overall result has been the adoption of stricter standards by the government, and more information is now made available to citizens about environmental conditions (Kim 1994).

17. As summarized by Ard-Am and Soonthorndhada (1994, 15), Wat Chonglom exhibited special characteristics even before the program:

> Wat Chonglom Slum was selected as a study and operational site for the Project on "Research and Development towards Self-reliance in Low-income Communities" due to its own desire to reach a better quality of life. The Project team visited about 20 slums or low-income settlements in Yannawa District. . . . Only Wat Chonglom's lead-

ers expressed their willingness to work on the project after 2-month consideration of our proposal.

The Citibank loan was interest free but required a repayment schedule amounting to only a few years. Although they were granted a grace period of three years, the community began repaying their loan immediately after each project was accomplished. Early repayment was symbolic of the community's sense of responsibility. Over the years all the money has been paid back by or even before the scheduled dates. No defaults have been reported.

Collective Action toward a Sustainable City

Citizens' Movements and Environmental Politics in Taipei

HSIN-HUANG MICHAEL HSIAO AND HWA-JEN LIU

Introduction

We begin with two stories of community mobilization in Taipei. The first is about defending living space. It involves a well-to-do middle-class community named Ching-Cheng, which indefatigably fought against the state-owned power company (Taipower), a large department store backed by overseas capital, and finally the city authorities.

From 1988 to 1989, this community faced the imminent construction of a nearby power substation. Residents found out later that the increase in demand for electricity in this district resulted mainly from a newly opened department store, which also planned to rent its basement to a brothel. Unhappy, the community's residents decided to implement a boycott. They fought the department store directly by calling it "a lousy neighbor" in the media. They protested against Taipower for selecting a site without having first informed or consulted them, but they ultimately were unable to overturn the decision. The self-organized Ching-Cheng residents were not defeated, however. In 1991 they successfully saved their community park from becoming a parking garage, and in 1992 they interrupted the municipal government's plan to change the area from a residential zone into a commercial one (Shen 1994). The case of Ching-Cheng, like many others in Taipei, stands in direct opposition to business interests and the top-down decision-making system of government. The statement that the community made was loud and clear: using economic growth to justify abusing citizen rights and the urban environment is no longer acceptable, even if it once was. The mixed success of the Ching-Cheng community over the years is the most frequently cited case of community mobilization among urban reformers and community advocates, and it has also become an exemplar for other mobilized communities in Taiwan.

The second story concerns the birth of a five-hectare city park, Nos. 14–15 Park. It illustrates the conflicting interests that can exist between the urban poor and other communities when improving the physical environment of a city as a whole is at stake. The predesignated park site was a Japanese-only cemetery under colonial rule and then was turned into one of the biggest slums in the city, the Kang-Le neighborhood, in the postwar development of Taipei.[1] Kang-Le slum was an enclave surrounded by five-star hotels and skyscrapers in one of Taipei's most prosperous areas. The graphic portrait of urban poverty and the cohabitation of living humans and the dead served only to surprise visitors and offend nearby business owners and middle-class neighbors.[2]

On March 4, 1997, despite strong opposition from urban planners and slum residents, the Taipei municipal authorities sent out bulldozers, escorted by police, and forcibly evicted thousands of slum dwellers, over one-third of whom were handicapped, aged, or extremely poor, and tore down their illegal but long tolerated shacks (Hsiao et al. 1997, 3). Overnight, 961 households and the community networks that supported their subsistence were destroyed. After the eviction, the first-ever freely and directly elected mayor of Taipei, Chen Shui-bian, proudly announced that citizens' urgent need for more green space would soon be satisfied.[3] One year later, the city administration revealed its proposal to name this park "International Plaza" and to use it to host carnivals and celebrations of such holidays as Halloween and St. Patrick's Day for foreign residents (Yang 1998). The whole process, as an example of the more vulgar side of "globalization," was praised by bureaucrats and certain media outlets as an effort to create a foreigner-friendly atmosphere and to enhance the visual presentability of the city.

These two vignettes illustrate both the successes and failures of urban environmental activism in Taiwan's capital city, Taipei. On the one hand, in the 1980s and even more in the 1990s the environmental movement epitomized mobilization from below in a society in which top-down politics had predominated since colonial times. On the other hand, community participation in this movement still reflected the inequalities of the society at large. Middle-class communities were often able to protect or even improve their quality of life, even in the face of the ecologically blind developmental programs pushed by the state and private business groups. Poor and slum communities were as likely to be the victims of the environmental movement as they were to be its beneficiaries.

This chapter attempts to chronicle the contradictory history of urban environmental activism in Taipei. We begin by describing the pattern of development to which the protesters were reacting. We then outline the varieties of community-based environmental activism during the eighties and nineties and its impact on environmental policies. Finally we return to the issue raised by the two vignettes: the relationship between sustainability and social justice.

In the first section, we trace Taipei's development from a commercial town to one of the leading cities in the Asia-Pacific region. Even though Taipei has a distinctive pattern of development in which industry and industrial pollution have never played the dominant role, we argue that the long-dominant practice of capital accumulation and a growth-oriented bureaucracy, usually admired as the midwife of Taiwan's "economic miracle," have yielded significant degradation of the urban environment. This discussion sets the stage for the central focus of the paper, which is on the environmental movements themselves and their consequences.

In the next two sections, we portray the emergence of Taipei's environmental movement against the imperatives of the market and bureaucracy and the subsequent positive governmental responses resulting from electoral competition. In the wake of Taiwan's democratization in the late 1980s, affected citizens and communities—with diverse class and ethnic backgrounds—have taken advantage of favorable political opportunities and have allied themselves with other social actors (nongovernmental organizations and political parties) to counter the negative effects of urban development and to push for a citywide sustainability agenda.

In the fourth section we identify the limitations of Taipei's environmental struggle. First, from the perspective of class division in social protest, middle-class communities, compared with poor communities, occupy a better strategic position in the bargaining process and enjoy a higher availability of resources; they therefore can achieve relatively satisfactory results. Second, environmental NGOs, mainly dominated by middle-class members, show either reluctance or indifference on the issue of the urban poor. And finally, the improvement of the urban environment sometimes takes place at the expense of the livelihood of marginalized groups, such as the urban poor and ethnic minorities.

The main purpose of our chapter is to analyze diverse environmental protests in the context of Taipei's urban growth and Taiwan's political transition toward democracy. In this way we identify the dual character of Taipei's urban environmental movement: in the name of sustainability, it empowers citizens to fight against the whim of bureaucracy and developers, but it does not properly address and respect the interest and livelihood of the urban poor. Reflecting upon the inadequacy of this dual character, we argue that the ideal of a sustainable city should not be decoupled from the realization of social justice.

Urbanization and Environmental Crises in Taipei

Every city has its own experience of environmental degradation incurred by rapid urban growth. Usually, a city starting its "developmental career" as a manufacturing center accepts the costs of industrial production: noise from mechanization, soil and water pollution, harmful fumes, and damage to the landscape beyond remedy (Mumford 1989, 458–74). Even if the rise of a service economy and the reduction in manufacturing gradually cause change in the industrial structure in the later stages of urban development, early industrial pollution has already left permanent scars on the urban landscape. Classic industrial cities such as Detroit and Manchester have paid for their unsustainable land use by falling in the world city hierarchy and finding themselves incapable of reviving their economic prominence even with enormous reinvestment (Friedmann 1997). But that has not been the case with Taipei.

In contrast to another major metropolis in southern Taiwan, Kaohsiung, Taipei has suffered relatively little harm from extensive industrial pollution because, over the past hundred years, Taipei never developed into a manufacturing city. Industrial products accounted for 88.7 percent of the total products manufactured in Taipei between 1938 and 1940, but they came from the relatively nonpolluting sectors of food and tea processing and rice milling. In fact, in the fifty years of Japanese colonial rule (1895–1945), aside from its political function as the colony's capital city, Taipei served as only a light industrial center, processing and exporting agricultural products to boost the Japanese economy (Chiang and Hsiao 1985, 194).

When the Kuomintang (KMT) took over Taiwan in 1945, 75 percent of the industrial infrastructure had been destroyed as a result of World War II, and the engine of industrialization had to be restarted (Huang 1983, 489). In contrast to the exporting of agricultural commodities under colonial rule, the pattern of industrial development was shaped by ISI (import-substituting industrialization) in the 1950s and EOI (export-oriented industrialization) between 1960 and 1972, then shifted to the second ISI and second EOI strategies from 1973 onward (Gereffi 1990, 17–18; Haggard 1990, chapter 4). Along the path of development, the picture of the domestic economy dramatically changed. The drastic decline of the agricultural sector mirrored the significant expansion of the industrial sector, and nationwide environmental degradation has in general been triggered by the growth of certain industries, namely steel and petrochemicals, that were encouraged by state sponsorship during the second ISI phase. While the coastal areas and cities of west and south Taiwan have suffered greatly from these two environmentally devastating industries, however, Taipei has been spared.[4]

If Taipei has benefited from the absence of extensive industrial pollution, then what is damaging Taipei's eco-social system? It is fair to say that the single-minded pursuit of economic prosperity, under pressure from competition to achieve regional economic hegemony during global economic restructuring, and as mediated through local mechanisms of politics, should be held responsible. Since the early 1980s, Taipei has been made into "a real estate profit machine" and is a "world city" candidate in the Asia-Pacific region that, much like its cohort cities (Hong Kong, Singapore, Seoul, Manila, Bangkok, Kuala Lumpur, and Jakarta), strives to attract global capital, expand its hinterland, and invest in vast urban construction projects (Berner and Korff 1995; Douglass 1998a, 1998b; Friedmann 1986; Knight 1993; Boon Thong Lee 1998; Machimura 1992; Yeung 1996).

The prosperity of the real estate market started with Taipei's demographic growth. In 1946, the Taipei metropolitan area (including Taipei city and Taipei county) had a population of less than eight hundred thousand (Tseng 1993, 85), but that figure had jumped to 6.1 million by 1999, amounting to nearly 30 percent of the total population of Taiwan. With such a concentration of population, the problem of housing and the demand for urban infrastructure soon loomed large. Unfortunately, because Taipei is situated in a basin, the geographical nature of the surrounding environment imposes limits on urban growth (Chiang and Hsiao 1985, 203). The sacrifice of environmentally sensitive areas to unbridled urban growth became "inevitable" (Chang 1993,

450). Though more than 70 percent of the hillsides around Taipei had been assessed as "improper" places to pursue construction work, a "mountain-removing, then town-building" movement still took place (Sun 1997, 76).

As major developers, the conglomerates and local factions, mainly consisting of political bosses in town, initiated the first wave of purchasing hillside lands around the Taipei basin in the early 1970s. In the next ten years, by working through their political connections, they played with the loose hillside-development regulations to change the designated land use from observed to developable lands, and they acquired permits to build. Though the national government implemented stricter hillside-development regulations in 1983, the new bylaws did not apply to those permits that had already been issued. Since the late 1980s, in response to the booming housing market around the Taipei metropolitan area, developers have sidestepped the new regulations, insisting their old permits still stand, and actually have built large hillside housing projects.

In the Taipei metropolitan area, the total investment from the private sector on hillside development projects in 1997 alone was estimated at more than 360 million U.S. dollars, an amount almost identical to the total expenditure on environmental protection from national revenue in the same year. It also was estimated that solely in one subdistrict of Taipei county, more than a hundred thousand housing units would be built through the hillside development projects approved in the previous ten years (Chen and Chen 1997). However, this massive amount of investment and development could not guarantee the quality of the housing units being built. Because of the corruption and incompetence of contractors and government officials, many newly built estates became life threatening. As people moved into the new hillside housing in the mid-1990s, tragedies followed. Incidents involving collapsing buildings were widely reported during the wet season each year. The two most notorious tragedies happened in 1997 and 1998. A mudslide in August 1997 took twenty-eight lives, injured fifty people, and completely or partially destroyed two hundred housing units (Wan 1998). As a result, twelve government officials received five- to nine-year prison sentences for their abuse of power in illegally facilitating improper hillside development (Chen 1998). In October 1998, more than ten thousand households in Taipei county suffered from mudslides and floods, and three lives were lost. The cost of urban expansion—land subsidence, deforestation, landslides, soil erosion, disturbance of the watershed, flooding, air pollution—was paid for by the suffering of ordinary citizens.

Unsustainable urban expansion does not happen naturally but is mediated through specific political mechanisms—namely, the unholy alliance between a pro-development state and the agents of the market (conglomerates and local factions). Tracing the history of the strategic coalition between the KMT government and conglomerates and local factions, formerly clients and now competitive partners of the KMT, one finds a clear pattern of "trading political loyalty for economic privileges." In certain economic fields, such as real estate, the government exclusively opened political channels for conglomerates to seek economic advantage in exchange for their political support (Chu 1989, 151; Hsiao and Liu 1997, 51; Chen 1995). Under such circumstances, public goods are inevitably privatized. Without the politically motivated laissez-faire attitude of an authoritarian regime toward land and housing policies, it is hardly possible that the investing of conglomerates and local factions in the real estate market could be so extensive and unconstrained. Taipei is a case in point.

In the last decade, one-fifth of the top 100 conglomerates in Taiwan have invested in the housing market, and local factions in Taipei county, on the outskirts of Taipei city, have owned a total of 161 construction companies and become involved in at least 230 large-scale development projects (Chen 1995, 161–67, 207). In 1998, 42 percent of Taipei county-council members (twenty-seven out of sixty-five) were directly engaged in real estate, redevelopment, and construction.[5] By controlling the urban planning and land use committees, council members affiliated with local factions and conglomerates facilitated unsound development projects, which brought in huge profits for the businesses of politicians and these local factions and conglomerates. The real estate coalition gained huge profit margins by obtaining title at low prices to protected areas not included in urban development plans (hillside or waterfront land, or tillage), then having the land status changed to residential or commercial; bidding for and obtaining newly released public land through political connections; and purchasing land adjacent to designated zones for national construction projects (public transit systems, highways, industrial parks) in advance.

Through manipulating urban planning agencies, conglomerates and local factions have been actively involved in the real estate market since the 1970s (Hsiao and Liu 1997, 46–53). The value of land multiplied by 184.7 times from 1952 to 1975, while the overall value of goods increased by only 4.2 times during the same period (Mi 1988, 112–13). From 1973 to 1981, the index of family income increased by only 3.1 times, but housing prices multiplied by four to five times, and land value increased by more than thirty times (Hsu 1988, 171). But these figures are not the worst part of the story. The most dramatic instance of speculation in Taiwan's history occurred in the late 1980s. The market price of housing multiplied by 2.5 times in various districts of Taipei between 1987 and 1988 alone.[6] A typical two-bedroom apartment would cost a middle-income white-collar worker more than twenty years' salary (Hsiao and Liu 1997). Constrained by rising real estate prices, urban slums became the solution for low-income families to satisfy their need for affordable housing.

Taipei's land-speculation fever in the late 1980s is an excellent example of the maximizing of urban land use at the expense of social and ecological considerations. This value-maximizing ideology is perpetuated in Taiwan's shift from a labor-intensive economy to a capital- and brain-intensive economy. It is also embedded in the concept that, according to the national plan of APROC (the Asia-Pacific Regional Operations Center, a project involving multiple cabinet-level agencies), Taipei is projected to change its role from the leading city in a single country to a regional economic capital whose hinterlands include Taiwan, part of Southeast Asia, and the coastal area of China. It aims to host the headquarters of transnational corporations, provide advanced services such as high-speed information exchange, and be capable of competing with and then superseding Hong Kong and Singapore.

In Taipei, as in other cities that strive to climb the hierarchy of world cities, both national and municipal governments have invested trillions of dollars in transportation infrastructure since the late 1980s: public transit systems, high-speed trains, expressways, connection lines to airports and seaports, and much more. Though environmental impact assessment procedures, required by Taiwanese environmental laws, were conducted in all cases, not one project was turned down. Moreover, the quality of public construction projects was no better than that of private development. Some major projects, such as the public transit system and highways, were filled with rumors of scandals and corruption that disgusted most Taipei residents.

As with profit-oriented hillside development initiated by the private sector, the single-minded ambition of the Taiwan and Taipei governments to gain a bigger share in global prosperity has caused numerous nightmares. Excessive construction has not only heavily changed the physical appearance of the city but also altered its cultural and social landscape. In recent years, several officially designated cultural heritage sites (archaeological sites, landmarks or architecture with historical significance) have been legally and illegally damaged, if not totally destroyed. For example, the city administration once intended to tear down a first-class national relic, a fortress dating back a hundred years, to facilitate the construction of an inner-city highway. After strong protests, the building was finally saved, but a strange, even heartbreaking, juxtaposition of the highway and the relic has resulted—the highway was built directly over the roof of the fortress, and a fifty-centimeter distance between the two has been left to safeguard the integrity of the building.

Furthermore, to fulfill the requirements of a world city, regulations on land development and urban zoning have been loosened to create space for high-tech science parks; trade centers; locations for financial, banking, and other service industries; "smart" buildings; and exposition sites for hosting major world events. Not surprisingly, because of the government's redevelopment and rezoning efforts, traditional economic activities and residential areas have been disregarded to make way for developers, transnational corporations, and public agencies. In the process of urban restructuring stimulated by global economic forces, there have been within the last two years numerous public and private development and redevelopment projects, changing large-scale residential zones into commercial zones (Chi 1997).

Despite the increasingly detrimental impact on the environment of traffic congestion, overcrowding, and noise brought about by such changes, the billions of dollars in profits behind them made them attractive to the city government's policy makers. Still, it is because of this very urban restructuring process that the social and economic map of Taipei has been redrawn and that many urban dwellers either have undergone a painful loss of cultural identity or have been totally rubbed off the map. Some development projects commenced with the eviction of a whole village or community that had existed for an extended period of time. In most cases, monetary compensation was provided, but usually without a proper resettlement plan. While the material needs of the city are being met, the social bond, a rare treasure in an overcrowded human setting, and one that residents built over a long period, is in jeopardy and may even be lost forever.

Local Resistance: The Profile of Taipei's Environmental Movement

As a result of urban restructuring, a perception that living in this city has become both difficult and unbearable is widespread among its residents. For those who are affluent enough to own a house, buildings might crumble overnight thanks to wet-season landslides. Among those who have lower incomes, inadequate housing and LULUs (locally unwanted land uses) are prominent issues: the city authorities have threatened to sue the residents of slums for illegally occupying public land, and facilities that have raised health concerns (landfills, incinerators) have been situated near poor communities (see chapters 2, 4, and 5 for similar stories). Regardless of wealth, air pollution causes respiratory diseases across all generations, and particularly among children. To satisfy the booming demand for office space, recreational area is minimized and skyscrapers are built one after another. Furthermore, within the city proper everything is either overcrowded or under construction. Feeling suffocated by a lack of open space, urbanites desperately look for somewhere with green space and fresh air. Their search usually yields two results: first, such a place is hard to find, since the slopes of the hills surrounding the Taipei basin have been cleared on a massive scale; second, the traffic on the way to assured green spaces is appalling, as reflected in the statistic that the number of vehicles in Taipei increased from 772,297 in 1987 to 1,443,630 in 1996 (Department of Budget, Accounting, and Statistics 1997, 458–59).

Public concern over hillside development was also raised by the frequent mudslides and floods. According to a nationwide poll conducted in 1998, 93 percent of interviewees considered Taiwan's hillsides in general to be overdeveloped; 67 percent believed the government and the developers should be held responsible for the detrimental effects of overdevelopment; and 77 percent supported stricter development regulations. In another poll conducted that same year among Taipei residents only, 68 percent urged the government to completely prohibit further development on the Taipei metropolitan hillsides, and 70 percent believed that governmental officials and developers jointly engaged in land speculation (Tung 1998; Fei 1998). All of these factors—hyperurbanization, horrendous air pollution, traffic congestion, housing shortages, inadequate transportation, insecure housing conditions—have led to a diminished quality of urban life in Taipei and increased physical and mental stress for the city's residents.

Alienated and blasé city dwellers—as Simmel might say (1971, 329)—have found ways to collectively vent their pain and anger by taking part in nationwide environmental struggles. It is well noted that during the 1980s, Taiwan experienced a surge of massive civil protests in which citizens attempted to gain political rights (freedom of speech, association, and demonstration) repressed under colonial and authoritarian rule for nearly a century and to express their concerns on pressing social issues such as the environment, gender inequalities, labor, welfare, and human rights. Collective action against environmental deterioration is no doubt one of the "early risers" in the process of democratization and has played a critical role in both demonstrating "the vulnerability of authorities" and diffusing "a propensity for collective action" to other social groups with different concerns (Tarrow 1994, 155). From the perspective of protest cycles, local environmental protesters have severely questioned the state's pro-development and growth-centered policies and have fully developed a repertoire of collective action, which includes sit-ins, hunger strikes, blockades, religious parades, and theatrical performances. Environmental protests soon became a model for other movements to follow, playing a role similar to that of the civil rights movement in the United States (McAdam 1988, 1999).

As part of the nationwide environmental movement, hundreds of protests took place in the Taipei metropolitan area between 1980 and 1996, and citizens have made explicit demands for a livable environment and a higher-quality urban life. Based on Hsiao's previous studies (1988; 1994; 1997b), we have compiled a comprehensive table to compare environmental protest "cases" at the municipal and national levels (see Table 3.1).[7] Most striking about the figures in Table 3.1 is the tremendous increase in the total number of environmental protest cases, with the number in 1991–1996 being more than thirteen times the number in 1980–1985. This national trend toward an explosion of protest over environmental issues as democratization took hold is fully reflected in the experience of the Taipei metropolitan area. Between 1980 and 1996, more than one-fifth of Taiwan's 1,210 environmental protest cases took place in the Taipei metropolitan area. The number of protest cases in the peripheral area (Taipei county) was almost four times that of the city.

As Table 3.2 shows, of the 274 protests in the Taipei metropolitan area between 1980 and 1996, 46 percent concerned government-sponsored development projects; 16.8 percent opposed development and construction projects proposed by the private sector. Protests

TABLE 3.1
ENVIRONMENTAL PROTEST CASES
IN TAIWAN AND TAIPEI, 1980–1996

	Taiwan Total	Taipei Metropolitan Area		
		Taipei City	Taipei County	Subtotal
1980–1985	75	3	6	9
	(100)			(12.0)
1986–1990	131	7	33	40
	(100)			(30.5)
1991–1996	1,004	46	179	225
	(100)			(22.4)
TOTAL 1980–1996	1,210	56	218	274
	(100)			(22.6)

SOURCE: Hsiao 1988, 1994, 1997b.
NOTE: Parenthetical figures represent percentages.

against all development projects in Taipei amounted to more than 60 percent of total protests.

Looking at Table 3.2, it is clear that the evolution of protest in the Taipei metropolitan area tracks the changing macroeconomic context described in the previous section. Despite the nonindustrial characteristic of Taipei's economy, the chief target of environmental protests in the early 1980s (55.6 percent) was industrial pollution from the private sector, especially the chemical industry. Between 1986 and 1990, the percentage of protests against industrial pollution remained high (60 percent), but the private business sector no longer was the sole target (32.5 percent): state-owned enterprises and public construction projects emerged as other important adversaries (27.5 percent).

In the 1990s, protests began to confront the attempts of real estate developers, politicians, and bureaucrats to mold Taipei into a world city. The percentage of protests against specific industrial pollution dropped significantly, but protests against development projects, whether state sponsored or private, increased from around 40 percent in the late 1980s to nearly 70 percent between 1991 and 1996.

Though the issues and the strategies of each protest case may have differed, local and community-based mobilization is nevertheless the common characteristic. This confirms the repeatedly highlighted significance of "locality" in environmental movements worldwide (Castells 1997; Diani 1995). The citizens' "war for survival" mainly responds to

TABLE 3.2

SHIFTS IN TARGETING OF POLLUTERS BY ENVIRONMENTAL PROTESTS IN TAIPEI METROPOLITAN AREA

	Development and Construction Projects		Industrial Pollution by Specific Enterprise		Other Targets	Total Protests
	Public[a] (Government-Sponsored)	Private[b]	State-Owned[c]	Private[d]		
1980–1985	3	0	1	5	0	9
	(33.3)	(0)	(11.1)	(55.6)	(0)	(100)
1986–1990	12	3	11	13	1	40
	(30.0)	(7.5)	(27.5)	(32.5)	(2.0)	(100)
1991–1996	111	43	18	32	21	225
	(49.3)	(19.1)	(8.0)	(14.2)	(9.3)	(100)
TOTAL 1980–1996	126	46	30	50	22	274
	(46.0)	(16.8)	(10.9)	(18.2)	(8.0)	(100)

SOURCE: Recalculations from Hsiao's original data, 1988, 1994, 1997b.
NOTE: Parenthetical figures represent percentages.
[a] Power plants, public transit systems, highways, industrial parks, sewer systems, dams, Sungshan airport, incinerators, sanitary landfills, unlawful waste dumping.
[b] Housing, golf courses, mining, graveyards.
[c] Taipower, Taiwan Water Supply Corporation.
[d] Cement, bitumen, and concrete production; clandestine quarrying; trucking services.

excessive development and the obvious deterioration of the urban habitat. In the context of Taipei's struggle, the conflicting interest between
citizens and global-domestic capital surfaced, and the tension over re-
distributing spatial resources among diverse social groups exploded. Citizens openly claimed their right to control over their immediate environment and strove to discover and elaborate on the meaning of
community.

By means of these protests, Taipei residents have not only expressed
their discontent over a deteriorating urban environment, but also challenged the top-down political structure that has long deprived urban
dwellers of their right to participate in the decision-making process of
public affairs. In most cases, the residents were "informed" by the government about changes in the designation of land use or about the introduction of locally unwanted facilities *after* the decision had been
made. The citizens were outraged not only by the perceived immediate
threat brought about by these development projects, but also by the
undemocratic, top-down decision-making machinery that had approved
them. Thus, these protests also reflect the residents' demands for institutional change toward participatory democracy in the city's public life.
In the process of struggle, local communities have served as agents of
environmental action, reflecting not only the immediate interest of their
communities, but also the potential for their action to contribute to a
more sustainable and just urban environment overall.

Community and Governmental Responsiveness

In responding to the negative effects caused by urban restructuring, communities rebelled. Ching-Cheng and Kang-Le, both protest cases cited
at the beginning of this paper, articulated the idea of "a city for citizens"
and aimed to defend their living spaces. Both the middle-class neighborhood and the slum community were pressured by urban redevelopment and the overdue need for public facilities and infrastructure. Other
communities also have been sensitive about hillside development and
landscape preservation issues. Wan-Fang, another middle-class neighborhood, campaigned to prevent the Public Housing Office from situating a large-scale housing project on a nearby hillside that experienced
landslides during the wet season. Chihshan Yen, with a high proportion
of female residents who are members of the Homemakers' Union Environmental Protection Foundation (a female-dominated national environmental NGO), showed strong opposition to the construction of a

gas station that, it was feared, might severely damage a historical ruin nearby and lower the quality of life of the community (Yu 1994, 43–56).

The rise of the community-based protests illustrates the efforts of community residents to preserve social bonds and place-specific identity, and to fight against unwanted development projects that usually favor the few over the many. Their demands for stricter environmental sanctions, cultural preservation, livable habitats, and institutional access to decision-making processes have put enormous pressure on government at all levels and finally changed the landscape of local politics. Facing ongoing direct action from these communities and electoral competition among political parties in Taiwan's fledgling democracy, the incumbent parties of both national and municipal governments could not afford to ignore these explicit demands to halt unwelcome urban development and unsound land use on hillsides.

At the national level, island-wide environmental protests have directly contributed to a wave of legislative and institutional reform since the late 1980s. The Pollution Disputes Resolution Law and Environmental Impacts Assessment Act were passed, and the Environmental Protection Basic Law is being reviewed in the legislature (Chi, Hsiao, and Wang 1996). Also, the Environmental Protection Administration (EPA) was upgraded to a cabinet-level agency in 1987. Due to pressure from lobbying by many environmental NGOs, stricter environmental regulations were adopted. In the case of deforestation and landslides, for example, the Ministry of Interior lowered the permitted angle of hillside development twice in one year and thus largely reduced the total area permitted for development.

At the municipal level, party competition in each local election has increased voter sensitivity (note the campaign slogan from various candidates, "citizen first"). This new trend has been more salient since the December 1994 change from appointment by the national government of the Taipei city mayoral post to direct election of this official. Any dubious connection with conglomerates and other local business interests is now viewed as a liability, if not poison, for a candidate in any local election. "Greening" the political platform has become inevitable, and it accurately reflects the rising public demand for a higher quality of urban life. As a result, in the first direct mayoral election, a pro-environment candidate from the Democratic Progressive Party (DPP, the biggest opposition party in Taiwan) was elected. At the same time, in the city council election, quite a number of candidates who had never been involved in plutocracy defeated the longtime representatives of or collaborators with conglomerate interests. The political efficacy of community protests is thus being successfully channeled through the system of representative politics. The question, then, is: What do elected officials do to prove to their voters that they are working toward a livable city? The magic answer is: Build more city parks.

According to a statistic from 1993, the area of park per citizen in Taipei at the time was 2.5 square meters, smaller than in other metropolises such as New York City (13.95), Paris (12.70), Seoul (8.70), and Tokyo (4.70) (Hsiao et al. 1997, 12). It is thus not surprising that in almost all campaign packages in recent elections, city parks have been one of the favorite topics of all candidates. With the urgent need for open space, a formula of "parks equal votes" was adopted. The current and previous mayors have strenuously worked toward building city parks during their tenures, no matter what conflicts the process might attract. The construction of the No. 7 city park in the early 1990s resulted in the eviction of thousands of slum dwellers, as did the Nos. 14–15 Park. Between 1991 and 1996, the two mayors built sixty-seven parks, and the total area of parkland increased from 805.8 hectares to 979.4 (Department of Budget, Accounting, and Statistics 1997, 452). The city government was also expected to add at least ten more parks in 1997 (Yang 1997).

In addition to city parks, several pro-community programs were set up. Following his election victory, Chen Shui-bian appointed the first environmentalist with a national reputation to take charge of the local EPA. Also, the city government's Department of Urban Development proposed various redevelopment projects that showed concern for the preservation of traditional landscape and historical architecture. For example, two old and historically significant districts of Taipei city (Tihua Street and the Tatung District) are expected to be economically revitalized and to attract cultural tourism. Each year, ten to fifteen communities are officially sponsored to improve their physical environment and to build stronger community networks. Tougher measures also have been enacted to regulate hillside development at the city government level.

Protest, then, has affected the political arena both by changing the character of political discourse around environmental issues and by forcing modification of the formal rules governing urban development. The municipal government has indeed responded to demands of urban environmental protests, stressing community autonomy and the importance of protecting environmentally sensitive areas by initiating various programs to facilitate community involvement. These effects, however, must be considered only a first step toward making Taipei more livable. Changes in rules and discourse do not necessarily mean changes in practice and behavior "on the ground." Equally important, efforts in the direction of livability continue to have very different implications for poor and middle-class communities.

The Politics of Protest

At first glance, it seems as if citizens' concerns over urban land use were addressed through the tougher measures adopted to inhibit hillside development and by several other governmental initiatives. Tempered by democratization, the top-down nature of urban planning has somehow been softened by the creation of new mechanisms for community participation. The mayor and county magistrate, pressured by the consideration of reelection, must take community voice into account and prevent urban-planning bureaucrats from exhibiting behavior unfriendly to communities. However, after closer examination, one finds that problems still remain. Unequal treatment of communities prevails, the government's capacity to implement its new policies is highly problematic,[8] the "development first" mentality still lingers, and the vision of becoming a world city has yet to be realized. The positive policy responses toward environmental causes have been tempered by an increasing number of huge infrastructure projects and district redevelopment plans that were approved and quickly and aggressively commenced.

In this section, special attention is given to class divisions in Taipei's environmental protests and the relationship between the class composition of a mobilized community and the likelihood of it achieving its desired outcomes. We also examine the limited role of translocal NGOs in Taipei's environmental movement and the relationship among community interest, sustainability, and social justice.

Social Class and the Efficacy of Mobilized Communities

Since urban environmental protest is location-specific and community-based, the social attributes of each community to some extent affect its bargaining power with the authorities and adversaries in the course of protest. From various case studies of Taipei's community and environmental movements, it is clear that the class composition of a community is closely associated with the readiness of available resources, the span of information networks, the extent of media coverage, and the level of government responsiveness (Shen 1994; Yu 1994). Middle-class communities are usually in a better strategic position to attract media coverage and to generate public support. They are also more likely than poor communities to receive a fast government response and to seek assistance from outside NGOs. The case of Chihshan Yen community demonstrates a link between the community group and translocal NGOs resulting from an overlap of activists in their membership.

A middle-class community enjoys more bargaining power because of its members' economic prosperity and social networks. But it would be misleading to maintain that their protests are guaranteed to succeed. We often find a mixed or compromised success in the outcome of middle-class community protests. The Ching-Cheng community won its park back but was defeated in the fight against the power substation. Though the Chihshan Yen community could not stop the construction of a gas station, its request to preserve historical ruins nearby received an enthusiastic response from the municipal government. A middle-class background does help to bring public attention to pressing issues through more efficient access to the press, governmental bureaucracy, and voluntary associations, but that too does not automatically guarantee a successful outcome. To achieve its objectives, the community must also depend on strategic interactions among the numerous social groups involved, who all will have articulated different interests within the system of political representation.

In contrast, a poor or slum community is indeed more vulnerable when it encounters powerful social institutions. If poor communities get any attention from the media, it is likely to take the form of distorted and negative coverage, and they are much less successful in dealing with the authorities. Let us take as an example the case of the Kang-Le community. In opposing the eviction of thousands of residents, Kang-Le formed a self-help organization in 1992 and desperately looked for a way to balance the citywide demands for public parks and the needs of slum residents. Before the professors and students from the Graduate School of Architecture and Urban-Rural Planning Studies at National Taiwan University got involved to help organize the anti-bulldozer campaign in early 1997, very few media outlets had paid attention to this story. When the press began to look into the dispute, the government authorities occupied center stage in the news coverage and marginalized the voice of the shantytown residents.[9] Some municipal government officials even used the media to distort the Kang-Le community's image.

Slum residents were portrayed as a group of "greedy rich people" who had illegally resided on public land for a long time and who were going to be generously paid up to 52 million U.S. dollars in compensation out of the taxpayers' pockets. They were also criticized for having deprived decent citizens of the right to a park.

Similar problems have been faced by urban Aborigines. Throughout the history of Taiwan, the Aborigine rights to land, natural resources, and cultural heritage have been largely ignored. On the one hand, the officially "reserved" homelands of the Aborigines have borne the weight of public construction projects (mostly dams and, in the case of Orchid Island, a nuclear-waste storage facility). Aboriginal opposition to these projects resulted in very few concessions from the state. On the other hand, having undertaken the process of rural-urban migration in the hope of escaping the troubled mountain economy, urban Aborigines still face the nightmare of eviction. Aboriginal migrants who moved to Taipei illegally built their ethnic settlements either on riverbanks or on hills, where the natural environment was similar to their homeland. These small, scattered ethnic settlements suffered from extremely poor living conditions; some were even without electricity and water, let alone more luxurious amenities. The rationale to evict the Aboriginal shantytown dwellers was quite similar to that which evicted the Kang-Le community: public safety, the retrieval of state-owned property, and the need for public works (in this case, high-speed trains). The Aboriginal struggle with the government received even less media coverage and public attention than did Kang-Le's, and the government response to their concerns was very unfavorable.

In sum, although in principle environmental protests have consistently advocated the right of people to have a say regarding their immediate environment, in practice the claim to that right by different communities is weighed unequally by politicians, the media, and the public. The way each community's requests are dealt with depends very much on the status of the community in the pyramid of power, which is structured around class and ethnicity.

The Minimal Involvement of Translocal NGOs

It is intriguing to note that translocal NGOs, whose membership mainly consists of the middle class, have played a limited role in the urban struggle, in contrast to the aggressiveness of local communities. According to a survey of environmental organizations conducted in 1997, roughly one-third of Taiwan's environmental NGOs had established their headquarters in Taipei, giving this metropolis the highest density of organizational networks in Taiwan (Hsiao 1997a).[10] However, three-quarters of Taipei's NGOs identified themselves as "national organizations" that focus on broader issues, and they are therefore inattentive to local affairs and urban protests in Taipei. Only a few NGOs had half an eye on urban environmental issues. The major interests of these NGOs were recycling, vehicle usage, and hillside development, and furthermore, they unanimously adopted soft-line approaches to change, such as lobbying, instead of actively allying themselves with local communities. Even in the case of the Chihshan Yen community, the involvement of the Homemakers' Union Environmental Protection Foundation derived more from an overlap in membership than from a primary concern on the part of the NGO for the preservation of Taipei's cultural landscape.

It is not unusual that a division of labor exists between translocal NGOs and local communities within the larger picture of environmental movements. Over the years, Taiwan's NGOs, backed by lobbyists and by think tanks consisting of academic recruits, have played a translating role to reframe local concerns into significant issues in the public sphere. In many cases, combining NGO access to the political system with the pressure derived from residents' direct action has yielded effective and favorable results. For example, communities in southern Taiwan and translocal NGOs have allied with one another to fight successfully against an incoming petrochemical and steel-refining industrial park, to secure the livelihoods of local fish farmers and fishermen, and even to protect endangered wetlands and a threatened species of bird, the black-faced spoonbill. However, there is no link between NGOs and mobilized communities in Taipei's urban struggle.

Eighteen out of thirty-three of Taipei's NGOs said that the quality of the urban environment was not even one of their major concerns. Why have Taipei's NGOs shown negligence on urban environmental issues and maintained such a distance from urban communities? What has made Taipei a special case in contrast to the alliances between NGOs and anti-pollution communities elsewhere? To answer these questions we need to consider the following issues: the pro-DPP sentiment among environmental NGOs and these NGOs' perception of "what counts as an environmental issue."

In Taiwan, visible nationwide environmental NGOs fall into roughly two categories: research-oriented groups that specialize in public policy and present their perspective through moderate means such as lobbying and environmental education campaigns, and action-oriented groups that engage in community mobilization and are prone to express their environmental concerns through noninstitutional and confrontational strategies. Both types of group have similarly decent annual budgets and a membership disproportionately made up of academics, but the real difference lies in organizational size. The first type, usually with an elite membership of fewer than fifty, acts as a body of consultants for policy makers and never directly participates in local protests. The second type, with a much larger membership pool, tends to bring local concerns into higher-level policy debates and actively engages in protests against large, government-sponsored development projects.

During the struggle against the authoritarian KMT state in the early 1980s, DPP and many action-oriented NGOs developed and cultivated an issue-based comradeship and an overlapping membership. It is well documented that many outspoken leaders of these NGOs are in fact members or supporters of the DPP (Weller and Hsiao 1998). In the 1990s, when the DPP and its incumbents occasionally did not maintain their firm stand on environmental causes, those action-oriented NGOs found it difficult to fight against old friends, except in extreme cases. For example, a DPP county magistrate was strongly attacked because the construction of Taiwan's seventh naphtha cracker (an industrial complex where crude-oil products are refined into the precursors of plastics), a project that environmental NGOs had strongly opposed for years, proceeded partially at his discretion. Besides this extreme case, most NGOs have been friendly toward DPP administrations, and the cooperation between the two has been pervasive. In Taipei's case, instead of working with protesting communities, quite a few environmental NGOs came forward to support DPP mayor Chen Shui-bian's campaign to increase green space. They also endorsed a citywide recycling project and community improvement plans proposed by the city government.

To most environmental NGOs, urban restructuring and changes in urban land use are not really environmental issues but rather technical matters related to urban planning. Compared to the concern of NGOs for forests, rivers, the ocean, wetlands, wildlife, and much more, the urban habitat is rather orphaned—a point that has been nicely elucidated by Harvey (1996, chapters 13–14). While making a firm stand against hillside development because of resulting deforestation and soil erosion, NGOs still have difficulty placing other urban issues, such as slum clearance, on their list of priorities. It is thus not surprising that they have remained silent on issues relating to the urban poor. Attentive to a narrowly defined "natural environment," NGOs somehow neglect the "unnatural" urban setting and remain largely uninvolved in many crucial urban battles. It is rather ironic to note that a movement and numerous NGOs, which "exhort the harmonious coexistence of people and nature, and worry about the continued survival of nature (particularly loss of habitat problems), somehow forget about the survival of humans (especially those who have lost their 'habitats' and 'food sources')" (Harvey 1996, 386).

Community Interest, Sustainability, and Social Justice

The third and probably the most important issue in the politics of protest is how Taipei's locally driven protests relate to the long-term sustainability of the city. Is it hypocritical that middle-class communities oppose highway construction and refuse to sacrifice their community parks for parking garages while their residents intensify their use of private automobiles? Is it narrow-minded to boycott the nearby construction of incinerators while the quantity of garbage that each citizen produces increases every year? Is it selfish for slum dwellers to try to save illegal shacks from being torn down regardless of the need for green space? Is it a public-safety problem that Aborigines build their ethnic settlements on the riverbank? In other words, are local communities waving the flag of environmentalism just to protect their own interests? Or can local interest be congruent with ecological concern across a city? On the road toward a more livable city, how is it possible to balance the subsistence of the urban poor and the sustainability of the city?

To praise all community protests as heroic and progressive is as problematic as to blame them for being insular and self-serving. Either romanticism or cynicism may generate an emotional response, but neither provides us with a vision. The motivation behind local protests might be led by self-interest, but once channeled through proper means, these local interests may be translated into larger issues of public concern. The fact that most local protests are interest-driven does not necessarily prevent them from contributing to urban sustainability. Let us take highways and parking garages as examples. As Friedmann has put it (1997, 18): "for an Asian city to replicate Los Angeles' love affair with freeways . . . is to commit collective suicide." In a city like Taipei, with an average density of 9,586 persons per square kilometer (Department of Budget, Accounting, and Statistics 1997), and with some districts even reaching

25,000 persons per square kilometer (Chang 1993, 432), to protest the excessive construction of highways and parking garages is to try to rein in the overuse of private vehicles and encourage the use of more environmentally sound methods of mass transportation. The same reasoning may apply to incinerators. When people refuse to accept an incinerator as their neighbor, we should not immediately denounce them as engaging in NIMBY behavior or as selfish, because their recalcitrance could point to better ways of solving the garbage problem. Instead of endlessly building incinerators and landfills, a task that Taiwan's EPA has been undertaking, one can argue that in the face of insufficient garbage processing facilities, it is more sensible to strengthen the system of recycling and to persuade citizens to voluntarily reduce their garbage output. It is undeniable that public discussion of stringent controls on private vehicles and a citywide recycling plan was aroused in the wake of these "selfish" community protests.

Another issue concerns the conflicting interests of the urban poor and society as a whole. In order to shed light on this sensitive issue, we would first like to go back to the conception of "sustainability." Regardless of its wide variety of connotations, one basic point of consensus on the meaning of sustainability is the concept of "intergenerational justice": in pursuit of a livelihood, the happiness of future generations should not be compromised or sacrificed (Friedmann 1997; Piccolomini 1996). If the pursuit of sustainability should take into account the quality of life of those who are not yet born, then the subsistence and quality of life of the urban poor should not be disregarded in satisfying the needs of other citizens. Like two sides of a coin, in theory or in practice, sustainability should not and cannot be separated from a more just social system. To increase the area of green space might help to mitigate a city's air pollution, but to use that as the justification for dismantling a poor community in its entirety is untenable.[11] If it does not take into account the unequal distribution of economic goods and power among different groups in a society, an ostensible environmental or ecological solution might unintentionally lead to dreadful social consequences (Beck 1995; Harvey 1992, 1996; criticisms on thoughtless slum demolition projects are also detailed in Gans 1962).

By reexamining the case of the Kang-Le struggle, we discover that the effort to balance both social and environmental demands has failed and that, even more serious, a fast-food approach to improving the urban environment has overwhelmed considerations of social justice, a value that must be maintained on the path toward a sustainable city.

Learning from the classic case of Orcasitas, in Madrid, the urban planners who supported the Kang-Le community's cause made a proposal that would have kept the city park project on course but also saved the community. They said that "the occupants of the illegal shantytown settlements who were . . . responsible for utilizing the area and increasing its value should be the first to benefit once the area had been redeveloped" (Castells 1983, 253). In this proposal, 6 percent of the designated park area would have been used to build affordable government-sponsored housing to relocate the aged and poor residents living on the same site, and the design would have turned the park into an eco-museum, evoking memories of the area's past by including features of the Japanese cemetery and slum architecture. However, the proposal was turned down by the city's top officials. Their refusal rested on the argument that the resettlement proposal favoring slum dwellers had no legal basis and would only stir up "unrealistic expectations" among slum dwellers in other areas. Immediately after the demolition, there was a 15 to 20 percent increase in rental and land value surrounding the Nos. 14–15 Park (Coalition against the City Government Bulldozers 1997, 11). This further confirms that an ecological vision such as a park system "was easily co-opted and routinized into real-estate development practices for the middle classes" (Harvey 1996, 427).

Conclusion

We have tried to set out the central dynamics of the evolution of Taipei's environmental movement, showing both how the movement reflects the changing character of the larger Taiwanese political economy and how the character of the movement itself limits the kinds of changes that it can achieve. The task of enacting change has not been an easy one, since the movement's overall character emerges out of myriad small, heterogeneous actions. Nonetheless, we have tried to show that there is an overall logic to the movement, one whose limitations must be balanced against its undeniably positive potential.

A simplified version of Taipei's struggle can be described as follows: Both the national and municipal governments engaged in a large project of urban space restructuring in order to attract foreign capital, and the KMT government was keen to provide the private sector with incentives to maximize land use on hillsides.[12] Residents later found out that this impressive government-inspired project promised everything but a livable urban environment. Foreign and domestic capital was placed in the "growth machine," leading to assaults on the natural environment, historical buildings, and the living space of various groups of residents. Feeling betrayed and hurt, unhappy residents mobilized neighbors, friends, and relatives to call their local representatives, to vote for other parties, and even to demonstrate in the street. Some translocal environmental NGOs noted this trend and passively participated in a few cases of community mobilization.

Though the governments initially had been unresponsive in meeting resident demands, the voice of the community grew too powerful and the threat of political backlash was serious; thus, several policy revisions were made. Both the national and municipal governments decided to inhibit excessive hillside development, but vast urban infrastructures would proceed as planned. To meet rising social grievances, the municipal government tried hard to build more city parks as an extra bonus for citizens. By doing so, it turned slum dwellers into the victims of urban improvement. Figure 3.1 summarizes this complex process—plus the larger one, led by the APROC, of transforming Taipei into a world city—in schematic form, identifying major actors and pinpointing the adversaries and the conflicts among them.

Taipei's experience of urban deterioration is by no means unique. Leading cities in East Asia have been haunted by land speculation and unsound land use. They compete among themselves in the construction of attention-grabbing but wasteful urban infrastructure projects. What makes Taipei special is that civil protests against these macroeconomic processes are facilitated by Taiwan's democratization. Institutionally consolidated party competition provides various communities with more means to address their locally driven interests. Through these means, mobilized communities were finally able to put the long-neglected issue of "urban sustainability" on the national and city agendas. The responsiveness of both the national and municipal governments has proven the political efficacy of community action. In turn, community mobilization has been encouraged by a more responsive and democratic regime—that is why the number of protest cases has increased with time.

One benefit of democracy has been that the voice of Taipei's residents has been heard. However, because of the inequality of power between different social groups, the demands of some communities have been met and those of others blocked. If modern cities are usually portrayed as the center of wealth, power, information, and cultural production, we should not forget that the sharpest disparity between the rich and

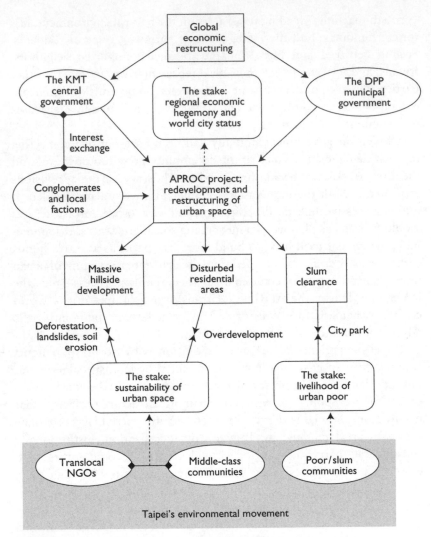

Figure 3.1.   The global-local nexus of Taiwan's APROC project.

the poor and between the powerful and the powerless also takes place in urban settings. While demands in the form of environmental protests for a higher quality of urban life have brought positive institutional and legal reforms, poor and slum communities have suffered. The extent to which these pro-environment decrees can restrict excessive public and private development is still unknown; in the meantime, shantytown settlements have already been torn down and traded for city parks.

The dynamics of Taipei's urban environmental struggles have important implications for other Third World urban centers that aspire to be "world cities." In order for their environmental movements to pursue a broader vision of livability, they must structure their actions and their ideology to incorporate more horizontal links between mobilized communities and NGOs. The NGOs themselves need to acknowledge the central importance of dealing with complex urban systems. Most important, the livelihood of poor and slum communities must be incorporated into the concept of sustainability; the broader ecological movement must be more sensitive to equality. The idea that the improvement of the urban environment cannot be divorced from the realization of social justice must become a more integral part of movement ideology. In the end, a city cannot become more sustainable without also being more just.

Notes

The authors' names are in alphabetical order, and each author contributed equally to this collaboration. We thank Peter Evans, Mike Douglass, Dungsheng Chen, and two anonymous reviewers for their constructive comments. We are also grateful for editorial assistance from Martin Williams and Fan Chang.

1. Ironically enough, the actual meaning of "Kang-Le" in Chinese refers to mirth and prosperity, everything opposite to the image of a slum.

2. An excerpt from a speech of Mayor Chen Shui-bian may accurately capture such a sentiment: "When a superstar like Michael Jackson stays in the Grand Formosa Regent, which is right next to the slum, it really is a shame to let him see thousands of people sleeping in a graveyard. This place brings shame on our citizens, it is a tumor of the city" (Coalition against the City Government Bulldozers 1997, 7).

3. Chen lost the reelection for the Taipei city mayoral post in 1998. His eviction of Kang-Le residents was a major target of attack during the campaign.

4. The squeeze on the manufacturing sector and the dominant role of the service sector set the structure of production in Taipei apart from the general mode of Taiwan's development as a whole. In contrast to the abrupt increase of employees in the manufacturing sector at the national level, the percentage of Taipei city's labor force in this sector has continually declined, from 25 percent in the early 1970s to 15 percent in 1995. The service sector grew steadily from 60 percent to 75 percent during the same period. It has also been found that the predominant status of the tertiary sector in Taipei is long established and was not challenged by the booming industrial sector during postwar development in Taiwan.

5. Information on council members is from http://teputc.org.tw/issue/mountain/9801115о4.htm.

6. This meant that the money that could buy a two-bedroom apartment in

1987 could afford to buy only the living room of the same apartment a few months later. Around that time, jokes such as "My life's savings aren't large enough to buy a bathroom" or "One square foot in this part of town is worth far more than I am" became common.

7. In Hsiao's series of studies, the definition of a "case" is the aggregation of incidents between a specific polluting facility (or group of facilities) and opponents (composed of local residents, concerned intellectuals, environmental activists) during the conflict-resolution process. The events contained in a case may be petitions, public meetings, picketings, demonstrations, blockades, obstructions, collective violence, attacks on property, clashes with police, or legal action. There are simple cases with only a few combative encounters between parties that are settled in a rather short period of time, and there are complex cases that may last for years and contain hundreds of incidents, such as the case relating to the building of Taiwan's fourth nuclear power plant. Thus there exists a wide variety of qualitative differences among cases, and the number of cases is not identical to the frequency of protests; nevertheless, that number can be regarded as a deflated figure of the total number of protests.

8. Gatekeeping procedures and tougher measures do not guarantee an exhaustive implementation, judging from past experiences. Within the pro-development national government, the EPA is burdened with enormous political pressure from above and "usually finds itself opposed to more entrenched parts of the bureaucracy" (Weller and Hsiao 1998). In order to maintain its integrity within the state apparatus, gatekeeping procedures such as the EIA have become a field of compromise between the EPA and other executive branches and are widely questioned by many environmentalists (Hsiao 1997a). Furthermore, the local EPA is not under the direct supervision of the central EPA but rather is under the jurisdiction of individual local governments. Thus, whether or not pro-environment measures are locally implemented depends, to a great extent, on the political inclination of each city or county government. It becomes inevitable that the extent of implementation varies from place to place and from incumbent to incumbent in the same local government, even when the same environmental codes are supposed to apply.

9. For a general discussion of media reliance on statements by government officials and other certified authorities, see Gitlin 1980.

10. The population of this survey included Taiwan's 232 environmental NGOs. Thirty-three out of ninety-six organizations that responded were based in Taipei.

11. Jacobs (1961, 91) argues that the concept of parks as "the lungs of the city" is solely science-fiction nonsense because "it takes about three acres [roughly 1.2 hectares] of woods to absorb as much carbon dioxide as four people exude in breathing, cooking and heating."

12. Though both the national and municipal governments experienced power transfer in 1998 and 2000, different incumbent parties still share the ambition of regional economic hegemony and world city status.

:: 4 ::

Community-Driven Regulation

Toward an Improved Model of
Environmental Regulation in Vietnam

DARA O'ROURKE

Introduction

Vietnam aspires to follow in the footsteps of the "Tiger" economies of Asia. Over the last ten years, the government has focused significant financial and political capital on advancing rapid economic development and on building modern, job-providing cities. But even with a strong development bias Vietnam has been forced to recognize that rapid growth can have potentially ominous environmental implications—as seen quite clearly in the neighboring cities of Bangkok and Taipei (see chapters 2 and 3). While representing the potential for successful development (although even that has been called into question recently), countries like Thailand and Taiwan also present models of urban environmental problems to be avoided. And as Vietnam begins along this development path from a base of 1950s-vintage, highly polluting heavy industry, accompanied by the recent expansion of export-oriented light industry, and acknowledging the state's limited capacity for environmental regulation, Vietnamese cities have the potential to become not just as bad as Bangkok and Taipei, but perhaps even worse.

Currently, Ho Chi Minh City and Hanoi are growing much more rapidly than either Bangkok or Taipei. While Vietnam as a whole has experienced GDP growth of more than 8 percent per year, with industry growing by 13 percent per year throughout the 1990s, Vietnam's urban centers have grown at twice that rate (Economist Intelligence Unit [EIU]

1997). Even in 1998, amid the Asian economic crisis, when Vietnam's overall GDP growth slowed to approximately 5.8 percent, Vietnamese industry continued to expand by more than 11 percent, slowing only to approximately 8 percent in 1999 (EIU 2000). A massive inflow of foreign direct investment, which also slowed in 1998, has been driving a process of rapid urbanization and industrialization concentrated primarily around Hanoi and Ho Chi Minh City. Much of this investment focuses on the crude exploitation of natural resources and cheap labor, leading to pollution intensities that are predicted to increase faster than industrial growth itself (World Bank 1997).

Past policies to control urban growth, such as restrictions on migration, planned decentralization of industry, and the development of New Economic Zones in the periphery, are becoming less effective or being abandoned altogether. Rapid population growth in cities is overwhelming existing infrastructures and exacerbating environmental problems. Vietnam's urban population is currently estimated at 15 million people, or 20 percent of the total population. However, urban populations have been growing by 4.5 percent per year, more than triple the rural population growth rate (United Nations Development Programme [UNDP] 1999). Traffic congestion (and the associated air pollution), residential overcrowding, unplanned land uses (including the siting of highly polluting factories next to residential areas), uncollected municipal solid waste, and polluted rivers and lakes are the most visible signs of infrastructural inadequacy and regulatory breakdown.

These trends would seem to indicate that Vietnam is on the path to repeating the unsustainable development patterns of its Asian neighbors. But are there forces that might move Vietnam's cities in the direction of greater livability? For instance, is the government applying international lessons to prevent Ho Chi Minh City from becoming another Bangkok? Are international financial institutions or NGOs pressuring for more "sustainable development" practices? And what about other potential actors?

At first glance, the picture would appear grim. The persistence of single-party communist rule in Vietnam raises the specter of environmental disasters similar to those perpetrated by socialist governments of Eastern Europe and the Soviet Union (see chapter 5). Can the Vietnamese state be expected to do better? In many ways it might be expected to actually do worse. It lacks the economic base that Eastern European states had to work with. A lack of funds, trained personnel, and political influence severely constrains the effectiveness of environmental agencies. The continued failure (or, more optimistically, the high costs and slow pace) of traditional environmental policies and regulations highlights the limits of simple command-and-control (CAC) strategies for environmental protection in Vietnam. State environmental agencies on their own simply have not been able to control the adverse impacts of industrialization and urbanization

What about other actors that might contribute to livability—communities, NGOs, or social movements? Again, at first glance the prospects seem grim. Communities cannot count on competitive electoral politics to give them leverage in demanding action from the state. Essentially all protests in Vietnam are illegal. There are no truly independent Vietnamese NGOs, and the NGOs that do exist are severely limited in the roles they play, appearing much weaker vis-à-vis the state than NGOs in other Asian countries. Linkages between NGOs and communities are also relatively underdeveloped.

Surprisingly, however, research on this challenging (and somewhat depressing) situation has revealed some promising strategies for responding to the environmental impacts of industrialization and urbanization, and for achieving a better balance of development and livability. Over the last five years, I have analyzed existing processes for mitigating the adverse environmental impacts of industrial development in Vietnam. This research shows that dynamic processes do exist that can motivate pollution reduction. In the cases I analyzed, community actions played a key role in pressuring the state to take action against polluting firms. Of course not all communities were able to mobilize effectively, and when community pressures were absent, traditional regulatory policies were largely ineffective in reducing pollution. Nonetheless, some communities were able to mobilize, pressuring the firms and the state and securing important pollution reductions.

Cases in Vietnam point toward the outlines of an improved model of environmental regulation that I call community-driven regulation (CDR). Under CDR, communities directly pressure firms to reduce pollution, monitor industrial facilities, prioritize environmental issues for state action, pressure state environmental agencies to improve their monitoring and enforcement capabilities, and raise public and elite awareness of environmental issues and the trade-offs between development and the environment. CDR represents the conjunction of local-level social networks and state-level agencies, advancing potential synergies between communities and state actors. With a clear focus on local pollution reduction, the different actors in CDR represent examples of Evans's "agents of livability."

The cases I use to illustrate the CDR model are focused on questions of combating industrial pollution. While the outlines of the CDR model might be applied to questions of reducing household pollution or improving the delivery of collective goods such as sewers or waste collection, my research is more specific. The cases consist of struggles between six firms and the communities that are affected by their pollution. These firms vary in size, location, technology level, and ownership; they include a Taiwanese joint-venture textile firm, a state-owned fertilizer plant, a state-owned chemical plant, a state-owned pulp and paper mill, a locally owned chemical factory, and a Korean multinational shoe factory producing Nike shoes.

My research involved semistructured interviews with factory managers, workers, community members, and government officials. I conducted waste audits to assess factory environmental impacts and sources, and I reviewed media reports, environmental impact assessments (EIAs), inspection documents, fines, compensations, and other government actions. The cases provide a wealth of evidence regarding processes of state and community action around pollution issues, the effectiveness or ineffectiveness of these processes, and the factors contributing to either outcome. Despite their broad variation, including cases that highlight how these actors are often "imperfect" agents of livability, they point toward a number of interesting dynamics. Before turning to the individual cases, however, it is worth elaborating on the CDR model.

The CDR Model

The basic premise of the CDR model is that community action can and sometimes does drive environmental regulation. Although my research sought to examine three dynamics—state pressures, market pressures, and community pressures on corporations—as the research unfolded, it became clear that community action was the key dynamic underlying state actions and corporate initiatives to reduce pollution in Vietnam. This is not to say the state is not also crucial. However, it is the ability of communities to pressure the state that creates incentives for firms to reduce pollution. From my interviews with government regulators it is clear that the vast majority of regulatory actions in Vietnam have occurred only after community complaints. For instance, staff at three of the most important environmental regulatory agencies—the Departments of Science, Technology, and Environment (DOSTE) in Hanoi, Dong Nai, and Phu Tho—admitted that all inspections to date had been driven by community complaints. Representatives of the National Environment Agency (NEA) similarly acknowledged that the inspections conducted up to the time of my interviews had been instigated after community complaints. Staffing weaknesses in these agencies, the absence of a system for prioritizing inspections, and the strength of community demands have led to a situation of essentially community-driven inspections.

While it might be expected that communities will complain about pollution and that these complaints will sometimes motivate the state to take action, it is not at all clear why certain communities mobilize when others do not, and why some mobilizations are effective while others fail. Reality is much more complicated than a linear model of community-state-corporate action. And community mobilizations alone do not explain successful outcomes. Environmental processes are influenced by pollution impacts, community strategies and actions, state interests and actions, and corporate responses. The state is clearly not monolithic, with agencies varying in level of authority and interest; internal state conflicts and contradictions often influence regulatory implementation. Other actors are also involved, including local and international NGOs, the scientific community, consumers (who may be local or international), and the media. These actors make up a complex "ecology of agents" around pollution controversies.

Still, community mobilizations influence both the occurrence of state regulatory actions and the effectiveness of these actions. Community pressures (combined with extralocal pressures) have contributed to the generation of new environmental laws in Vietnam and the practical implementation of these laws. Analyzing the relations between community actors and state agencies, among state agencies, and between state agencies and firms is critical to specifying how agents of livability interact and how CDR really works.

The CDR process leads to more than just pro forma state actions. Community members in general are much more interested in results— that is, pollution reduction—than in inspections, reports, EIAs, or even agreements to build treatment plants. Mobilized communities thus serve as an expansive team of monitors to follow up on inspections and promises of improvement. This is particularly important, as monitoring and follow-up are the Achilles' heel of traditional top-down environmental regulation.

CDR can help overcome other common limitations of traditional environmental regulation as well. For example, among the tensions that always exist within the state regarding environmental regulation, the most basic is the conflict between the desire to promote accumulation (either by attracting foreign firms or supporting state-owned enterprises, or SOEs) and the countervailing pressure to regulate the adverse impacts of industry. On a micro level, there are significant incentives (both direct and indirect) for government inspectors to *not* enforce environmental regulations. There also are often severe constraints on staff and funds, which make regulation difficult even for the most committed inspectors. Community participation in the regulation process helps to tip the balance of this equation toward enforcement. At a minimum, community actions make it more difficult for firms to bribe local officials or to falsely claim problems have been solved.

While CDR is quite dynamic and varied, successful cases follow a generally similar pattern: (1) communities identify environmental problems and instigate action to solve them—usually through complaint letters to a local government agency, letters to the firm, or protests; (2) the state responds by investigating, gathering data, and analyzing the past performance of and existing requirements on the firms; (3) the state may also impose fines or require technical changes inside the factory; (4) the community monitors (albeit through unscientific means) the state's actions and any changes in the performance of the firm; (5) if pollution is not reduced, the community escalates its pressure on the firm and challenges the state to fulfill its legal mandate, often turning to extralocal actors such as the media, NGOs, or higher governmental bodies to support their claims.

This pattern of environmental regulation differs in a number of regards from both traditional command-and-control regulation, common in the United States, and simple public participation. Under CAC, a "patrol" model is employed in which the state sets environmental standards, establishes inspection systems, patrols for violators, and then enforces its solution (Gottlieb 1995; Fiorini 1995; Kraft and Vig 1990).[1] The CAC system assumes that the state can patrol corporations effectively. Even when CAC works, however—and it often does not in developing countries—it has many limitations, the most important being in monitoring and enforcement (Afsah, Laplante, and Wheeler 1996; Desai 1998). Under CDR, the community in essence determines its own set of environmental priorities and inspection needs, serves as an additional inspector, monitors progress, and increases the accountability of state-corporate negotiations.

In traditional public participation programs, government agencies allow communities to provide input into environmental issues, but the state sets the agenda for discussion and creates the forums for participation (Canter 1996; Fiorini 1995). Governmental agencies also sometimes use participation as a means to protect firms and the state from outside pressures (Taylor 1995). Vietnam has a complex and often indirect process for public participation. There are no procedures for public review of EIAs, new legislation, or state environmental reports. However, communities have been granted formal rights to demand protection from pollution under the Law on Environmental Protection (passed in 1993).

Community efforts—to monitor factory performance, target problems, demand results, and verify improvements—support state actors who are interested in implementing effective environmental policies. A unique feature of community-driven regulation is the drive for continuous improvement: although the state may set minimum environmental standards, community members are interested in reducing emissions to the point where their lives and health are no longer affected. This combination of a baseline standard with steady improvement has numerous advantages over command-and-control regulation. In the best case, CDR can result in a "virtuous circle" whereby community actions pressure an environmental agency to take action, which results in pollution reduction, thus bolstering community demands and agency capacities, which in turn leads to further community actions and state responses.

For CDR to be effective, community, state, and corporate actions must converge in a synergistic manner. Communities must mobilize effectively, they must have a point of leverage within a state agency, and firms must be responsive to state and community pressures. These characteristics and actions are influenced by history, political opportunities, and existing structures of mobilization and regulation, as well as by the relations developed among firms, communities, and the state.

The Actors in CDR

There are four key actors in community-driven regulation: (1) community members affected by the pollution from a factory; (2) officials within state agencies responsible for regulating and promoting that factory; (3) extralocal actors such as the media, NGOs, and consumers; and (4) the decision makers in the factory itself. The characteristics of these actors, their interests, and their interactions—in other words, the "ecology" of actors and interactions—shape the effectiveness of environmental regulation and are critical to whether such regulation is effective.

In this chapter I seek to move beyond the general model laid out in the introductory chapter and to specify the dynamics that characterize the interactions of these actors when environmental conflicts are focused on degradation caused by factories. While the concrete sequences of my cases are obviously specific to the Vietnamese context, the analytical dynamics are potentially relevant well beyond Vietnam. Before going into the six specific cases, it would be useful to consider some of the characteristics and interactions central to the CDR model and the conditions under which they unite to advance pollution reduction and livability.

Communities   Community characteristics and their relations to firms and the state determine whether communities mobilize, how they mobilize, and whether their actions are effective in pressuring for pollution reduction. To begin with, communities have different capacities, different levels of understanding when it comes to the impacts of pollution, their legal rights, and even knowing where to direct complaints. These basic differences have been observed by a number of analysts, who have hypothesized about the influence of general education and income levels on community mobilization around environmental issues (Afsah, Laplante, and Wheeler 1996).

In order to understand whether capacities are likely to effect change we have to start by recognizing that communities, like the state, are not monolithic. Even in the small communities that were the focus of this analysis, people living in the shadow of a factory could be both cohesive groupings of individuals with similar interests and goals, and opposing forces with different levels of power, wealth, and education who battled to advance their own interests. The question of whether division or cohesion predominates when communities confront other actors is therefore crucial to the CDR model. Strong social ties within the community help overcome obstacles to collective action and aid in the mobilization of resources. Vietnam's socialist past and its system of local People's Committees have strengthened this social cohesion. As Fforde and de Vylder argue (1996, 49), "It is almost impossible to overestimate the importance of [the local collective] to Vietnamese society."

Linkages, meaning external ties to state agencies and extralocal actors, are also critical if community mobilizations are to be effective (cf. Portes 1995; Woolcock 1998). The establishment of the National Environment Agency in 1993 and the provincial Departments of Science, Technology, and Environment in 1994 created a focus for community efforts to influence state environmental decisions. The DOSTEs in particular not only implement national policy, but have also become targets for community demands and thus are pressured to communicate those demands to state decision makers. Linkages to extralocal actors such as the media are also useful for advancing community demands and for reaching higher government authorities.

In short, if communities are endowed with a certain amount of capacity and cohesiveness, as well as certain linkages, the prospects for successful community-driven regulation are much greater. Even though in practice most communities are in possession of these resources only partially, my cases show a clear relationship between relative endowments along these dimensions and relative success.

State Environmental Agencies   State environmental agencies are both coherent actors and arenas for competing interests, and there are many reasons why these agencies do not regulate forcefully.[2] Environmental agencies have internal political conflicts, must cooperate with other state agencies and higher authorities, and must respond to external pressures. What's more, questions of capacity are as crucial for state agencies as they are for communities. They need to have the basic organizational, fiscal, and human capital to enforce environmental laws. Unfortunately, most environmental agencies are underfunded and understaffed. Relative to the firms that they are trying to control, environmental agencies are weak, and they know it. What, then, can push these imperfect agents to take action to protect the environment?

Clearly, finding points of leverage and applying pressure on the state are critical to advancing environmental protection during rapid development. Again, linkages are key, and here I refer to the social and political connections between state officials and civil-society actors that foster effective communication and feedback. Social relationships are at the heart of regulation. State agencies operate at many levels and interact with civil society actors in diverse ways.[3] Because of the important role of linkages, local-level agencies (particularly those that have strong community ties) are more successful than provincial or national agencies in implementing state policies. Of course, social relationships can also be sources of pressure that impede an agency's effectiveness: factory managers interested in protecting their interests will also attempt to build and activate ties to the local agency. Linkages must therefore be balanced by state autonomy.

Extralocal Actors   At the local level, it is common for community members to lose in political battles. In these situations, effective communities often turn to extralocal resources to strengthen their campaigns. The most obvious of these are the media and environmental nongovernmental organizations (NGOs). Vietnam is somewhat unique in the kinds of extralocal resources that are available to communities. There are still no truly independent NGOs working on pollution issues there. Given the limited presence of NGOs and other independent intermediary organizations in Vietnam, one might argue that this category of actor could be dropped from the analysis. My final case, however, demonstrates that translocal NGOs can have a substantial impact, even in Vietnam. The key is connectedness—or linkages once again. NGOs can be embedded not just in a set of provincial or national connections, but in a set of global networks that can, under certain circumstances, provide extraordinary leverage on behalf of local livability and create a window of opportunity for local regulation.

Firms   Finally, of course, there are the firms themselves. In my cases, they are primarily agents of degradation, but they are also potential agents of livability. It is therefore crucial to try to conceptualize the characteristics that make firms more or less likely to respond positively when they are put under pressure by communities, state agencies, or extralocal actors to reduce their pollution. Having the capacity—in the form of technological and fiscal resources—to reduce pollution creates the possibility for corporations to become agents of livability, but motivation is usually more important than capacity.

Linkages, particularly in the form of social ties between a firm and the community, can be instrumental in motivating the firm to take action on pollution problems. How a firm is connected to the local community, such as through its workers, consumers, suppliers, or just as a neighbor, influences how it responds to community complaints about pollution. In cases where community members can influence decisions that affect the firm, such as approving the use of local water supplies, corporations become particularly responsive to local demands. As in the case of state agencies, however, close ties can work both ways. For instance, in a "company town," or when many jobs are at stake, threats of capital flight, layoffs, and loss of tax revenues can protect firms from community and state demands. Linkages to other groups may be equally important in determining corporate responses. Linkages to the state can increase the firm's willingness and ability to resist community pressure. On the other hand, connections to environmentally sensitive customers can increase the price of pollution if consumers become aware of the firm's behavior.

A Schematic of the CDR Model

Figure 4.1 presents a simple schematic of relationships between key actors, showing that a number of routes can be taken to influence firms to reduce pollution. Communities can pressure firms directly. Communities can work with the media and NGOs to pressure firms. The state can pressure firms on its own, as can extralocal actors. And communities can pressure the state to pressure firms.

In my cases, the most effective process involves a dynamic in which communities pressure the state to pressure a firm. In the most successful cases, communities are cohesive and connected, state agencies are capable and responsive to community pressure, and firms are accountable to consumers or the state and in a strong market position to respond. There are also cases in which communities are divided and isolated from state authorities, state agencies are insulated from and unresponsive to community needs and corrupted by ties to firms, and firms are insulated from all pressure and are motivated only to externalize pollution costs. Nonetheless, it was most often pressure from communities, exerted via the state, that produced results. The conclusion is easy to state, but the complex dynamics that lie behind it can be appreciated only by examining individual cases.

Six Case Studies of Community-Driven Regulation

Specific case studies are the best way to understand the complexities of the process of community-driven regulation. The cases that follow are drawn from a larger investigation, which involved reviewing data from a wide sample of factory-community relations, conducting more than

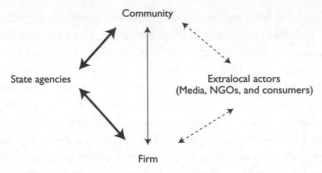

Figure 4.1.   A schematic of the CDR model.

150 interviews, and making site visits to forty factories. The six cases
illustrate what I consider to be a broad range of outcomes in instances
of community efforts to force factories to change their polluting behavior.

All of the cases must obviously be situated in the context of the par-
ticularities of Vietnam's history and current structure of political and
economic power. Vietnam's political system, in which the government
is controlled by a single party, influences the way community members
access and pressure the state. The country's socialist past has left important marks on the landscape of industrial environmental issues, from
the mechanisms that have evolved for responding to community demands (through the People's Committee system), to the development of
a strong state role in production (through state enterprises), to land-use
rights and land tenure. Vietnam's recent transition to a market economy
and the internationalization of the economy have also altered opportunities open to firms and the state.

Table 4.1 summarizes the basic features of the firms in the case studies. The cases themselves are drawn from both the north and south of
Vietnam, which historically have had very different political systems.
They focus on state-owned enterprises, foreign multinationals, and centrally and locally managed firms.

Case 1. Pollution in the Pews:
Organizing around Dona Bochang Textiles

Local regulators say the air pollution from the Dona Bochang Textiles
factory is really not all that bad. The neighboring community, however,
does not seem placated by the thought that other communities have it

TABLE 4.1
OVERVIEW OF FIRMS AND POLLUTION IN THE SIX CASE STUDIES

	Dona Bochang	Lam Thao	Viet Tri	Tan Mai	Ba Nhat	Tae Kwang
Product	Textiles	Fertilizer	Chemicals	Paper	Chemicals	Shoes
Ownership	Taiwanese-Vietnamese joint venture	Ministry of Industry	Ministry of Industry	Ministry of Industry	Hanoi Department of Industry	Korean
Pollution	Boiler gases, soot, dyes	Acids, sulfur dioxide, sulfuric acid	Chlorine gas, sodium hydroxide	Black liquor (pulping chemicals), boiler gases, fibers, dust, biochemical oxygen demand, chemical oxygen demand	Calcium carbonate dust, noise	Boiler gases, solvents
Location	Dong Nai Province (new urban)	Phu Tho Province (rural)	Phu Tho Province (semiurban)	Dong Nai Province (new urban)	Hanoi (urban)	Dong Nai Province (industrial estate)
Established	1990	1962	1961	1963	1968	1995

worse. In their view, pollution from the factory (a joint venture whose majority owners are Taiwanese) is a continuing assault on the neighborhood, affecting people's daily lives, disrupting special occasions, even defiling their center of worship—the local Catholic church. Pollution impacts such as respiratory problems, corroded roofs, and blackened plants have led to an escalation of community actions that have included writing regular complaint letters, throwing bricks at the factory, working with the media, and developing a long-term campaign to either make the factory a better neighbor or move it altogether.

As the Taiwanese managers soon found out, the people living around Dona Bochang are a tightly knit community. Approximately 95 percent of them are Catholics who moved to the area in 1954, fleeing the Communist victory in the north. As Catholics, they were first protected by Ngo Dinh Diem, the former president of South Vietnam and himself a Catholic; after the unification of the country under the Communists in 1975, they were politically marginalized. However, throughout Vietnam's political changes, they have retained a distinctive identity as Catholics in this overwhelmingly Buddhist country. The community's solidarity and internal social capital has been strengthened by more than forty years of church organizing around religious and community issues (although not political ones). The residents along the factory's back wall live together, work together, socialize together, and worship together. Each time I went to interview an individual household, fifteen to twenty people would be gathered in the house within ten minutes, all telling their stories.

Situating a highly polluting factory in this community is a glaring example of unplanned urban development and the absence of zoning in Vietnam. The factory (which was taken over and expanded by the Taiwanese company in 1990) and the local residents are separated by no more than a three-meter-high wall and a dirt road that runs along the perimeter of the factory. People live cramped together in small houses along the back wall of the factory; the community church is along another wall. The factory's air emissions, when not blowing across the back wall into the residential area, often blow directly into the church. Unfortunately for the parishioners, the church is an open-air building with little more than a roof, an altar, and rows of pews.

With regular pollution incidents affecting the church, this tight-knit community has a focal point for discussing and organizing around pollution issues. Although the parish priest claims he does not organize community actions, he admits that the community cannot help but discuss the pollution while at the church. Indeed, in church the affected families have a chance to mention their concerns to the chair of the local *phuong* (or ward) People's Committee, who also happens to be Catholic and lives near the factory.

In my interviews, one family stood out as leaders of community action. They seemed fairly well educated and quite well off for the community, running their own small household enterprise finishing wood furniture. Living and working just a few feet from the factory wall, the family had collected a thick file on the factory's pollution, including press clippings, letters they had sent to various government agencies, the responses they had received, and photographs of pollution impacts. They regularly drafted letters for others to sign. They had been on the official delegations to the factory and to government meetings. They had even made a video of the pollution. In many ways, they seemed fearless in their quest to end the pollution, a quest they have yet to finish.

After several years of having their complaints ignored, an incident served to ignite community action in 1993. On the day of a local wedding (for a different family), pollution from the factory coated trays of food laid out for the reception in a layer of black soot. A large number of community members considered this the last straw, marched to the front gate, and threatened to tear down the wall and shut down the factory if the manager did not come out to talk to them. Some young people went so far as to throw bricks at the factory, highlighting how serious the community was in their determination to force a response.

On that day a factory representative asserted that they were doing all they could and promised the problems would be solved. The community forced the manager to sign a statement attesting to the level of pollution. Photographs were taken of the pollution impacts. Several months later, when nothing had changed, the community brought its complaints, the pictures, and the signed statement to the Dong Nai Department of Science, Technology, and Environment and to the media. After newspaper reports questioned the failure of the government to regulate the pollution, the DOSTE agreed to take action. It responded to the community complaints by organizing an inspection team and several meetings between community members and the factory. The community, however, criticized the inspection process, charging that because it was a planned inspection, the factory would be able to turn off the polluting equipment before the inspectors arrived. Community members argued that their daily experiences were more accurate than the data collected from the inspection. Later, when pollution levels resumed, the community sent more written complaints to the government and the media. This renewed pressure motivated more meetings and finally resulted in the factory agreeing to install equipment to reduce its emissions.

By the fall of 1997, the neighbors of Dona Bochang had achieved a qualified victory over the factory. Since the wedding party incident, the factory had made three changes to reduce its air pollution. First, it built a taller smokestack—the classic solution to local environmental problems. When that did not reduce the local impacts, the factory changed its practice of "blowing the tubes" from its boiler (that is, forcing the built-up soot out of the smokestacks), which was a major source of the black soot people complained about. Finally, when the problems still were not resolved, the factory installed an air filtration system to capture the pollution. This process took several years, but it resulted in a significant reduction in air emissions (according to the firm itself and the Dong Nai DOSTE). The community agrees that there have been improvements, but it continues to pressure for further pollution reductions.

The state's role in this case is complicated. As the factory is a joint venture, the Dong Nai People's Committee owns 10 percent of it. Community action is thus in conflict with the short-term economic interests of the provincial People's Committee, which controls the DOSTE. The community members' perception that they had to overcome this conflict of interest led them to extralocal actors such as the National Environment Agency and the media to help address their problems. It also strengthened the community's resolve to keep pressure on the factory and on the provincial authorities. Community members did not trust the state to take action without repeated pressure. At the same time, the fact that majority ownership of the factory was foreign may have worked to the community's advantage: Vietnamese government agencies appear extremely sensitive about public perceptions that the state is privileging foreign capitalists over common people.

The Dona Bochang case represents a clear success of CDR: A cohesive and connected community united to pressure a state agency, sounding repeated alarms and monitoring state and corporate actions; in response the state took action on the polluting firm. By using official complaint procedures as well as unofficial tactics (protests, threats, media pressures), a tight-knit, capable community was able to exert significant influence over pollution issues.

As much as the improvements at Dona Bochang are due in large part to the strength, organization, and persistence of the community, however, it should be noted that the community on its own was not able to change Dona Bochang. Letters and meetings with the factory owners did not result in pollution reduction. Success came through the community's exerting pressure on local and national government agencies both directly and through the media. For instance, during my research it was common to read headlines in the Vietnamese press such as "Dona Bochang Factory Continues to Generate Pollution." The community's linkages to local government officials and extralocal reporters were as critical as its own cohesiveness to generating this kind of press attention and to its ultimate success in motivating state and corporate action.

Case 2. Lam Thao's Bitter Tea: The State as the Polluter

A woman in her sixties led me and a group of neighbors to the wastewater canal they said was the source of many of their illnesses. With the skill and strength of a lifelong farmer she dug down several feet into the soil to expose a leaking pipe. Farther on, several men used a crowbar to pry open the cement cover of the wastewater pipe to show more leaks and to illustrate how the wastewater had literally burned away the cement cover. So acidic it often has a pH value of one, the wastewater has leached into the community's drinking water supply and contaminated it. Even their tea, the lifeblood of the Vietnamese day, is now bitter. The positive side, one woman joked, is that they don't have to add any spices to make sweet and sour soup.

Unfortunately, acid in the wastewater is only one of the environmental problems faced by the communities living around the Lam Thao fertilizer factory. Lam Thao, built with Russian assistance in the 1960s, stands as a monstrous example of disregard for the environmental impacts of industrial development. Air pollution from the factory's production of sulfuric acid and superphosphate fertilizer carries sulfur dioxide, sulfuric acid, hydrochloric acid, hydrogen fluoride, and other toxins to the surrounding villages. Although community members complain that they have been living with the pollution since the factory's opening in 1962, they assert that the pollution increased substantially in 1992, after the plant was expanded. In one hamlet, the People's Committee chair explained, "We did not realize [how bad the pollution was] until the disease rates became high and some environmental organizations investigated." He asserts that the death rate in his hamlet doubled in 1992, the year the factory increased its output (personal interview, April 18, 1997).

Other health problems associated with the factory's pollution include "swollen skin, rashes, [and] people losing teeth [they become loose and fall out from drinking the water]. The rate of cancer has increased recently, and children have problems with their throats." A local nurse notes that air pollution has caused high rates of lung illnesses, and "swollen throats are very common close to the factory" (personal interviews, April 18, 1997). Pollution from the factory also regularly damages crops. Water and air pollution kill rice, banana trees, and coconut trees. Fruit trees that survive gradually decrease their yield. Accidental leaks from the wastewater pipe regularly destroy nearby farmers' crops. One commune alone claims to lose 300 million dong's (about twenty-two thousand dollars') worth of rice per year to pollution damage.

Communities around the factory have no problem assigning blame for the health and economic impacts they face. However, they differ in their strategies for taking Lam Thao to task for its actions. Two communities (each containing several hamlets) are severely affected by Lam Thao's pollution: the factory's wastewater primarily affects the community next to the factory, and air pollution affects the one across the Red River. Despite similarities in terms of community cohesiveness, however, differences in capacity and linkages strongly affect each one's ability to counteract the factory's threats to local livability.

The members of the community next to Lam Thao are better educated than their counterparts across the river; they hold regular meetings and have applied direct pressure on the factory, including letters, demands for meetings, and complaints to government authorities. The community across the river is made up of very poor farmers, with no electricity, a high incidence of child malnutrition, and few connections to the hierarchy of the district People's Committee. The first community has been successful in getting Lam Thao to build a new wastewater canal, cover the canal with cement, and build neutralization tanks for the wastewater. It also has pressed the factory to pay compensation for crop damage, amounting to more than eighty thousand dollars in 1996 alone. The second has won only small monetary compensations each year, which it claims pay for only about 5 percent of its crop loss.

Both communities appear to be relatively cohesive. The second is in fact the more tight-knit, with less migration in or out and a higher percentage of farmers who are affected by the pollution. However, despite divisions in the first community, which has members who work in the factory, it has been much more successful in pressuring Lam Thao to change. Much of the community's success has resulted from using its ties to local government officials (several of the community members are actually former officials) to demand compensation from the factory. It has documented impacts from the air and water pollution, made the information available to government officials and local media, and demanded official monitoring of pollution levels and impacts. Its effectiveness at winning cash compensations for damaged crops and water supplies has in fact motivated Lam Thao to invest in solutions that are cheaper than compensation. The second community, on the other hand, has waited for the government to analyze the problems and provide fair compensation.

The first community is also much more sophisticated than the second about its legal rights, recognizing the power of the Law on Environmental Protection in guaranteeing the legitimacy of community demands to be protected from pollution or at least compensated for its impacts, and focusing pressure on the state to enforce the law. Thus, the first community benefits not only from its sophistication but also from its greater linkages, in this case its more developed ties to provincial authorities. The second community, on the other hand, is both physically and politically cut off from provincial decision makers.

Conflicts within the state also influence the Lam Thao case. Two ministries are responsible for promotion and regulation of the factory: VINACHEM, the Vietnam Chemical Corporation, a division of the Ministry of Industry, owns and operates the factory; the Ministry of Science, Technology, and Environment (MOSTE) is responsible for regulating it. MOSTE's lack of autonomy vis-à-vis the Ministry of Industry seriously hampers enforcement: the Ministry of Industry is strong enough to effectively veto environmental regulation that MOSTE attempts to advance. Community members have thus focused their complaints on the provincial People's Committee and the DOSTE, demanding local protections from centrally controlled industry.

The Lam Thao case demonstrates that community cohesiveness is by no means enough to win environmental improvements, particularly with regard to state enterprises. In this case, the community that is more cohesive nevertheless lacks capacity and linkages and ends up gaining very little in its struggle against the well-connected factory. Only the community that combines cohesiveness with capacity and linkages (in the form of connections to higher authorities) is successful. The divisions within the state (central versus local, industry versus People's Committee) highlight how the state can be pressured to take action, but only when the community can find a point of leverage in the state to counter pro-industry interests.

Case 3. Growing Up with Pollution: Environmental Change at Viet Tri Chemicals

Viet Tri City rises up out of the Red River delta as a testament to Vietnamese industrial development. The town was created in 1963 as a base for industry away from the obvious wartime target of Hanoi. Virtually everything had to be imported to make Viet Tri into an industrial center: Technicians from China and Russia designed and built the factories. Workers came from around the Red River delta to begin the process of proletarianization. Raw materials were floated down to the confluence of the Lo and Red Rivers, where a town was quickly being constructed. Viet Tri is an example of intentional government policies meant to decentralize the location of industry while continuing central management.

In the rush to create an industrial complex in Viet Tri—which came to include a paper mill, a sugar mill, a beer factory, a particle board factory, a nearby fertilizer plant, and the Viet Tri Chemical factory— little attention was paid to the environmental impacts of industrial activities. Soon, Viet Tri became known as the most polluted city in Vietnam; stories of the dusty, dirty town spread throughout the country. By the end of the 1980s, Viet Tri's factories had gained well-founded reputations for being major polluters, and Viet Tri Chemicals became known as one of the most egregious polluters in an increasingly "unlivable" city. In 1988 city authorities went so far as to petition for Viet Tri Chemicals to be shut down.

With this past, it is surprising to learn that by 1993, Viet Tri Chemicals had been "recognized as having made the most positive contributions to [a] cleaner environment" of any chemical plant in Vietnam (Nguyen 1993). During tough economic times, the factory management succeeded in securing a loan from the central government that allowed them to significantly upgrade their sodium hydroxide production equipment, plant 230,000 trees near the factory, institute an emissions monitoring program, and train their workers in better environmental practices. While the factory had by no means solved all its environmental problems, it significantly reduced emissions in four short years.

Asked why these actions were taken, the vice-director of the factory explained simply that the changes were necessitated by community pressure. This is likely an oversimplification, but it does highlight the importance of community pressures in the transformation of a seemingly insulated state enterprise. The factory justified its capital investments in equipment changes by pointing to both economic and environmental benefits. Switching from graphite to titanium electrodes in the electrolysis process helped the factory substantially reduce its energy costs, thereby lowering overall production costs. At the same time, the change reduced lead emissions and accidental releases of chlorine gas. Later, after a round of particularly vocal community complaints, the company established an emissions-monitoring program.

In 1995 Viet Tri Chemicals took another step that no factory in Vietnam had ever taken, giving tours of the factory to concerned community members. The tours were prompted by community complaints at a meeting of candidates for local elected office.[4] The candidates turned the idea of touring the factory into a campaign promise that has since been honored by tours once or twice per year. The factory has also set up a program to reward workers for coming up with ideas to reduce waste or improve the environment. In 1996, the factory awarded workers a total of 50 million dong (about thirty-six hundred dollars) for ideas that were implemented.

Living with pollution over the last forty years, the community around Viet Tri has developed a strong awareness of environmental issues. Half of the workers from the factory live nearby, raising the awareness level and technical knowledge of the community. The acting director lives only two hundred meters from the factory gates. Community members, including some who work in the plant, have written numerous complaint letters about the pollution problems to the factory and the local People's Committee. The community around Viet Tri Chemicals thus has a high level of capacity for responding to environmental problems.

Because of the gravity of pollution problems from Viet Tri Chemicals, and because of the proximity of their homes to the factory, workers and managers seem to take these issues quite seriously. Because the factory used to experience frequent releases of chlorine gas, the workers became intimately aware of the health impacts of the factory's pollution. Groundwater pollution was also hard to ignore, as it contaminated the wells of many of the workers who lived nearby. The community around Viet Tri, although including groups with very different interests—workers, managers, farmers, and other residents—is fairly unified on pollution issues. Awareness, and close connections to the impacts of emissions, have led the community to exert significant pressure on the factory over the years. In 1996, when a late-night spill from the factory's detergent line killed fish in a cooperative fish pond, community members were at the factory gates the next morning with evidence and demands for compensation. Several government officials mentioned these spontaneous "gatherings in front of the factory" as a major pressure on Viet Tri Chemicals.

There are, however, divisions within the state regarding the factory, which is a centrally managed state enterprise. The profits from Viet Tri (if there are any) go to Hanoi, while the problems stay in the community. The few benefits from the factory accruing to local officials seem to be counterbalanced by community complaints and the fact that the factory continues to stain the city's reputation. It is thus somewhat understandable that local officials would support the factory's closure or at least stricter regulation.

The very real threat of being shut down, driven by both local calls for the factory's closure and poor economic performance, has led the management to take seriously the need to change. One manager intimated that the factory's bad reputation was one reason they were not getting government loans. Viet Tri Chemicals thus did not respond to pollution complaints by simply building taller smokestacks or installing waste treatment systems, but instead chose to significantly upgrade its production methods. Changing the production process helped change the company's environmental reputation, which helped the factory in several other regards.

As in other parts of Vietnam, community members in Viet Tri submit complaints to the local People's Committee, which then forwards the complaints to the responsible agencies. However, two differences seem to be at work in this case. First, when community members complain about Viet Tri Chemicals, it is the factory that has the burden of proof to show it is not guilty, because of the long-standing awareness about its pollution. This is the opposite of virtually every other case I examined in Vietnam. For example, in the fish kill from the detergent spill, it was the factory rather than the community that requested the DOSTE to inspect the situation. The factory felt it needed data to show it was innocent. Most factories would be presumed innocent until proven guilty. This shows the strong linkages and trust the community has developed with the state. Second, while Viet Tri Chemicals is a state enterprise, local government officials have made clear that they are willing to challenge the central government to resolve problems at the factory. Local elected officials appear to consider this an issue they cannot ignore. This cleavage between state agencies provides a political opening for community demands.

Viet Tri Chemicals shows that SOEs can be regulated under certain circumstances. A connected community with strong capacities was able, over a number of years, to put the factory on the defensive. Through changes in state concerns and conflicts between local and central agencies, a previously insulated factory became vulnerable to community complaints. Community members were successful in establishing an effective system of alarms, and vulnerable factory managers then turned these pollution concerns into pollution prevention strategies that had both environmental and economic benefits.

Case 4. Living Off Pollution:
The Divided Community around Tan Mai Paper Mill

Just meters beyond the outer wall of Tan Mai paper mill, a thriving industry exists in the shade of coconut trees. In ponds where rice fields used to lie, local villagers stand chest deep in wastewater from the factory. Young men strain to lift nets out of the ponds, filled to the brim with the catch of the day: paper fiber emitted in the mill's wastewater.

As one part of this community literally lives off wastewater, selling recovered fiber to low-grade paper makers in nearby Ho Chi Minh City, other people pay the price in damaged crops, polluted drinking water, and dead fish. The Tan Mai case is an example of a divided community that both depends on the factory's pollution for income and is injured by its activities. Some community members work in the factory. Others complain of losing an entire year's crops with no compensation.

Although Tan Mai had been causing pollution since the 1960s, it was not until the factory increased its production in 1992 that community members organized as a group to demand recourse for dead fish and damaged crops. Between 1992 and 1996, community members wrote letters to the DOSTE, the media, and the factory management. The DOSTE investigated the claims of the community but never showed the results to community members and never awarded compensation for lost crops or fish.

Few people argue that Tan Mai does not have serious environmental impacts. The factory managers acknowledge that they need a new waste treatment system. Even the people who make their living off recovering fiber express their concern about the impacts of the factory's pollution. Local farmers cannot eat the rice they produce, using it only to feed to their pigs. Community members complain of nausea from air pollution; undrinkable well-water; nose, eye, and skin problems; and lower yields from their fruit trees.

However, the community around Tan Mai is both physically and emotionally divided. One group of families lives next to the factory's back wall, collecting the paper fibers; another group grows rice in fields nearby; a third lives in company-built apartments on the urban side of the factory; and a fourth lives in fish-raising houseboats on the river into which Tan Mai discharges its wastewater. The People's Committee has a young and dynamic chair who is quite open about the environmental impacts of the factory on the community and equally open about his frustration with not being able to change the situation. Through this local official, the community has submitted formal complaints to the factory and to provincial authorities. But, as he explains, "The people in this area have children working in the factory. They can use electricity and water from the factory. So of course there are losses and benefits from the factory, but they don't want to complain much" (personal interview, June 6, 1997).

Tan Mai is owned and managed by central state authorities and is at the same time under the regulation of the National Environment Agency. Either through corruption or a concerted policy, the state has worked to block criticisms and demands for environmental improvements at factories such as Tan Mai. For instance, after complaints from the community, the DOSTE took measurements of water pollution at Tan Mai, but they were taken in a way that covered up the real pollution levels: some samples were actually taken upstream from the factory, where the water was relatively clean. The DOSTE then issued a formal memo stating that the factory was in compliance with environmental standards. Everyone involved in this case recognizes that Tan Mai is nowhere near compliance with environmental standards, yet this document is now accepted as proof of Tan Mai's performance. Once Tan Mai received the DOSTE memo, neither the community nor local government authorities were able to fine or seek compensation from the factory.

Community members have thus resigned themselves to the factory's continued pollution, seemingly giving up on further complaints. They gave different reasons for no longer writing complaint letters, including "they have no effect," "they only result in DOSTE coming out, measuring, and then disappearing," and "they get you noticed by the authorities." This discouragement is not uncommon. Other communities I studied also feared that complaints would be ignored or cause more trouble than they were worth. Nonetheless, some persevered and were sometimes successful. The community around Tan Mai, however, has been unable to overcome internal divisions and resistance. It is in fact endowed with a reasonable level of capacities, including a mix of educated young members and industrial workers. It even has some connections to local government representatives. Nonetheless, it has not been able to forge broader state or media linkages, and its internal divisions have weakened its ability to pressure environmental agencies to take action against the centrally managed factory.

Then again, perhaps more cohesion would not have much effect. Tan Mai is, for a number of reasons, an extremely well insulated company. The government has targeted the paper industry for expansion and is aggressively promoting the three largest pulp and paper mills in the country, including Tan Mai. Promotion and protection of Tan Mai thus win out over other interests (even tax collection) and block local regulation of its pollution. The firm in this case has such strong linkages with the state that virtually no amount of local pressure can motivate stricter regulation. Recognizing this, community members have given up even submitting formal complaint letters.

Case 5. Owner as Regulator:
The Frustrated Community around Ba Nhat Chemicals

When Mr. Tien left his window open, as people without air-conditioning are forced to do on hot summer days in Hanoi, within an hour much of his one-room apartment would be coated with a fine layer of white powder. For Mr. Tien, a retiree from the government, living next to the Ba Nhat Chemicals factory meant living with calcium carbonate dust, the noise of grinding rocks at all hours of the day and night, and the respiratory problems that haunted the neighborhood.

Ba Nhat had been producing chemicals in this area since the 1960s, when three small cooperatives were merged into a city-owned company owned by the Hanoi Department of Industry. Output at the small factory, which employed two hundred people, had grown over the years, as had the pollution that rained down on the apartment buildings just five meters from Ba Nhat's walls.

Pollution had been serious since at least 1987, when the community began complaining in earnest about the impacts of the factory's production. Over a period of twelve years, community members wrote more than a hundred letters to all levels of the government, including the National Assembly; submitted a letter to the courts, similar to a lawsuit demanding action on the factory; motivated journalists to write articles; and even wrote their own articles and paid to have them published. These actions were coordinated by the Committee against the Pollution of Ba Nhat, which met regularly to strategize about the factory and was headed by a retired professor.

Community members were successful in pressuring the government to commission a study by a university professor on the factory's pollution. The results found that three thousand people were adversely affected by the pollution, which included carbon monoxide emissions seventy times higher than permitted, dust ten times higher, sulfur dioxide four times higher, and other toxic gases five to seven times the permitted levels (Nguyen 1996). By the early 1990s, everyone seemed in agreement that the factory was a problem. Every level of government imaginable had been contacted. Data clearly showed the factory was in violation of environmental laws. Nonetheless, the factory continued with business as usual.

The community around Ba Nhat has all of the critical traits necessary to motivate action on environmental issues. It is cohesive, has a high technical capacity, and has good connections to government officials. It is the best educated of any I studied, made up of government employees and current and retired professors from the nearby Hanoi Polytechnic University. Residents are relatively well off, solidly upper middle class by Vietnamese standards. The community is in an urban area, close to the halls of power. It even has access to a wealth of damning environmental data. However, even with all of these critical characteristics, the community failed year after year to win changes at Ba Nhat.

City government agencies are at the center of the Ba Nhat decision-making process: the Hanoi Department of Industry (DOI) owns and manages the factory, and the Hanoi DOSTE is responsible for regulating it (although community members complain that responsibility for environmental management of the factory is not well defined). Both agencies report directly to the Hanoi People's Committee. Within this political system, the DOSTE is much weaker than the DOI. In fact, the DOSTE had not shut down or moved any of the DOI's two hundred factories despite repeated promises to do so.

What the community needed and failed for years to find was leverage over the DOI. For state-owned enterprises like Ba Nhat, environmental reforms necessarily involve one state agency pressuring another to make a change. As the National Environment Agency does not have jurisdiction over city-owned factories, this case boiled down to a political battle between the promoters and regulators of Ba Nhat within the Hanoi city government. Failing to motivate changes in the Hanoi bureaucracy, community members took their complaints to higher levels, petitioning the National Assembly and even the prime minister.

Finally, in late 1998, after more than ten years of community complaints, the Hanoi government announced that it would physically move the factory out of the city center to a rural area with an existing chemical complex. DOSTE staff explained in interviews that they had faced a series of battles to win this decision First, the DOSTE had to overcome the DOI's resistance to moving the factory. When it finally won approval to do so, it then had to begin the process of working with suburban and rural government officials and community members to convince them to accept the factory. These efforts were blocked twice before a rural community with an existing chemical plant finally agreed to accept the plant. Continued (and escalated) community pressures were critical to strengthening the position of the DOSTE and, I believe, ultimately tipped the scales toward moving the factory. As one government official explained, "Pollution was the key issue on motivating the move. There were many complaints from the public, and the National Assembly representative from Hai Ba Trung worked to push forward the decision. Ba Nhat is the first factory in Hanoi to be moved by force because of public pressure" (personal interview, December 26, 1998).

Once again, the Ba Nhat case shows clearly that community capacity and cohesion alone are not enough; it also illustrates the subtleties of linkages. This is by no means an isolated community, but its connections with the state were frustrated by other powerful interests for more than a decade. With no autonomy and little capacity, the Hanoi DOSTE is almost powerless to regulate polluting state enterprises that provide jobs and tax revenues to the Department of Industry. Only connections that were able to invoke a state agency or power *above* the Hanoi People's Committee, and extensive public pressure, were enough to overcome the dominant position of the DOI. However, this case also raises the specter of organized communities motivating polluting factories to move to less-organized, weaker communities.

Case 6. Global Production, Global Communities: Nike Shoe Manufacturing in Vietnam

In a single room the size of a football field, two thousand women sit hunched over sewing machines stitching sports shoes. Row after row of young women work eleven hours per day, six days per week at the production lines of the Korean-owned Tae Kwang Vina company. Most of the factory's workers (90 percent of whom are women) have traveled from northern and central Vietnam in search of these jobs. Trading rural rice fields for the new Bien Hoa 2 Industrial Estate, the women have left their homes and families for the prospect of forty dollars per month in the factory and a better life.

The vision of a better life is hard to conjure walking through this factory of ninety-two hundred workers. During the summer months the workers sweat in hundred-degree-plus temperatures at their assembly lines. They are exposed to toxic solvents and glues that often make them dizzy or nauseated (and that would be much more strictly regulated in countries such as the United States). Respiratory ailments are common, as are accidents in some of the more hazardous sections. And then there is the repeated verbal and physical abuse they experience at the hands of foreign managers.

More than seven thousand miles away, in cities such as Portland, San Francisco, and New York, human rights and labor activists have been strategizing on how to change the conditions inside factories like Tae Kwang. While the activists might not know the name of this factory, who its managers are, or who even owns it, they are clear on who is responsible for its poor labor and environmental conditions: Nike, Inc.

Nike is the world's leading producer of sports shoes and apparel, with $9.6 billion in sales in 1998, according to its annual report. It is also one of the world's leading innovators in global outsourcing. Nike owns none of the factories that produce its famous sports shoes. The five Nike factories in Vietnam, which employ thirty-five thousand workers, are owned by Korean and Taiwanese subcontractors. Nike still designs its shoes in Beaverton, Oregon, but prototype shoes are produced in Seoul or Taipei, and a final production run is likely to be done in China, Indonesia, or Vietnam.

For twenty years, this subcontracting arrangement was a win-win situation for Nike. The company was able to create competition between subcontractors, push down production costs, shift the risk of investing in factories and equipment, and avoid the difficulties of managing hundreds of thousands of workers. It was also able to use the subcontracting system as an excuse to avoid responsibility for environmental and working conditions in the factories that produce its shoes. As Nike neither owned nor managed the factories, it argued it could not be held responsible for their day-to-day conditions. Never mind that Nike staff are in the factories every day monitoring what is produced, how it is produced, and the quality of the final products.

Managers at Tae Kwang are careful to explain that they don't just sell shoes to Nike; they are "strategic partners" with the global power-house. T2, the parent company of Tae Kwang, has been producing Nike shoes in South Korea since the early 1980s. When labor costs began rising in South Korea, T2 set up shop in China and Vietnam.

Although Tae Kwang is one of the newer factories in Dong Nai province, it is already known as a bad place to work. In general, people from Dong Nai avoid jobs at Tae Kwang if they can help it. (Dong Nai is next to Ho Chi Minh City, so finding other jobs is a viable option.) Huge numbers of migrants thus serve as the labor pool for the factory. Tae Kwang is also known by government agencies as "uncooperative." Officials in the Dong Nai DOSTE say they get little response from Tae Kwang to their requests that it reduce its toxic emissions or clean up its polluted effluent. The factory seems to have learned a lot about navigating local labor laws and environmental regulations from its experiences in South Korea and China. For instance, the company has been able to avoid complying with national requirements for a wastewater treatment plant without suffering any consequences. It recently hired the son of the chair of the province Communist Party to help with these kinds of issues and to be a "problem solver" with the government.

Regulation of companies like Tae Kwang is difficult for the Vietnamese government. The state is in the bind of working to attract foreign capital (competing with countries such as China and Indonesia, where the bulk of Nike production occurs) while at the same time attempting to establish regulatory policies and mechanisms of enforcement. Clearly, a company responsible for more than thirty-five thousand jobs and fully 4 percent of Vietnam's total exports in 1998 carries a fair amount of influence with government officials.

Environmental laws are one example of policies that have been selectively enforced in Vietnam. For instance, Tae Kwang burns all of the scrap rubber from its production process in order to generate steam, and in the process creates thick black clouds of pollution. Despite requests by the NEA and DOSTE to reduce these emissions, in 1997 Tae Kwang actually purchased additional scrap rubber from other Nike plants in Vietnam to feed its boilers, thereby increasing the pollution. Because Tae Kwang is in the middle of an industrial estate, officially no one lives near the factory, so there is no community to complain about these problems. The people most affected by Tae Kwang's pollution—the workers—have little power to influence the company. The company union is controlled by the managers, who hand-pick all union representatives. The community that does exist around Tae Kwang has little capacity, cohesion, or linkage to external actors. The majority of the factory's workers are recent immigrants to the province, often straight off farms, who rarely stay more than a year or two at the factory before moving on. The residents of the area appear to feel few connections or allegiances to these workers.

Local efforts by either government officials or community members to influence Tae Kwang have thus had little effect. However, powerful external pressures do appear to have influenced the company. NGOs in the United States and Europe have been successful in pressuring Tae Kwang to change its production practices and have helped to build the capacity and linkages available to workers and community members. Activist campaigns regarding labor conditions in Nike plants have gained worldwide media attention. In October 1997, groups in more than ten countries organized protests, pickets, and informational campaigns regarding Nike's production practices. In April 1998, protests and pickets expanded to even more cities and countries across the United States and Europe. NGOs in the United States such as Global Exchange, the Campaign for Labor Rights, Vietnam Labor Watch, and Press for Change have coordinated to pressure Nike to force its subcontractors dispersed across Asia to improve their environmental performance and working conditions. These groups have used the media to educate the public about conditions inside Nike plants. Some have called for boycotts of Nike products, while others have begun lobbying government bodies to force Nike to change (Benjamin 1998; Bissell 1998; Shaw 1999). My own research on Tae Kwang has been used by these groups to pressure Nike to improve conditions in its Vietnamese plants (O'Rourke 1997; Greenhouse 1997).

For Tae Kwang, extralocal pressures have led to regular visits from Nike's labor and environmental inspectors, as well as monitoring by third-party accounting and health and safety firms. The first goal of these inspections has been to reduce worker exposures to toxic solvents and glues. In May 1998, the company announced a major initiative to eliminate the use of organic solvent-based cleaners and glues, pledging to comply with U.S. workplace laws in all of its factories. By December 1998, workplace health and safety conditions had been substantially improved at Tae Kwang (O'Rourke and Brown 1999). Pressure from Nike—which has been driven by media and NGO pressures back in consumer markets—is now having more of an impact on the reduction of air pollution and workplace hazards than local government or community pressures could have had on their own.

The Tae Kwang case is obviously quite different from the other five. There are no neighbors living next to the factory, and the workers have no cohesive community to represent their environmental and health concerns. Instead, a network of NGOs and activists outside Vietnam has worked to pressure Nike directly and to indirectly pressure the Vietnamese government to increase enforcement. This coalition of international actors has then worked to build links to local community members and workers. In this way, extralocal actors are actually working to support and build the capacity of local community members and are providing room for state agencies to more effectively regulate a multinational corporation.

This last case demonstrates that even in an environment that leaves little space for NGOs and other intermediary organizations, these groups still can play an important role. Taking advantage of global linkages, they can exercise leverage on behalf of local livability that trumps the power of firms like Tae Kwang, which appear invincible in the local context.

Summary of the Cases

The six cases presented here offer compelling evidence of the importance of community capacity, cohesiveness, and linkages in solving pollution conflicts in Vietnam. Table 4.2 summarizes the key characteristics of the cases and their outcomes.

In the cases in which the communities had basic capacities, were relatively cohesive, and had linkages to the state (Dona Bochang, Viet Tri, and Ba Nhat), the community was successful in pressuring for pollution reductions. However, even with these characteristics, changes can be blocked or delayed for many years by powerful state interests. Linkages alone can win partial victories (first Lam Thao community and Tae Kwang). But a lack of cohesion (Tan Mai) or of linkages (second Lam Thao community) can block a community from successfully organizing for pollution reductions.

TABLE 4.2
SUMMARY OF THE SIX CASE STUDIES

	Dona Bochang	Lam Thao		Viet Tri	Tan Mai	Ba Nhat	Tae Kwang
		First Community	*Second Community*				
Key dynamics	Capacity	Little capacity	Little capacity	Capacity	Some capacity	Capacity	No capacity
	Cohesiveness	Divisions	Cohesiveness	Some cohesiveness	Strong divisions	Cohesiveness	Divisions
	Linkages	Linkages	No linkages	Linkages	Some linkages	Linkages	External linkages
Outcomes	Success	Partial success	Failure	Success after many years	Failure	Success after many years	Partial success

Conclusions

Vietnam offers a hard test of the ability of community-driven regulation to push urban-industrial environments in the direction of livability. Regulatory allies within the state are much weaker than state agencies for whom accumulation is not just a priority but practically the only priority. The power of communities is circumscribed by legal rules and the nonelectoral character of political power. NGOs and translocal social movements are largely excluded from the political landscape.

Given this context, the fact that three of the six cases (Dona Bochang, Viet Tri, and Ba Nhat) show substantial reductions in industrial pollution—or, indeed, elimination (by inducing the factory to move elsewhere)—as a result of community pressure must be read as a strong endorsement of the efficacy of the CDR model. The cases are also useful in clarifying some of the broader characteristics of key actors within the Vietnamese context and the sources of variation among particular struggles between communities and firms.

The first thing that is striking in terms of the overall landscape of the Vietnamese political context is the surprising vibrancy of communities as political actors, even those communities that have not been successful. For example, the community closest to Lam Thao exhibited a remarkable level of mobilization and fighting spirit despite a clear appreciation of the odds against them. Overall, the picture of Vietnam is very much at odds with the stereotypical image of state-socialist societies in which civil society is crushed and moribund under the overwhelming weight of the state. Vietnamese communities appear just as mobilized and combative as their counterparts in ostensibly democratic Mexico or Brazil. Determining whether that is due primarily to historical traditions of community activism or to differences between the structure of Vietnamese political organization and the similar structures that formally existed in Eastern Europe and the Soviet Union lies beyond the scope of this chapter. What is clear, however, is that a close look at Vietnam demonstrates the importance of avoiding presuppositions about the power of macropolitical regimes when thinking about potential agents of livability and local ecologies of political actors.

At the same time, the Vietnamese case does seem to confirm one of the standard disadvantages attributed to state-socialist regimes, as far as environmental politics are concerned. The cases confirm that when both regulators and industry managers are part of the same state apparatus, regulators are likely to be hamstrung. Again and again in these cases, the state agencies that own and profit from the operations of industrial polluters negate the ability of state environmental agencies to work as allies of mobilized communities. In this respect at least, increases in private ownership in Vietnam should open up opportunities for more effective regulation and greater livability.

Variations in success among the cases generally tracked well with my expectations from the CDR model. The cases show that when a community has strong internal social ties and external political linkages, it is much more successful in advancing environmental demands. When state agencies can act autonomously and are responsive to community needs, they are much more likely to enforce environmental laws. And when firms are both vulnerable to external pressures and situated in a strong market position, they are more inclined to reduce their pollution. The cases also show that community action is a necessary but not sufficient condition for pollution reduction in Vietnam. In more than one of the cases, mobilized communities that had taken a wide range of actions against a local polluter still failed to motivate the firm to reduce its pollution.

While there is no prototypical community that succeeds at CDR, a number of features of successful communities stand out: cohesiveness within the community; capacity as manifested both in strong leadership and an overall level of skills and sophistication; and linkages, particularly in the form of connections between the community and local government authorities. Essentially, successful cases involved communities with strong internal social ties and strong external political ties that forcefully and strategically pressured a state agency to take action.

While three of the cases indicate that CDR can work, all of them illustrate the variety of factors that can stand in the way of effective community action. Divisions within the community, poor organizing, and the inability to find leverage over a recalcitrant state agency can undercut possibilities for achieving greater livability. Sometimes, communities themselves can be arenas of conflict or otherwise incapable of mobilization. Firms and government agencies can capitalize on these divisions to ignore community concerns.

Even when communities organize successfully, their capacity can limit what they demand and achieve. With little data and no training, community members often end up complaining only about pollution problems that they can see, smell, or feel. This results in a focus on purely localized, short-term, acute impacts of pollution. Although that type of pollution likely accounts for a significant percentage of industrial pollution in Vietnam, such a narrow focus severely limits the range of environmental issues that become priorities for state action. With no knowledge of technical alternatives, communities tend to push for pollution control rather than prevention simply because their main concern is stopping local emissions. Another potential problem with CDR is that when stronger communities force factories to clean up or move, or when they scare off dirty factories from siting in their area, pollution is gradually shifted to areas with the weakest communities.

The clear limits of community capacity and the potential inequity of a system driven purely by community pressures underscore the importance of strengthening the capacity and roles of allies within the state apparatus. At present, environmental agencies at all levels in Vietnam are young and weak. Strengthening basic environmental procedures at the national level, such as instituting national environmental monitoring of ambient pollutants, national collection of environmental data, and state-sponsored research on environmental priorities thus remains extremely important. More fundamental, however, is the political position of environmental agencies within the state. Simply put, in internal government battles, environmental agencies generally lose. One of the optimistic implications of the CDR model is that community actions may actually help state environmental agencies to overcome these weaknesses.

Public and media pressure regarding pollution issues is gradually raising the profile and the bargaining power of environmental agencies and making the state a better agent of livability. Community pressures can help overcome agency resistance to implement laws that affect other state actors. (For example, in a case similar to that of Lam Thao, community pressure might help the provincial DOSTE prevail over the Ministry of Industry.) Community pressure can also motivate inspectors to simply do their jobs, a not insignificant feat, as most inspectors are overwhelmed by their tasks, ill-prepared for their duties, and underpaid. Community action also helps shine light on local-level corruption and increases transparency in all state environmental actions.

At the same time, state actions help support community mobilization. For instance, passage of the Law on Environmental Protection served to legitimate community complaints regarding pollution, even while state agencies were unable to enforce the specifics of the law. Creation of the National Environment Agency and the provincial DOSTEs provided a target for community complaints, even though these agencies initially couldn't do much. An emerging state environmental infrastructure thus serves to support community actions and demands.

Potentially, the CDR process can create a kind of virtuous circle of environmental regulation. As communities make demands on the state, environmental agencies are forced to improve their inspection and enforcement capacities (in order to retain legitimacy). As inspections and enforcement improve, communities are buoyed by successes to make greater demands on the state. In three of my cases, state agencies played pivotal roles in supporting and legitimating community demands for pollution reduction. Successful community action requires identifying and focusing pressure on the right actors within the state. When successful, this dynamic supports a process in which state agencies and civil society actors develop and grow and strengthen their roles as agents of livability alongside one another.

Evans (1996b) argues that "linking mobilized citizens to public agencies can enhance the efficacy of government" and that synergy occurs when "civic engagement strengthens state institutions and effective state institutions create an environment in which civic engagement is more likely to thrive." The outlines of CDR in Vietnam display this dynamic of mutually reinforcing interactions. At the minimum, these cases point to the *potential* for state-society synergy in industrial environmental regulation.

Again, the Vietnamese case should be considered a hard test of the community-driven regulation process. The successes that we have see in Vietnam occurred in a context with no independent local NGOs, no free press, no vulnerable elected officials, weak environmental agencies, and significant poverty driving development imperatives. Under more supportive circumstances, CDR would have much greater chances of success.[5] At the minimum, the cases in Vietnam attest to the value of exploring the CDR model elsewhere.

While only in its embryonic phase, CDR already shows potential to significantly improve environmental regulation in Vietnam. Policies and programs that formalize mechanisms of community input into state environmental decision making, create greater legitimacy for community demands, educate citizens about their rights, and support local monitoring efforts would move community-driven regulation forward and go a long way toward meeting the challenge of balancing industrial development with environmental and livability concerns.

Notes

The author sincerely thanks Peter Evans and two anonymous reviewers for insightful comments on this chapter. The author would also like to thank the many researchers, government officials, workers, and community members in Vietnam who made this research possible. In particular, the author recognizes Dr. Dinh Van Sam and Dr. Tran Van Nhan for their tireless support and assistance.

1. McCubbins and Schwartz (1984) discuss models of congressional oversight in the United States, which they call the "patrols" model and the "alarms" model. In the patrols model, Congress establishes systems to regularly evaluate implementation of legislation. Under the alarms model, Congress creates systems that trigger action such as congressional monitoring.

2. See Rueschemeyer and Evans (1985, 48) for a discussion of the tendency of states to be simultaneously corporate actors and arenas in which conflicts are played out.

3. As Ferguson (1998) points out, states should be viewed "not in opposition to something called 'society,' but as themselves composed of bundles of social practices, every bit as 'local' in their social situatedness and materiality" (p. 13).

4. While Vietnam remains a one-party Communist state, the government has initiated "democratic" reforms including local-level elections of People's Council representatives and National Assembly members. To date, little competition exists in these elections; however, the scope and power of elected officials (particularly National Assembly members) appear to be increasing.

5. Recent studies of environmental initiatives in the Philippines (the Eco-Watch program), Indonesia (the PROPER program), and Mexico indicate that there is significant potential for greater community participation and state-society interaction in pollution control programs.

:: 5 ::

Social and Spatial Inequalities in Hungarian Environmental Politics

A Historical Perspective

ZSUZSA GILLE

Introduction: The "Strong State, Weak Market, and Abused Nature" Paradigm

"The Best Earth Day Present: Freedom," the title of an article by Laurence Solomon in the *Wall Street Journal* on April 29, 1990, was a most succinct expression of the prevalent hopes for Eastern Europe's environmental redemption after 1989. After listing the infamous cases of environmental destruction in former socialist countries, Solomon summed up the bright future awaiting postsocialist citizens: "[n]ow all this [environmental pollution] is being swept away by democracy and economic rationality." That democratization and a switch to a market-oriented economy will automatically turn environmental matters for the better has been advocated implicitly or explicitly for decades both by the Western scholarly literature on the environmental crisis of existing socialism (Goldman 1972; Taga 1976)[1] and by reformist economists within state socialist countries (Szlávik 1991; Veress 1982; also see DeBardeleben 1985). While the economic argument blamed the socialist state for suppressing the market, thereby preventing it from motivating production units to use natural resources more sparingly and with greater care, the political argument blamed it for monopolizing knowledge and denying accountability for pollution it allegedly caused single-handedly. Naturally, when the problem is constructed as being a result of too much state intervention, the only logical solution seems to be the liberation of both markets and citizens.

While a few studies are now expressing doubts about such economic hope and are beginning to explore the failure of the prediction that the "Westernization" of the economy would reduce environmental destruction (Andrews 1993; Gille 1997, 1998; Kaderják and Powell 1997; Manser 1993), the primary object of this paper is to shed light on why the political prediction also falls short. Through a Hungarian case study I will demonstrate that securing "freedom from"—in the sense of freedom from oppressive, undemocratic state control—does not necessarily imply attaining "freedom to"—in the sense of freedom to pursue autonomous collective goals. In other words, banishing the state does not automatically enable or empower citizens concerned about their health and environment to do anything about it. Rather, the premature and excessive retreat of the state may leave them without the institutional infrastructure necessary to enforce environmental interests, ultimately producing political and environmental effects that contradict the accepted euphoric expectations. In order to understand these developments in Eastern Europe's environmental transition we must unpack the notion of extreme state power under socialism. In so doing we must provide a more nuanced and much more sociological reading of the kinds of "freedoms" that not only existed but also determined how environmental problems were produced and distributed, and that defined some of these problems as worthy of the socialist state's attention.

The second objective of this paper is to start locating the agents of livability and sustainability. This goal cannot be met without meeting the first one: since the present does not start with a tabula rasa, only by seeing the historical legacies clearly can we answer questions about the conditions under which more positive outcomes can be expected in the future.

I have chosen a Hungarian case study to tackle these tasks: a case study of an agricultural, relatively underdeveloped and ethnically heterogeneous region in the southern part of the country that found itself incapable of defending its environmental interests both under state socialism and after socialism's collapse. If one is to draw conclusions from this story, one must understand that while for this region the outcome of environmental politics might be similarly negative before and after the collapse of state socialism, the reasons for failure are markedly different.

This case study was not chosen for its representativeness of socialist environmental problems—although an increasing volume of evidence indicates that it is indeed quite reflective of a particular section of the Hungarian socialist economy—but rather for the shock value of its apparent exceptionality. In the literature on socialist environmental pollution, the culprits are invariably large, out-of-date, noncompetitive, state-nursed enterprises in heavy industry, primarily metallurgy and the coal-based energy sector, which indeed constituted a major source of air pollution. Emissions from these industrial dinosaurs, however, account for only a part of the disastrous environmental legacies of state socialism. Environmental problems caused by a newer generation of industries and their rapid growth—such as electronics, the nuclear energy sector, and especially the chemical industry—were becoming ever more significant in Eastern Europe during the final decades of state socialist rule.

Many former socialist countries could boast a modern, competitive chemical industry that often relied on Western technology and know-how and cultivated strong ties with the world market. While the industry's associated environmental and public health burdens are very serious, and it is a well-documented fact that hazardous wastes are produced overwhelmingly by the chemical industry, its pollution has never been treated as somehow "representative" of the ancien régime. That may have to do with the convenience of blaming environmental degradation entirely on the dinosaurs of coal-based heavy industries. Such reasoning gives the illusion that if only these factories went out of business or were modernized, the problem would be solved. That effectively disarms attempts to politicize the environmental problems created by the nascent economic order, to which the successful chemical industries would have much less difficulty transitioning.

When I started this research in 1994 one of my original hypotheses was that chemical industries would keep posing a significant and even intensifying environmental threat after 1989. This hypothesis has now been confirmed by empirical evidence.[2] There is therefore an urgent need to subject chemical industries to social-science scrutiny, both because they have been ignored as nonparadigmatic polluters in Eastern Europe and because their environmental effects are on the increase. The case of the Budapest Chemical Works (BCW) and the Garé toxic waste dump undertakes such a study.

Beginning in 1978, BCW dumped about 15,500 tons of tetrachlorobenzene—a highly toxic substance generated in its pesticide production—in the vicinity of Garé. Garé is a small agricultural village in Baranya County, a relatively underdeveloped and multiethnic region of

southern Hungary. For decades, the dump has contaminated groundwater and soil, emitted a constant foul odor, caused excessive numbers
of diseases and deaths among domestic animals, and prompted complaints of elevated cancer rates among the villagers. When the leaking
toxic waste started to threaten the nearby spring and the health and
livelihood of an entire region, the company was ordered to eliminate the
dump site. However, when it made plans to do this by incinerating the
accumulated waste in a facility that would also be built here, it sparked
greater controversy and sharpened divisions among the surrounding villages. Many fear that the incinerator's emissions would be perilous to
their health, and since it would be built with mostly French capital, many
also worry that it would soon begin to burn toxic wastes imported from
abroad. In the six years since the controversy began its course through
numerous public hearings, demonstrations, petitions, and lawsuits, it
has caused the resignation of public officials and become Hungary's
most covered and most divisive environmental pollution case.

Despite the site of the conflict, the case is not about a rural problem.
In fact, the waste dump of Garé constitutes an *urban* problem, in a
double sense. First, it hosts the wastes of agricultural chemicals, a key
technical foundation on which, through a decreasing demand for an
agricultural labor force, urbanization rests. Second, and most directly,
Garé's open space–turned–waste dump has been functioning as a catalyst of industrial growth based in Budapest. Without land where the
irresponsibly accumulated wastes of industry could be placed out of
sight and out of mind, industrial accumulation would have been in
jeopardy.

For a theoretical understanding of this relationship between city and
country, industry and land, market and nature, one might turn to Karl
Polanyi (1957), who considers land not an actual commodity, since it
is not produced for the market, but rather a "fictitious commodity."
Nevertheless, in "self-regulating" market economies it is treated as if it
were a commodity, which inevitably results in the destruction of nature,
of humans and their social fabric. O'Connor (1988) borrows the notion
of fictitious commodities from Polanyi and rephrases it as the "conditions of production." These conditions include human beings and their
labor power, natural resources, and the environment in general, as well
as urban and rural space.[3] We might also turn to William Cronon's 1991
conceptualization of the city-country relationship: In *Nature's Metropolis,* a title that aptly expresses his understanding of Chicago's rise,
Cronon describes the lands west of the emergent city as its hinterland.

Without the natural and social conditions of this more rural hinterland, the city could not exist; in turn, the metropolis's development and power irrevocably reshape those natural and social conditions. While these conceptualizations were born of studies of capitalist societies, in the absence of better terms elaborated specifically for state socialist societies one might still adopt them to provide a critical understanding of Garé's history. Garé's land thus might be called a condition of production for the increasingly muscular Hungarian chemical industry, as well as the hinterland of two large industrial cities, Budapest and Pécs. Garé's case is thus a cautionary tale about how efforts to create livable cities can be made at the cost of rendering rural hinterlands unsustainable. As such, it is also a call for approaching the goal of sustainability relationally.

As I will show, the fact that Garé's case got this far, and this far out of hand, has a lot to do with certain agendas of the state under socialism. Let us therefore review the history of the case from this perspective. In what follows I will analyze the nature of the state's presence or absence in two areas during three historical periods. The two areas are production, more precisely the production of waste, and regional development, more concretely the development of wastelands both in the figurative and in the literal sense. The historical periods are those under state socialism, during the "transition" (1987–1990), and in postsocialism (that is, the present).[4]

State Socialism

State Presence in Production

In state socialism, the state exercised control over production in several ways. As owner of the means of production and the employer of a great majority of the economically active population, it had exclusive disposition over all the economic conditions of production. It redistributed resources and goods through plans of various time frames and decided about subsidies and credits through the national bank. Planning and redistribution, however, were primarily tools of macromanagement, which thus had to be complemented by microlevel management through various political organs, such as the party and the union, just to mention the most decisive ones.[5]

The connection between the two levels of control was crucial. Based on the monthly "mood reports" party secretaries submitted to the next higher level of the party, a hierarchy of firms was established. Enterprises with good political records were those whose management gave prominence to party members and officials when it came to making decisions, or encouraged party membership, ideological education, and participation in various political campaigns.[6] Firms with bad political records were those whose management preferred not taking the advice of party officials in economic decisions about investment or remuneration, or made promotion decisions based on work performance rather than a good political résumé, or were less than willing to carry out witch-hunts for "ideologically unreliable" employees. The managers of such firms were in constant danger of losing their positions unless they proved themselves irreplaceable in the economic sense. That, however, was quite difficult, because they lacked political leverage and thus encountered difficulties in securing subsidies, credits, or extra funds for social welfare goals.

The Budapest Chemical Works was a firm whose political profile was always looked at with suspicion. Its longtime manager was far too reform minded: he protected intellectual and professional employees from Stalinist witch-hunts during the 1950s, he was already advocating Western-style teamwork and economic incentives such as bonuses or other monetary rewards in the early 1960s, and he successfully fought the idea of his firm's building a huge and most likely inefficient replica of a Soviet chemical plant in the 1970s. No wonder he failed to secure the goodwill of party and ministry officials, consequently depriving BCW of subsidies and loans.

Since BCW's management knew that its political performance remained dubious, it had to compensate with its economic performance. BCW was not only a main supplier satisfying Hungary's pesticide and fertilizer needs,[7] but thanks to its ability to overfulfill the state's plans, it won the "champion factory" title eighteen times between 1948 and 1968. From 1968 on, when the old indicator of economic performance, plan fulfillment, was replaced with a monetary indicator, and in particular hard-currency earnings through exports, BCW scored high on this index as well. Thus, the company's economic success effectively demonstrated its management's irreplaceability.

This success, however, came with its own set of contradictions. In 1967, Hungary, like many countries, ceased production of DDT because of its recently discovered effects on public health. Not only had DDT production constituted an important part of BCW's production (according to my rough estimates, 7 to 10 percent), it had used as its primary input the main product of one of BCW's plants—chlorine. Since there was no demand for chlorine elsewhere in the country at the time, BCW had to find uses for it, lest a third of its production come to a halt. Such a setback would have shaken the security of BCW's management, previously supported by the company's economic excellence. The solution lay in cooperation with an Austrian firm. BCW struck a deal to barter tetrachlorobenzene (1,2,4,5-TCB) with ÖSW, a firm in Linz, for a herbicide the latter produced out of TCB. For the TCB delivered in excess, BCW, or more precisely the Hungarian state, received hard currency.[8]

Evidence

This seemingly rather advantageous deal had its opponents. A former middle-ranking manager and a foreman questioned the large amount of waste that TCB production entailed: the ratio of waste to final product was as high as 45 percent, or almost one to two, a high percentage even among the usually high waste ratio of aromatic compounds. Indeed, the waste product (a mixture of paradichlorobenzene, other isomers of TCB, and hexachlorobenzene) turned out to be a major headache for the company, a problem that still, after thirty years, has yet to be solved.

Under state socialism, not only did the official discourse treat waste as a useful material, but firms had to deliver their wastes according to plan.[9] Efforts to reduce waste at its source thus remained quite ineffective, which, together with already existing systemic tendencies of centrally planned economies toward wasteful production, made large waste-ratio production the rule rather than the exception.[10] In the face of these forceful economic and political mechanisms, any objection to contracts such as the one between BCW and ÖSW, especially in the face of the promise of hard currency income, remained futile. Even the more conscientious engineers, who cared about the fate of waste products, expected that they could quickly find a use for the by-product soon to be generated in annual quantities of hundreds, and later thousands, of tons. It was not only the aforementioned official waste credo that maintained such an optimism; the engineers' belief in their own science also helped minimize worries about the waste problem. Given the excellent fungicide qualities of the by-product, for example, BCW's researchers thought they would eventually find a way to reuse it (personal interview, Emil Valovits, 1997).

BCW approached numerous research institutes and companies, and two reuse possibilities emerged. One, the plan to reuse the waste materials as a fungicide, failed because researchers found the toxic qualities of the by-product too dangerous to human health (BCW archives 1968). The other option was more successful: the Hungarian State Railways used the by-product, with its fungicidal qualities, as an impregnator for its wooden sleepers, to prevent the wood from rotting. But the railroad's needs were too small compared to the amount of waste produced, and its later switch to concrete sleepers eliminated even this demand.

BCW, however, did not restrict its search to prospects for reuse; in 1968 it started looking into the technical possibilities of storing or eliminating the by-product. One proposal was to store it in waste drums in abandoned mines, but the locations suggested would have endangered nearby underground drinking or thermal water sources. The other proposal was to dump the waste drums into the Black Sea. This, after a few deliveries, was stopped by a minister himself, probably fearing the international political consequences of dumping waste in a neighboring country.[11]   *Evidence/Reason.*

State Presence in Regional Development

Why could not BCW store its waste in its yard or elsewhere in Budapest? This question leads us to consider the state's interests and authority in assigning land uses—that is, in regional development. For in-factory storage, the volume of waste was obviously prohibitive, and permits for a dump or for a temporary storage place in Budapest would have been rejected even if BCW had requested them: from the 1960s on, a new direction in regional development policies prohibited the siting of new industries in the capital and called for relocating many of the existing plants to the countryside. The rationale behind this prohibition was to alleviate overcrowdedness and to improve the quality of air in Budapest.[12]

Interestingly, it was exactly such a relocation project that provided *Evidence.* temporary relief for BCW's waste problems. In 1969, BCW transferred its glue plant to a former briquette plant in Hidas, a small town in Baranya County, and it immediately started transporting its waste drums there for storage.[13] However, the drums' corrosion and their imminent leakage made it clear that this was only a temporary solution.[14] BCW was, therefore, happy to be invited as a partner in establishing a waste-dump site in the nearby village of Garé in 1978.

Let's look at the local antecedents of this dump. In the 1970s, Pécs, the seat of Baranya County, was struggling with the same environmental problems as Budapest. It faced serious air pollution; in addition, its local factories produced unwanted wastes, which were being dumped in municipal waste sites on the outskirts of the city. In 1976, local water authorities reported an impending danger to the city's drinking water sources caused by one of these dumps. Simultaneously, plans were being drawn up for a park with hiking trails and a picnic ground in the same area, which "could make possible active daily or weekend recreation, useful leisure activities, and the protection of health for the urban population" (Agricultural and Food Department of the Executive Committee of the Council of Pécs 1976, 1).

As a result, the dumping permits for two of Pécs's most significant firms, the Pécs Tannery and the regional subsidiary of a nationwide meatpacking enterprise, were withdrawn even before a new dump was sited and established. As the city government strove to distribute more environmental public goods (clean water and a greenbelt), the two enterprises were faced with the problem of finding a new location for their wastes. They turned to the local seat of the Hungarian State Geological Institute (MÁFI). By this time, MÁFI had already completed the so-called pollution vulnerability maps of the entire region of Southern Transdanubia, initiated by its forward-looking director in 1974, and could thus point scientifically to those areas where a bed of clay would protect the groundwater from contamination. I have not been able to find concrete answers to the question of how Garé was chosen among many such areas, but I have been able to find factors that made Garé a likely choice.

First, Garé, only eighteen kilometers south of Pécs, was close enough to keep the waste transportation costs of the tannery and meatpacking plant from rising considerably. Second, the site had to be land with insignificant economic value; it certainly could not have been in an area that had any industrial potential. Garé had none, since the region's proximity to Tito's Yugoslavia had discouraged planners from industrializing it in the 1950s and 1960s. However, it was also important to choose land that did not have any agricultural potential either. Since the county had an interest in increasing production (so it could bargain for more state resources), it could not allow potentially productive lands to be used for nonproductive purposes, such as a dump site. That the county had to deliberate and approve of the proposed site from a developmental point of view is reflected in the minutes of the meeting in which the siting was officially approved by the various interested parties. County officials and representatives of the Pécs Tannery concluded, "the assignment of the territory for disposing the waste does not interfere with the county's developmental interests" (Archives of the Council of Baranya County 1978).

The best choice of land for the dump site was land that either had been withdrawn or was likely to be withdrawn from agricultural production. This was indeed proposed for many Garé-like villages, whose hilly plots were unsuited to mechanized cultivation. On the land assigned for the dump, for example, production had become so inefficient that the value of the produce grown had been, in the words of the mayor, "practically zero." Obviously, this was important not just from the state's or the county's point of view but also from that of the enterprises, which could therefore acquire the land at low cost.[15]

Garé and its vicinity easily fulfilled the criterion not only of economic insignificance but also of political insignificance. Its rapidly aging peasant population and the large ratio of ethnic minorities, primarily Croats, Germans, and Romani (better known as Gypsies), coupled with the retirement of and lack of replacement for old village leaders in the 1970s, eroded the political clout of residents, leaving them ill-equipped to defend themselves from the centralizing efforts of socialist regional development.[16] Garé found its agricultural cooperative merged with that of Szalánta in 1974, which justified the fusion of the two villages in 1976. Administratively, this implied the closure of Garé's council (or local administration) and the use of joint budgets for the sole benefit of the superordinate village, Szalánta. Two years later the joint council issued the permits for the new dump. A village that lacked its own administration was obviously seen as an easy target for such LULUs (locally unwanted land uses) as a toxic waste dump. The prehistory of the dump demonstrates that Garé and its vicinity had become a figurative wasteland before transforming into one in the literal sense.

State Presence without State-Society Synergy and Inequality in Environmental Claims-Making

Reviewing the state's role in the areas of production and regional development reveals that its strong presence did not facilitate a synergy between itself and society. But was this really a consequence of the overwhelming nature of the state's presence? Furthermore, did this lack of synergy and the state's indifference, if not hostility, to environmental protection prevail universally, or were there certain issues, places, or social groups with particular environmental needs that received more attention from the state? In this section I explore the actual mechanisms of state-society communication about environmental matters under state socialism and illustrate that certain groups and certain issues were in fact favored by this mechanism.

The process for a socialist enterprise to ask for the state's help in environmental matters first involved a letter to one of the ministries, most likely to the firm's superordinate ministry. This might have been paralleled with letters to scientific institutions and authorities. BCW had to take a surprising amount of initiative to resolve its waste problems. It approached two ministerial departments; seven land, water use, and public health authorities; three scientific institutes; and five enterprises just within a year of contracting with ÖSW. Yet it failed to win the state's commitment to help.

Reason ⌐ Residents, as individuals, had even less leverage over state authorities to make them respond to environmental problems. Most complaints were probably silenced, but newly opened archives indicate that in exceptionally critical situations the local party organization took up the issue with the relevant ministry.[17] I have found only one such instance between 1948 and 1982, in the ninth district of Budapest—the district where Budapest Chemical Works is located. In 1960, the first secretary of the Political Committee of the party's Ninth District Organization wrote letters to the head of the Council of Budapest (the municipal government) and the minister of heavy industry, stating that "the population of the neighborhood was concerned about the sulfur dioxide and chlorine gas emissions and ore dusts caused by BCW" (Political Committee of the Ninth District Organization of the Hungarian Socialist Workers' Party 1960). The party secretary, rather than demanding immediate action, humbly asked the head of the Council of Budapest and the minister of heavy industry to incorporate ameliorative tools into the already planned reconstruction of BCW.

That environmental concerns were raised by residents is also suggested in the People's Patriotic Front (PPF) taking up environmental concerns in 1973. The PPF was an umbrella organization of the party, but its orientation was more pragmatic than explicitly political. Issues tackled by the PPF were typically those of health, the status of women, and peace, a catchall profile that picked up whatever the party plans could not or would not prioritize. The PPF presented itself as a mass movement, a voice from below, but its political function was, of course, to co-opt the messages of outspoken individuals and to show that problems were being dealt with. That environmental protection received just such treatment is indicated by a speech made by a member of the Executive Committee of the Council of Baranya County in 1979: "The organs of the PPF have been dealing with issues of environmental protection since 1973. One often hears desires and wishes, which have to be disarmed"[18] (Archives of Baranya County 1979a). Residents thus did voice environmental concerns, and local party organs and council governments did undertake to address them; however, they did so only in order to demonstrate that people's concerns were being addressed and thus to prevent dissatisfaction from becoming louder.

If enterprise managers and residents as individuals were equally powerless in realizing their environmental interests, how do we explain the success of certain claims? Where did calls for environmental protection have to come from in order to be heard? My research in Hungary suggests that it was experts in various decision-making positions and at various levels of authority who could occasionally exert pressure on other authorities to take certain ameliorative steps. How and why were they able to do so?

Until the late 1970s and 1980s it wasn't their expertise that made the difference. Rather, as suggested by several engineers I interviewed, who had designed environmental facilities or policies or had written environmental studies, they knew of the many urban-industrial problems but found that their "expert" opinions didn't go very far in the face of bureaucratic or political agendas. One of the experts, who worked in the Wastewater Department of the National Chief Water Administration, illustrated this by saying that even after emissions standards were established in 1961, if his department initiated proceedings to fine a particular offender based on those standards,

> the penalty was canceled if the plant proved that it had no money to pay it, or if the party secretary of the plant was on good terms with the director [of the Water Administration]. [Or] the party secretary of the county just had to call over and the director ended the procedure of the Wastewater Department. As a result, it was exactly the large enterprises [thus, those with the most significant emissions] which they let go, because these were the ones that had the highest contacts (personal interview, anonymous engineer, summer 1997).

If this engineer found himself to be successful, as in one instance in which he persuaded a firm manager to build a new wastewater treatment facility that he had helped design, it was not because of his expertise but because of his contacts in ministries and other offices. When he had such resources, he said, the "whimper of the 'technical ones'" found open ears."[19]

That engineers and "technical ones" were the most successful advocates for environmental causes is further supported by the studies done on industrial waste problems in the 1970s and 1980s: they were conducted on the initiative, within the framework, and with the support of the Alliance of Technical and Scientific Associations (METESZ), a national organization that united various groups of technical intelligentsia. The first national waste-dump register, also initiated and completed by METESZ, further indicates the importance of professional contacts for gathering data and making claims. When I asked the director and designer of this project how the idea for it had occurred to him, he responded that everywhere in the country engineer acquaintances had pointed out to METESZ members their waste disposal problems, until finally there were so many complaints and requests from so many enterprises that METESZ leaders decided to carry out a survey that would compare the location of existing waste dumps with the location of geologically safe soils (personal interview, Miklos Kassai, spring 1996). They managed to get state funding for it and to incorporate it into the plans of the MÁFI. Having found that about half the existing dumps were established on soils through which the wastes disposed could reach and pollute groundwater, their next task became to draw up plans to relocate the inappropriately sited ones. BCW's landfill in Garé was the prototype of these "scientifically sited" dumps.

While the technical intelligentsia's contacts in various sectors of the economy and with various decision makers, and the information accumulated from these various channels, positioned them particularly well to push authorities to take ameliorative steps, the justification of such steps still needed a certain rhetoric. Experts found that complaints about causing health problems and air and water pollution were not nearly as effective in and of themselves as they were when couched in terms of their implications for fulfilling the party plan or for industrial development in general. As one of the engineers described the prevalent view on industrial waste and emission: "They started dealing with waste problems more seriously in the case of those water resources that were mostly important for industry. . . . [The concern was] to achieve a water quality that would not cause troubles for industry, and it was of secondary importance that it wouldn't cause trouble for people" (personal interview, anonymous engineer, summer 1997).

The party secretary of the ninth district, for example, did not find it sufficient to claim that the red ore dust from BCW was "exceptionally harmful to health"; he had to put special emphasis on the damage the air pollution caused to other factories, whose machines were being corroded by the dust and gas emissions. BCW itself, when asking for help from the state in solving its waste problems, similarly argued,

The solution of the waste disposal problem is a rather urgent task, because the current uncertain and not always professional practice could cause a lot of damage to water management and impedes production and its development. The proposal of the chemical industry administration to bury the waste in the proposed manner [in abandoned mines] could guarantee the [planned] rate of development for a long period (Archives of the Budapest Chemical Works 1968, 1).

I would conclude, then, that when various state agencies did address environmental issues, they were not responding to pressures from below—that is, to pressures directly by the affected residents—but rather to pressures by technical experts—if you will, to pressures from the "middle." This confirms previous studies that argued that in various state socialist countries the intelligentsia were the most salient, if not the only, proponents of environmental protection (Gustafson 1981; Hajba 1995; Jancar-Webster 1991; Szirmai 1993). This was as true for intellectuals within the state as for those outside. What mattered most was their connections or, more precisely, the fluidity with which information traveled back and forth between them. In the first period of state socialism, these experts, like the intelligentsia in general, suffered from marginalization resulting from the party's ideological suspicions about their class origins and sympathies. Because of their pragmatic involvement in industry, these intellectuals saw a lot—probably a lot more than was evident to untrained residents—and they tried to blow their whistles at the most egregious environmental assaults, but their suggestions had to be justified on the basis of their contribution to plan fulfillment if they were to get a green light from party and state officials.

Later, as a cautious political liberalization proceeded, and as the economy became increasingly dependent on knowledge-based industries (such as the chemical and electronics industries), and as reforms placed increasing emphasis on expertise in the management of the economy, the freedom and leverage of intellectuals with technical and scientific training increased considerably.[20] By the end of the 1970s and the beginning of the 1980s, purely ecological claims were becoming more acceptable. When asked about the causes of the new, more environmentally sensitive attitude that took hold in the 1980s, an engineer interviewee noted that the "relationship between the 'technical ones' and politics changed"—that is, that scientific arguments had gained more acceptance.

But how does the understanding of the social basis of official "environmentalism" help explain why Garé's backyard was transformed into a toxic waste dump while Pécs was sprucing up its own? I suggest that urbanites were more successful in cajoling environmental goods out of the state than were disempowered rural residents. First of all, the experts were more likely to be urbanites themselves; therefore, they were more exposed to and more familiar with urban and industrial environmental problems than with rural ones. Second, if environmental problems had to be dressed up as impediments to plan fulfillment and industrial growth in order to be heard, then clearly urbanites living near factories had a discursive advantage over residents living in agricultural areas. Third, the technical intelligentsia's services and contacts, so crucial in making environmental claims, were inaccessible to rural villagers. In sum, both the "software" (information and discourse) and the "hardware" (contacts, institutional positions) of environmental claims-making placed rural residents at a disadvantage.[21]

This is how it was possible for leaders in Budapest and Pécs to take measures to ensure safe drinking water and clean air for their constituencies while endangering and polluting the same for disempowered villagers. Budapest protected its air quality by prohibiting the siting of new industries in the capital and strongly encouraging the relocation of existing ones to the countryside, and Pécs's leaders revoked the dumping permits from the meatpacking plant and the tannery even before a new location was found, in order to keep drinking water safe and to create a greenbelt. In contrast, Garé received the by-products of urban "environmental protection" despite desperate attempts to prevent the dumping by its powerless leaders.

> The Meatpacking Plant, the Tannery, and the Hidas Chemical Works dump their filth and slurry here if they want to. It seems like there is no appeal against this. The population and the council both took steps but these somehow did not achieve anything. The bosses decide, and the village smells the stink. That's just how it is (Archives of Baranya County 1979b).

Not surprisingly, two of the largest pre-1989 environmental protests—not counting the national cause of the Danube dam—whose meaning and implications cannot be categorized along urban / rural lines were sparked by urban residents over urban industrial pollution. In 1977, residents of Nagytétény, an industrial district of Budapest, appealed to the local government to close a large metallurgical factory in order to stop the lead and other heavy-metal contamination of the soil that was causing horrible and mostly fatal diseases. The civil initiative,

which picked up speed in 1987, had been initiated by health professionals (pediatricians and a dental nurse) and intellectuals, one of whom is
now a member of parliament. They weren't successful at the time, but
the outrage, having grown into what they called the "lead scandal"
(Moldova 1995, 113), achieved the organization of residents' forums,
the first that were not immediately silenced—even the newspapers wrote
about them.

The 1984 protest against a planned incinerator in Dorog, a heavily
industrialized town about twenty kilometers west of the capital, was
also started by a pediatrician. Her knowledge of the plan, which was
naturally meant to be a secret, came from other intellectuals working in
the local government. She was soon joined by other professionals, and
the new group managed to collect two thousand signatures against the
plant. While it didn't succeed, the movement was able to force ministry
officials to sit down to negotiate with them, and as a result the company
implemented additional technical safeguards. Later, after 1989, a group
of experts was allowed to monitor the operation and emissions of the
plant. Even though neither urban movement achieved its goals, the availability of experts and their social capital evidently was crucial for both
to even make a claim. Also unlike rural concerns, both of these urban
cases were covered by the media, even if not in an objective manner.

Obviously, one reason why these protests, fervent by state socialist
standards, were sparked in industrial areas is the magnitude of the problems themselves. It is curious to note, however, that while close to a
third of Hungary's villages had to import drinking water by the end of
the 1970s because the old wells had become contaminated, and pesticide
application in agriculture claimed its victims from among villagers (and
their fauna), and illegally and clandestinely dumped toxic waste drums
kept turning up on former agricultural lands (Balogh 1982), no visible
protest was mounted in rural areas.

While in general, experts with the necessary social capital had a
greater chance of cajoling environmental goods out of the state, or at
least of making claims, urbanites were not equally successful. Polarizing
the urban-rural hierarchy even more was the *political* capital various
entities, firms, and villages possessed: it was easier for various arms of
the state (ministries, water authorities) to ignore the wishes of a politically blacklisted manager (as of BCW) and of a council president of a
small, doomed village (as of Garé), because they knew just how few, if
any, party strings these politically marginalized actors could pull if state
channels became unworkable. However, while Garé lacked social cap-

evidence

ital to defend itself, BCW, because of its economic power, could mobilize contacts; that is, it could transform its economic capital into social capital in order to secure a dump site even without the state's assistance.[22] In 1982, the State Plan Committee sanctified this "independent solution" when it approved Garé as one of the six planned regional waste dump sites for the country. Thus, the absence of state-society synergy in small, disempowered villages first of all meant that state authorities averted their otherwise watchful eyes from such "independent" solutions, which therefore helped maintain the state's ignorance of industrial waste dumping problems; and second, later, when such problems were finally being acknowledged, this missing synergy implied that they would be solved for urban constituencies at the expense of rural ones.

From Hopeful Transition
to the Postsocialist Retreat of the State

On November 13, 1996, the Open Media Research Institute reported the following:

> The Young Democrats on 12 November demanded the resignation of Ferenc Baja, minister of environmental protection and regional development, for failing to clean up pollutants around the waste dump of Garé in southwest Hungary, Hungarian media reported. Although ministry officials ruled out any threat of disaster, the party insisted that the fifteen thousand tons of hazardous waste, which were shipped to Garé by the Budapest Chemical Works more than fifteen years ago, have been contaminating the area. Baja said the ministry has made repeated attempts to break the deadlock over the matter and will order the chemical works to stop the spread of contaminants within fifteen days.[23]

What may seem to have been a deadlock, however, was instead a series of painful negotiations and a learning and unlearning process. Participants in the debate had to learn how to use new democratic institutions for their interests but simultaneously unlearn the idea that there was a state to assist them, since the state had been reduced to simply one of the negotiating partners—and, let's add, probably one of the weakest. This in fact turned out to be the most consequential development in the Garé case.

The year 1989 marked the first step in the withdrawal of the state from entire fields of social life. This was no different in Garé's case. It was, however, rather unfortunate for Garéans, because in 1988, their relationship with the state had started to become a two-way communication. Prior to that, in 1981, Garéans had already formed the Environmental Protection Committee, at first with the modest aim of "reporting unintended uses by the dump to the health authority" (Archives of Baranya County 1981). By 1987, however, they had acquired a surprising technical competence in matters of dumps and incinerators and had formulated their own suggestion to incinerate the drums in a cement kiln elsewhere or to transfer them to a newly established and modern toxic waste dump for Pest County, adjacent to the capital. Their formation and demand, however, did not make it into the news until after 1989.

There were several factors that made the formation and later radicalization of this civil organization possible and politically safe. First, the contents of the dump and especially of BCW's drums had become public knowledge. This knowledge came indirectly from a survey of the environmental conditions of the dump's vicinity and from several orders by various environmental authorities issued to BCW to repack the drums and to pay penalties for failing to start doing so by a specified date. The incidence of mysterious diseases and deaths among domestic animals also had prompted BCW to defend itself by providing a public explanation of the drums' contents and history.

Second, by the mid-1980s, the protest against the Gabcikovo-Nagymaros dam on the Danube on the border of Hungary and Czechoslovakia was gathering momentum, and other, smaller and lesser-known environmental groups were mushrooming. Environmental protection had become the only area where initiatives from below did not face an automatic and immediate coercive reaction by the state, for several reasons: *(a)* State representatives thought the call of these movements for better science and more professional economic management harmonized rather well with the reform discourse of the party, and therefore they didn't consider the initiatives as necessarily antiregime.[24] *(b)* After the Helsinki process took off, but especially after the Danube Circle received the Right Livelihood Award in 1985, the party leadership's image in the West would have suffered greatly if it had clamped down on environmentalists.[25] The country's reliance on Western loans having increased considerably, this image grew ever more important. *(c)* In some cases, environmental claims enjoyed the backing of urban municipal governments, which used the threat of leaking environmental secrets to cajole extra funds out of the state for infrastructural developments and social and welfare institutions (Szirmai 1993). While the party-state viewed environmentalism as something it could co-opt and

contain within its technocratically oriented reform policies, "greens"—
reform economists, scientists, activists, and to some extent local governments—started recognizing its sacred cow status and increasingly used
it as a Trojan horse, merely green on the outside but filled with substantive demands for market liberalism and democracy.[26]

Third, in general, the sense of impending political crisis, sharpened
by Chernobyl, made representatives of the state a lot more attentive and
flexible in issues that had previously been taboo (Pickvance 1996). A
contrast with a dumping attempt almost a decade after BCW began
removing its waste to the Garé site indicates the striking difference in
the relation between state and civil society: In 1987 the Hungarian state
started testing for the country's first nuclear waste dump site in Ófalu,
a small village about twenty kilometers from Garé. The village was economically, ethnically, and administratively in the same position as Garé
had been in in 1978, yet the villagers, supported by scientists and the
media, won the battle against the siting (Juhász, Vári, and Tölgyesi
1993; Reich 1990).[27]

In Garé the effects of this changing political climate were accentuated
by the arrival of a young, ambitious, and well-connected doctor in 1983,
whose presence upgraded the village's social and political capital.
Thanks to the efforts of Garé's Environmental Protection Committee,
now headed by the doctor, BCW terminated TCB production in 1987,
and in 1988 representatives of BCW, the Pécs Tannery, the meatpacking
plant, and various departments in the Council of Baranya County sat
down to negotiate with the committee. Not less important was the committee's success that same year in launching a criminal investigation
against BCW for endangering the environment.

With the start of the negotiating process, there was hope for a resolution that would satisfy all the surrounding villages and the environmental authorities. But the collapse of the state socialist order quickly
crushed those hopes. In 1989 the central police office of Baranya County
ended the criminal investigation as part of a general amnesty. Although
in 1990 BCW received an order to eliminate the dump by December 31,
1997, an order to conduct a survey of the environmental conditions of
the dump, and deadlines for turning in cleanup plans, the radical dis-
array of the legal system—or at least its momentary opacity—favored
BCW's time-buying tactics.

Like most everybody else, BCW was trying to get out of the state's
shadow. By mid-1992 the value of its assets had been assessed, and the
company was all ready for privatization. Uncertainties around what

form privatization would take, if not around the survival of the firm
itself, obviously did not encourage BCW's management to comply with
the cleanup orders. The management had two choices for the pattern of
privatization it would follow: the common practice of leaving the dirtiest
and least profitable departments and plants in state ownership (by letting
its Hidas branch plant take the dump), or the path of claiming liability
for Garé and using it as a springboard for a new, privately owned and
profit-oriented waste treatment facility. According to Hungarian privatization laws, the value of the assets of a firm to be privatized decreases
by the amount of environmental cleanup costs it faces; in Garé's case
the costs reached 2.6 billion forints (approximately 17 million dollars),
while BCW's assets were valued at more than 4 billion (approximately
27 million dollars). The fact that BCW decided to keep the dump even
though it meant a substantial decrease in the value of its assets indicates
that the incinerator, already past the initial stages of planning, was
looked at as a factor that could increase the firm's profit-making potential and thus its overall commercial value.

BCW, in full ownership of the dump, in 1992 became a private share-
holding company, and with that, the state ceased to be the owner of the
waste dumped in Garé. This was unfortunate to the extent that the
likelihood of using state money (such as the Environmental Protection
Fund) to solve the Garé problem, which would have been the quickest
solution, was reduced to practically zero.

Garéans, meanwhile, just like BCW, were quick to take steps toward
independence from the state and tried to undo the havoc wrought on
their village by four decades of centralized regional development policies. In 1990 they voted for their independence from Szalánta and, draw-
ing lessons from decades of state impotence in environmental issues,
including the amnesty given BCW the year before, also embarked on a
search for private remedies. In 1991 Garé's leadership proposed the village as the location of the incinerator BCW was planning to build. In
hindsight—given Garé's and BCW's shared experiences with the state
and their ambitions for independent solutions—the alliance seems less
surprising than it did at the time.

But whom did BCW turn to in order to secure enough capital to invest
in a profit-oriented incinerator? The obvious solution was, again, the
West. BCW and the Industrial Ministry put the incinerator project out
for bid; the winner was a French state enterprise. This firm, then called
Tredi, formed a joint venture with BCW under the name Hungaropec,
which would become the owner and operator of the Garé incinerator.

Szalánta's leadership was rightly scared, not just by the environmental consequences of a hazardous waste incinerator, but by the prospect of losing its economic leadership in the district, after having already given up its political leadership when formerly subordinate villages regained their administrative autonomy. Consequently, leaders and residents of Szalánta objected to the idea of the incinerator and turned to environmentalists for help. The greens, in turn, mobilized experts, their environmentalist networks abroad, and other towns whose survival depends on wine production and urban and thermal water tourism and whose reputations could easily be ruined by the incinerator.[28] In the years to follow, the debate between Garé, BCW, and Hungaropec on the one hand, and Szalánta, other villages and towns, and the greens on the other, evolved into a massive conflict, or rather a name-calling quarrel leading to libel suits. The divisiveness of the case is probably what is most responsible for its frequent media coverage. In this, the roles of the state, the public, and the market have become the key, albeit covert, issues.

When the state ceased to be the owner of the waste drums and lost its exclusive role in assigning uses for lands, BCW rewrote the history of the Garé dump and a new discourse on the resolution of the case emerged. To relegitimate itself in the region, which now had a say in the permit process for the incinerator, BCW shifted responsibility for the dump to the socialist state and portrayed itself as a victim of backward state politics:

> Hungary, as well as her Eastern neighbors, was characterized by the dumping of the hazardous by-products of industry, that is, by "sweeping the problem under the rug," due to the incorrect industrial policy of the past decades; while in Western European countries with a developed industry and with an ever higher concern about the environment the most widely accepted solution has become the utilization of industrial wastes by incineration, which is already applied in numerous densely populated areas of Western Europe (Switzerland, the Ruhr, the vicinity of Lyon, Strasbourg, etc.) (Hungaropec brochure 1992, 1).

At the moment the socialist state became the criminal, BCW became the victim; at the moment the state-dictated procedures for disposing of toxic waste were proved wrong, the private, profit-oriented solutions were embraced. The Hungaropec brochure continued: "It is obvious that a real solution is possible only *on an entrepreneurial basis*, so that the investment earns its costs in the long run, and that it provides the

population of the vicinity with new jobs, decent livelihood, and infrastructural development" (p. 1; italics in the original).

This change in the script, of course, automatically pushed forward
BCW as the sole legitimate problem solver in the Garé case. Opponents
of the incinerator, however, immediately noticed the effects of the
change on environmental decision making. They angrily argued that the
emphasis in the whole procedure of environmental hearings and other
deliberations had shifted from achieving the cleanup to authorizing a
profit-oriented venture. Indeed, BCW successfully evaded obeying orders to start cleanup or to stabilize the environmental situation by blaming the delay on the legal proceedings, or, more precisely, on the
opponents of the incinerator who kept appealing decisions favorable to
the company.

The state's role during this time never went beyond facilitating the
public hearings and deliberating at various geographical levels of authority. The first decision made by the Southern Transdanubian regional
environmental authority denied the permit for the incinerator; the second, made at the national level, granted the permit; and the third, which
was the result of a civil lawsuit against the national authority with
charges of endangering public health and the environment, obliged the
previous authorities to start the process of environmental impact studies
and public hearings all over. Presently, this decision is being appealed.
While under state socialism, waffling on planned investments usually
resulted from lack of funds allotted by the plan itself, in this case, it is
due to the political weakness of the state—more precisely, on the one
hand, to the reluctance of local administrators to face up to the political
consequences of their approval of the incinerator, and, on the other, to
the corruptibility of public officials.[29]

What the waffling and suggested illegal efforts to win the state's favor
might be telling us is that various actors, even as they turn to private,
entrepreneurial solutions or, alternatively, to grassroots ones, have a
strong need for the state's larger involvement, which it cannot provide.
In interviews I conducted, villagers from Garé and Szalánta seemed
equally weary of the various meetings, votes, and legal battles, leaving
them nostalgic for the seemingly simpler and faster, if not democratic,
decision-making system of state socialism. Many of those I interviewed
even said that if state socialism had not collapsed, the dump would be
long gone and the problem solved; but they rarely went as far as calling
for the present state's more direct involvement. This might indicate a

deep lack of trust in the state's capacity, but it might also indicate the effect of prominent antistatist, postcommunist ideologies.

Naturally, the liberal transition discourse does not make it easier for the state to take a more active role. Should the state do what a well-behaved state in capitalism is supposed to do—let the market run the show? Or, rather, should it step in, thereby committing the biggest crime of postcommunist states: a "capricious intervention" thus "weaken[ing] or undermin[ing] the operation of market actors and market forces" (Schöpflin 1995, 67)? These are the alternatives this discourse presents. If, for example, the state pushes through cleanup, either with a relatively drastic administrative action or merely by allocating state funds for it, it delegitimates the presence of a Western, profit-oriented business in Garé's vicinity. That would imply a familiar politics of closing Western capital out and manually operating the economy. However, one might argue that in Garé's case the Hungarian state has already opted for being a grade-busting student of liberalism, inasmuch as it let a Western incinerator firm keep forcing the idea of cleanup via profit-oriented incineration, thus delaying actual cleanup until a final decision based on the "rule of law" is made.

The retreat of the state from the terrain of production and regional development freed even previously disempowered and silenced rural communities such as Garé to organize politically around environmental issues. It also made it possible for environmentalists to come to the aid of villages such as Szalánta, which previously had not enjoyed the expertise of urbanites, and help them exercise their democratic rights in environmental decision-making processes. At the same time, these changes, which ostensibly increased the empowerment of local communities, reached the limits of what communities could accomplish on their own.

On the one hand, the alliance between Szalánta and the greens, just like the alliance between Garé and international capitalists, indicates the acknowledgment that local communities require coalitions with broader visions, expertise, and political capital in order to realize their environmental goals. On the other, the villages' tug-of-war, with no solution in sight, indicates that the state needs to take on a more active mediating role. Unfortunately, the uncritical acceptance of the argument that blames socialist environmental destruction on the absence of the market and on the state's intervention in the economy led to a fragmentation of the state's accumulated human and social resources.[30] As in the case of the METESZ waste dump survey, for example, 1989 meant a total halt to already begun and quite progressive projects. As the initiator of this survey told me, "The change in the political system stopped this process; the second stage, such as the test drills and control, did not materialize, the pool of experts was replaced, ideas were forgotten. It was as if we had lost several years from our lives" (personal interview, Miklos Kassai, spring 1996).

Without these state resources, the new freedom is paralyzing. The result is a nonresult: the deferment of the cleanup under the pretext of striving for entrepreneurial and democratic decisions. If state socialism was mostly characterized by power through the incalculable, professionally ungrounded, and politically unchecked decisions of the state, the present is characterized by what Gaventa (1980) would call power through the "nondecisions" of a fragmented state held in check by the private sector.

Conclusion: The Presence and Absence of the State

The history of Garé's dump offers a general lesson about what social and political dynamics prevent an environmental state-society synergy from developing but also offers us a vision of what sort of alliances and communications between agents are necessary for moving toward a synergistically created sustainable society. State socialism—under which the _reason_ state is active but its power is unchecked—and the present period of postsocialism—in which, by contrast, the state has retreated from a series of arenas and in which the private sector is strongly opposing the state's more active involvement in the economy and in local politics— equally fail to produce positive and democratic outcomes.

The transitional period between these two stages appears as a fleeting moment of hope both in national and local history. This was the time when the state finally acknowledged environmental claims for what they are, when it opened up channels of communication and even allowed its decisions to be overturned by popular resistance. It was also a time when the state was still willing to take responsibility for trying to resolve environmental claims and still seemed to have some capacity to do so.

BCW's case demonstrates that contrary to journalistic and academic accounts, according to which the state's routine intervention in the economy under state socialism was a key structural cause of environmental degradation, the source of waste and pollution is not necessarily the paradigmatic enterprise producing by state order and with state subsidies or loans. The wastes BCW deposited in Garé resulted from the firm's

Evidence

failure to rely on state subsidies and from pressures from the world market. That, however, does not mean that this case is exempt from the structural features and dynamics of state socialism. In fact, the decision to produce TCB and its tremendous volume of by-products was motivated as much by BCW's political need for economic success as by the market. Furthermore, the landing of this waste in the woods of a disempowered agricultural village followed not, as in the West, from the village's weak position vis-à-vis the market, but rather from the state's role in regional development—that is, its politically motivated decisions as to which settlements to develop economically; from a lack of democratic control over the state and over production; and from the pervasive informal, horizontal relations that BCW could exploit to secure a dump site. Both deprivation and disenfranchisement resulted primarily and directly from the state's unchecked power, which, unfortunately, left communities powerless vis-à-vis not just the state but also industrial enterprises.

However, this power was not simply abused by the state with the aim or the effect of ignoring environmental issues. Rather, Garé's case is evidence that the state attempted to resolve environmental problems, but its efforts reflected and reinforced fundamental inequalities in society. By scrutinizing the few communicative channels that did exist between the state and society regarding environmental protection, I have shown that urbanites, in this case residents of Budapest and Pécs, were able to access environmental goods at the expense of their rural hinterlands, in this case Garé and the surrounding villages. They managed to do so because they enjoyed a certain discursive leverage and the necessary social capital—expertise and a network of urban-institutional connections—for making successful environmental claims.

In the transitional period, from about 1987 to 1990, the state showed an unprecedented openness to environmental initiatives, and urban experts, now able to voice environmental concerns without having to justify them from a production or development standpoint, for the first time allied themselves with concerned residents and environmentalists. Taken together, these developments opened new communication channels between state and society, resulting in a number of successful challenges to the accepted norms of environmental stewardship, despite the still absent or barely established infrastructure of democratic control. These challenges increasingly voiced oppositional or dissident demands, and by 1989, environmental damage was explicitly framed as a systemic result of central planning and of one-party rule, which hastened the collapse of state socialism.

By 1990, however, environmentalism had lost its potential for filling in for other political issues, and many former environmentalists left the movement for party offices and parliamentary seats. In addition, the technical intelligentsia, now freed to sell its expertise on the market, allied itself with liberal forces that not only opposed but often ridiculed environmentalism. The retreat of the state gave local communities greater opportunity to defend themselves legally but at the same time left them without an institutional instrument capable of implementing solutions to their problems of environmental degradation. The early marginalization of an environmentally sustainable vision of the transition on the national level, coupled with the opening up of politics on the local level, has resulted in searches for local, individual, and privatized solutions to cleanup problems. Under such conditions, democracy does not foster dialogue and consensus among communities but rather their division and prolonged conflict.

What lessons does this history offer us? It is clear that state presence in itself does not facilitate state-society synergy; in fact, it might preclude it. But in state socialism that was not because the state insulated firms from the market; rather, the overwhelming state presence crippled the political capacities necessary for communities to defend themselves, therefore making it too easy and cheap for enterprises to pollute. However, the retreat of the state is a double-edged sword: it may set free communities at risk but it may also leave them in an institutional vacuum and therefore helpless. Clearly, local communities need allies who possess both the political capacity necessary to prevent or find solutions to local environmental problems and the organizational or economic capacity to implement them. Furthermore, such allies must have the political credibility to do so without antagonizing other communities. In democratic transitions in which nongovernmental organizations are still in the process of establishing themselves and in which their financial foundations are still weak, one of these allies needs to be the state. However, it is exactly in these transitional periods that states with compromised histories lack the credibility necessary for a state-society synergy to develop. The summoning of other, more credible allies—intellectuals, the media, political parties, and international actors—is necessary to push the state toward greater accountability and more active participation in working out a sustainable vision for the future, and toward

enforcing environmental regulations, regulating environmental investments, and solving environmental disputes. Only with such an alliance
can the cocoon of "freedom-from" metamorphose into a butterfly of
"freedom-to."

Notes

*Research for this paper has been supported by the International Research and
Exchanges Board, the Joint Committee on Eastern Europe of the American
Council of Learned Societies and the Social Science Research Council, the
Wenner-Gren Foundation for Anthropological Research, and the Project on Eu-
ropean Environmental History, Sociology, and Policy at the University of Cal-
ifornia, Santa Cruz. I have greatly benefited from Michael Burawoy's and David
Stark's comments and especially from the numerous stimulating dialogues I had
with Peter Evans.*

1. Often this suggestion follows from the authors' assumption that if enterprises in state socialism were more like their Western counterparts—that is, more
profit oriented and innovative—they would have fared better economically as
well as environmentally.

2. Based on their sophisticated statistical analysis Kaderják and Csermely
(1997) came to the conclusion that changes in Hungary's industrial sector indeed
have reduced the environmental damage, measured by emissions, of paradigmatic socialist industries, primarily metallurgy. However, other industries
exhibiting strong growth potentials, such as the oil and plastics industries, are
and will be responsible for major growth in burdens on the environment. With
respect to hazardous wastes, the authors similarly find that "oil, pharmaceutical,
sweets, and the meat industries will become growing 'producers' of hazardous
wastes" (p. 27).

3. O'Connor argues that there is a contradiction in capitalism not just between the forces and the relations of production but also between the forces and
relations of production on the one hand and the conditions of production on
the other.

4. Besides adding my name to the long list of scholars who reject the term
transition while feeling compelled to use it as a shorthand, I'd like to emphasize
that in this paper, my periodization and labeling are grounded in the history of
environmental politics in Hungary and, more concretely, of my case.

5. Burawoy (1985) describes the way these organs of the state worked together at the shop-floor level to constitute a distinct factory regime.

6. These included campaigns as diverse as Communist Saturdays, on which
workers worked without pay for some centrally decided political goal, or the
collection of signatures and donations for the people of Vietnam during the
Vietnam war, or for starving children in Africa.

7. In 1967, BCW produced one-third of the pesticides (including herbicides
and fungicides) and one-fourth of the phosphorus fertilizers used in Hungary.

8. At the time, Hungarian enterprises were obliged to exchange their hard currency earnings with the state bank.

9. Until the 1960s, plants were expected to produce a certain volume of wastes in order to meet waste quotas. See Gille 1998 for more information.

10. In the literature, these tendencies are usually documented indirectly with macro and micro indexes of material and energy intensity, as well as more directly with waste / GDP ratios. See Gille 1998 for an elaboration on the dynamics involved.

11. It is still a well-kept secret of BCW which country this was.

12. Industrializing the countryside was not a new idea in the sixties. However, while in the fifties the establishment of new factories in rural areas was encouraged for political reasons, namely, to break peasant majorities, in the sixties the goal was to achieve greater equality in living standards between villages and cities and to rationalize the geographical distribution of economic activities, as well as to improve urban air quality.

13. This move was doubly supported by the state's policies. First of all, Hidas was on the list of preferred relocation targets; second, coal-processing plants, because of the imminent exhaustion of Hungary's coal mines, were prioritized as facilities for which new industrial uses had to be found. Nevertheless, when BCW applied for the subsidies or preferential credits promised to companies that engaged in relocation projects consistent with these policies, the attempt was once again in vain.

14. Ironically, the premature corrosion of these barrels was a consequence of the socialist waste-reuse efforts. The brigade producing TCB replaced new barrels with used ones in an effort to perform well in one of the many industrial material-conservation campaigns.

15. The land had been partly in state, partly in cooperative ownership.

16. I am making Hungarian socialist regional development policies appear more seamless and their history more unilinear than they really were. The goals, rationale, and methods of regional development policies went through several changes, and the actual outcome of these policies often did not reflect the original intentions of the planners. Gábor Vági, who was most likely the best-informed and most theoretically and critically attuned sociologist on this topic, analyzed the changes as well as the relationship between central intentions and local outcomes in several essays (1982, 1991).

17. That BCW did not approach the party is yet more evidence of its tenuous relationship with the party ever since the 1950s.

18. In Hungarian, the word *leszerelni* literally means "disarmed," but it also has a connotation of toning down, attenuating, and disabling. To the extent that the audience for this speech was fellow apparatchiks, the Executive Committee member was probably seeking, albeit through deliberately obscure references, to keep environmental claims from within the party, or from scientists or important administrative officials, from seeming too critical.

19. "Technical ones" is the literal translation of the Hungarian *müszakiak,* and it is the official label for employees with degrees in engineering. In the early period of state socialism, people in administrative positions at state agencies usually did not hold science degrees.

20. Konrád and Szelényi (1979) put this change in terms of a shift in ideological perspective from *telos* to *techne,* comparable to a shift from substantive to formal rationality.

21. Gustafson (1981) interestingly finds that in the Soviet Union geographers and other scientists brought up agricultural interests in the defense of nature, particularly in their protest against hydroelectric power plants. Yet the mechanism was the same: the reason why they could be successful was that, from the 1960s, "hydropower . . . interfered with the leaders' new plans for expanded agricultural development in the European zone of the country—a fact that underscores the close link between the rise of environmental issues and the Brezhnev agricultural program" (p. 48).

22. By *social capital* I mean *(a)* an accumulated expertise that can be mobilized and made directly available to a particular community or social group, and *(b)* membership in a network of institutional and noninstitutional connections through which outside expertise and information can be accessed. By *political capital* I mean *(a)* a good political résumé (as of a community or other entity—a firm, for example), and *(b)* membership in close-knit networks of party officials or officeholders in other political organizations (unions, the PPF, communist youth organization, etc.). Finally, *economic capital* simply denotes the exploitable economic importance of a production unit for a particular locality or industrial sector. It can be based on sheer size (e.g., a significant employer, customer, or monopolistic provider of certain goods) or on income, especially in hard currency.

23. OMRI, an heir to Radio Free Europe, disseminates news about Eastern Europe and the former Soviet Union.

24. The media had been dealing with environmental concerns in quite a matter-of-fact fashion since the mid-1970s, and scholarly journals had been regularly publishing articles on one or another scientific aspect of environmental protection. The conclusion of these articles and reports was invariably the need for integrating environmentalism into economic management and technological innovation.

25. The increased dialogue and cultural exchange associated with détente started to take off in 1975, after the Helsinki Accord was signed. The signatories accepted the status quo of contemporary Europe—that is, they gave up territorial claims and respected existing borders—but the real impact of the accord came from its Human Rights Clause, which forced state socialist countries to grant more freedom to their domestic political opposition.

The Right Livelihood Award Foundation was established in 1980 by Jakob von Uexkull, a Swedish-German writer, philatelic expert, and former member of the European Parliament, to honor and support those offering practical and exemplary answers to the crucial problems facing the world today. It has become widely known as "The Alternative Nobel Prize."

26. Here I am borrowing Hungarian sociologist Sándor Berki's incisive metaphors (Berki 1992).

27. Teréz Reich, the leader of the protest, describes Ófalu in this way: "Ófalu is a small village of five hundred inhabitants. Only ten years ago was a road built to the village. There are no water pipes, and the only water is polluted.

Most inhabitants commute because they can't find a job in the village. Ninety percent of the people belong to the German minority. In the village, there is only one intellectual, but she doesn't work there. No teacher, no doctor, no other representative of the intelligentsia can be found there. There are three villages within ten kilometers of each other (Ófalu, Mecseknádasd, and Óbánya), that have only one governing body; they belong to one council" (Reich 1990, 59).

28. The most feared problems are the dioxin-containing air emissions of burning halogenous wastes and the creation of yet another toxic waste dump for the by-products of incineration. Greens instead suggest incineration in an already existing facility (abroad or, ironically, in the one that residents of Dorog resisted so strongly in the 1980s), biodegradation, or the safe dumping of the drums elsewhere.

29. Besides rumors, the only detectable signs of corruptibility are two sudden resignations: a high-ranking employee of the regional environmental authority, a key contact for BCW, resigned the day the permit was denied to Hungaropec; the head of the national authority that later granted the permit resigned unexpectedly as well, his last official signature being the one on the document granting Hungaropec the permit.

30. Nowhere is this more painfully seen than on the terrain of waste politics. After 1989, in the Ministry of Environmental Protection, numerous reductions in the staff dealing with industrial wastes were implemented, until finally the entire Waste Department was eliminated. Comparisons with cuts in other departments indicate that the Waste Department was dealt by far the most severe blow. In addition, the progressive waste legislation of the 1980s, such as the provision obliging enterprises to prepare material flow charts, so that wastes would be more easily detected and their amount determined, was cut from the new waste laws, and even the obligation to prepare material balances became severely limited.

:: 6 ::

"Water, Water, Everywhere, Nor Any Drop to Drink"

Land Use and Water Policy in São Paulo, Brazil

MARGARET E. KECK

Introduction

Without a dependable supply of clean drinking water, no city is livable. Safe, reliable disposal of sewage is just as fundamental. Yet for decades, engineers and politicians recognized that both the drinking water supply and sanitation infrastructure in São Paulo, the largest and most industrially developed city in Latin America, were precarious. The story of São Paulo's water supply and sewage facilities over the course of the twentieth century is a classic case of failure to move an emerging "world city" onto a trajectory of greater livability, despite the tremendous concentration of human, organizational, and economic resources that were centered there.

There are many reasons for the failure. Privileging accumulation over livability is a central part of the problem. The priority for water managers was always electrical energy to fuel the region's growth. Political factors are also at the heart of the explanation. Fragmented policy domains became self-sustaining, as technical agencies developed corporate interests they were reluctant to surrender. The pervasive clientelism of Brazil's political system, in which reaping the spoils of large projects was an important medium of political exchange, persisted through military and civilian governments alike (Hagopian 1996; Ames 1995). Since the system rewarded spending on problems more than resolving them, there was no reason to expect it would produce solutions. A growing panoply

162

of environmental laws were rarely enforced, large projects consistently failed to reach their goals, and by the end of the 1980s, the metropolitan area's water management system seemed headed for collapse.

It is important to stress that the cause was neither a lack of technical capacity nor a lack of alternative ideas. Both were readily available. For close to thirty years, critical voices within the technical agencies, sometimes allied with individuals and groups outside the state, made continuous, albeit often quixotic, efforts to keep the mismanagement of water resources and reservoirs in the public eye. By the middle of the 1980s, the networks of those contesting the existing system of watershed management cut across the jurisdictional and sectoral fragmentation that characterized official decision making. Their big opportunity came in the 1990s, when, with the support and encouragement of multilateral financial institutions, public agencies finally began to move toward dealing more comprehensively with water issues. Sanitation infrastructure that had languished half-finished for years was completed, and São Paulo went from having around 60 percent of its sewage collected to having more than 90 percent collected.

Despite the improvement in sanitation indicators, by the early 1990s most of Brazil's sectoral infrastructure autarkies (sanitation, electric power, habitation) were in bad shape financially, and the federal government was not prepared to rescue them in the form they held then. The governments of Fernando Collor de Mello and Fernando Henrique Cardoso pushed privatization as the solution to what they characterized as inefficient service delivery (although private investors wanted the firms cleaned up before they were prepared to bid on them). Along with privatization, decentralizing management and introducing market mechanisms into service delivery made up the policy prescription. All of these played a role in the story of São Paulo's water reform.

During the 1990s, São Paulo, followed by other states and the federal government, passed laws mandating a new regime of water resource management, in which users would pay for what had previously been a free good. The laws called for new institutions (watershed committees and agencies) to manage the complex relationships among producers, consumers, and the public. They implicitly understood water issues to involve political problems, rather than strictly technical ones, and thus to require (not simply allow) participation by organizations of civil society. These new institutions are still embryonic, in that parts of the reform still await enabling legislation. Until user fees are actually charged, they are not even fully functional. There also is no guarantee that even fully enabled, these institutions will not fall prey to the well-known pathologies of capture or immobilism. Nonetheless, we find some reasons for a bias toward hope in the persistence of the professionals and activists who have long waged the battle for livability.

This chapter asks three questions. Why, in the largest city of Brazil's most industrialized region, was the problem of ensuring drinking water and basic sanitation for its population neglected for so long? How did the definition of the problem and available solutions change between the early 1970s, when the first important anti-pollution laws were passed and major sanitation projects were launched, and the present? In that process of change, what were the respective roles of state actors and organizations within civil society in framing the issues and alternatives available, and how are we to understand the relationships among them?

Answering these questions requires a careful political history of sanitation and water policy, combined with an analysis of the persistent tradition of oppositional efforts to forge new approaches and a sociological understanding of the development of state-society networks that made these oppositional efforts possible. Networks are central to the analysis, both descriptively and as an analytical tool for analysis of state-society relations. Throughout, my account stresses ideas as well as people and organizations, since ideas play an important role as positional markers and bases for cohesion within the networks.

I begin with a brief historical-institutional analysis of where water resource and sanitation issues fit in the development of the São Paulo metropolitan area (see Figure 6.1). From there I set forth some of the guiding ideas about development, technical expertise, and participation that helped define the relationships among actors even when, under the 1964–85 military dictatorship, political arenas for dissent were very limited. I look at the kinds of organizations that developed to protest water pollution and the contexts in which they did so, and finally I explore the factors that led to the beginnings of a more integrated and participatory approach to water resource management in the region.

Communities, both middle class and poor, are important actors in this story—sometimes as agents of livability, sometimes caught between livelihood and sustainability. Local NGOs and political parties are also important. Community leaders create NGOs as organizational vehicles for pursuing projects of livability. Oppositional political parties also provide valuable resources to those working for better management of water and watersheds. State agencies are clearly part of the problem,

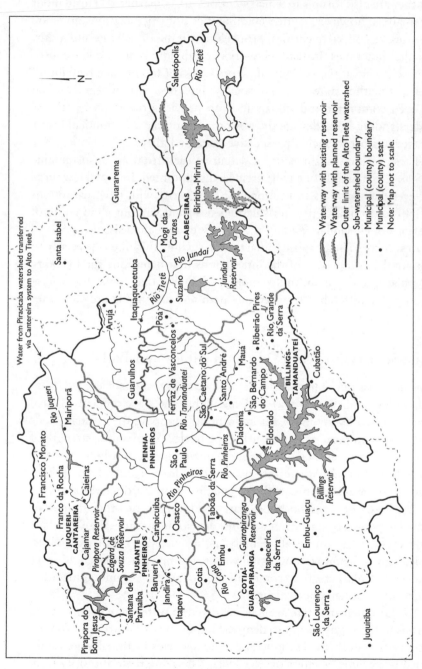

Figure 6.1. The Upper Tietê watershed, including metropolitan São Paulo. Source: Fundação Universidade de São Paulo, "Síntese do Relatório Zero," executive summary of *Relatório Zero* (São Paulo: Sistema Integrado de Gerenciamento de Recursos Hídricos do Estado de São Paulo, 2000), http://www.sigrh.sp.gov.br/sigrh/ftp/relatorios/CRH/CBH-AT/st0103.pdf.

but they are also forums in which solutions are constructed. Throughout the analysis, however, neither communities nor organizations nor state agencies, as collective entities, propel a reframing of debates and a shift in policy outcomes. Instead, networks of individuals are the key constitutive element in the ecology of actors working to enhance livability. I find that neither state, nor civil society, but the continuing interaction between committed individuals in both provides the richest path for understanding how, despite the powerful economic and political forces arrayed against it, such a perspective remained alive.

Those seeking in this story a definitive turn from an unsustainable path to a sustainable one will surely be disappointed. In Brazil few turns are ever definitive; its institutional history is rife with new institutions cobbled onto old, of new jurisdictions designed without elimination of previous ones. Understanding that is key to any analysis of a political process there. The purpose of narratives such as this one is precisely to capture the complexity of the interactions that determine the livability of a place, and the shifting ecologies of agents that make them. Frequently, the difference between one path and another is only a matter of inflection.

State-Society Networks in Good Times and Bad

This essay assumes interpenetration between state and society (see Migdal, Kohli, and Shue 1994) and highlights the development of pro-reform networks involving actors in both. Mapping these interactions is at least as important as measuring the relative or absolute strength of organizations or agencies. Individuals move among and between state agencies and societal organizations, and both formal and informal channels of communication can foster collaboration. Ordinary social networks, based on neighborhood, party, workplace, or other sources of shared experience, may affect network development more than the characteristics of an issue itself. Finally, policy debates begin with ideas, which can spur innovation, empower or disempower actors, and serve as encoded markers that communicate to others commonalities that might not otherwise be evident.

To claim that the state agencies involved in water management were porous in these ways is not to deny the importance of a strong corporate identity within them. Technocratic state agencies in Brazil were established to become "centers of excellence," deriving their authority from their superior know-how rather than their political connections. The circulation of technical personnel among bureaucracies that Schneider (1991) found in economic agencies, for example, is much less common in the water or sanitation agencies; more common is to find that most mid- to high-level water engineers and other technical personnel made their entire career in the same institution. Also more common, especially for the high-level management of these institutions, is elite circulation between public and private sectors, in particular large engineering firms that derive much of their revenue from government contracts.

Both of these characteristics—strong career-based organizational identities and close linkages with private firms active in the same field— support a status-quo orientation. Much of the time, that is a sufficient description. However, when aspects of the status quo are disrupted, even careerists become open to new ways of thinking about their roles. Such a disruption occurred in the 1980s, resulting from diverse factors: democratization of the political system, which created democratizing pressures within the technical agencies themselves; economic crisis, which reduced budgets and salaries; and a shift in policy by multilateral lending agencies away from their support of large engineering works, especially dams. How were the agencies to reconstitute their roles and legitimize their activities in these new circumstances? At such moments of interrogation, new ideas may find a hearing they would not otherwise have had.

Both activists and policy makers "frame" issues and alternatives, attempting to give them resonance in a particular political setting by describing them in relation to other desired values or goals, or to recognized social narratives (McAdam, McCarthy, and Zald 1996; Keck and Sikkink 1998a). This cognitive work is a central part of building political support. Framing an issue also frequently involves a causal story, a narrative that describes a problem and allocates blame (Stone 1989). Some frames *demobilize,* for example when policy makers convince people that an issue is too technical for them to understand. Thus, activists working on water and sanitation problems in the 1980s and 1990s increasingly framed their activities in terms of democratic participation and not just technical improvement of services.

Evans (1997b) is right to stress the heterogeneity of both state and society. Social movements and community organizations have always addressed the state at some level, either as challengers or more often through contacts with individuals holding elective or bureaucratic office. Reformers in public positions have often looked for support to community organizations whose demands could lend urgency to their ar-

guments. Professional organizations have also served as important channels of interaction.

These ongoing contacts—formal and informal—constitute networks.
In the main, such networks have been studied in their manifest form, as
policy networks or policy communities. During most of the period under
study here, the dominant policy networks in the sanitation arena look
like a classic case of agency capture—either by the electric company or
by big construction interests. But the opposition to the mega-project
approach to water and sanitation also acted, often self-consciously, as
a network. Like its much more powerful counterpart, it traversed the
state-society divide, its members sharing information and collaborating
to advance policy goals at favorable conjunctures, facilitating state-
society synergies. At less auspicious moments, actors in societal organizations and state agencies often coordinated efforts to modify or impede implementation of policies they opposed.

The more closely one examines the evolution of water management
in São Paulo, the more the role of networks becomes apparent. Over
the past thirty years, activists within and outside the state have formed
ties and shared ideas in community groups, environmental organizations, universities, and technical agencies, their loose linkages sustaining
a vision of water policy centered on preserving the quality of the water
supply and the contribution of local water sources to the metropolitan
area's quality of life. They lost most of their battles, but they managed
to preserve small institutional redoubts that enabled them to live to fight
another day. When reform became the order of the day, the reformers
were in place. Still, however encouraging their persistence may be, the
obstacles to livability in São Paulo remain dauntingly high.

Land and Water in Metropolitan São Paulo

São Paulo's water problems are a result of 130 years of rapid, essentially
uncontrolled population growth and urban sprawl (see Table 6.1). Already at the dawn of the twentieth century, the city's elites had begun
to push the tenements out from the crowded urban center, fearing moral
and physical infection (Rolnik 1994).

In the 1940s bus service spurred the growth of the periphery, and
workers built their homes, in their "spare time," on small lots without
urban services (Kowarick and Ant 1994, 64–71). Access to services became a frequent demand of social movements on the periphery and a
useful currency for politicians in search of votes (Kowarick and Bonduki

TABLE 6.1
POPULATION OF SÃO PAULO
(CITY), 1872–1980

Year	Population
1872	30,000
1890	65,000
1900	240,000
1920	580,000
1940	1,300,000
1960	3,800,000
1980	8,500,000

SOURCE: Lúcio Kowarick, ed., *Social Struggles and the City: The Case of São Paulo* (New York: Monthly Review Press, 1994), 41–45.

1994, 127–31). After the 1964 military coup, urban renewal acccelerated. São Paulo's mayors built boulevards and highways for private cars, while public transportation remained slow, overcrowded, and decrepit. Federal housing programs did not reach very-low-income families, and the numbers of *casas populares* (low-cost housing units) that were built were absurdly small considering the need.

Although expelling some of the slums from the city center kept São Paulo's elites from having to see poverty, disease, and malnutrition, the move to the periphery magnified the effects of these ills. The infant mortality rate, which had been falling in São Paulo as elsewhere in Brazil since the 1940s, began to rise again in the 1960s. By 1974, it had returned to the rate prevalent in the immediate postwar years, and around 70 percent of the cases were attributable to lack of water, poor water quality, or malnutrition. The percentage of households with running water dropped by five percentage points between 1950 and 1973, and only around 35 percent were connected to public sewers (Kowarick and Bonduki 1994, 137–38). The waste of a growing city flowed along gullies in the streets, ending up, untreated, in its rivers—the Tamanduateí, the Pinheiros, and especially the Tietê.

Rapid industrialization took as much of a toll on the watershed as the chaotic housing patterns that accompanied it. Until the 1970s, "developing" São Paulo's water resources meant generating electric power, organized via concessions to the Canadian firm Light (São Paulo Tramway Light and Power Company), founded in 1899, and the local firm

CPFL (Companhia Paulista de Força e Luz), founded in 1912. The centerpiece of the Light system in metropolitan São Paulo was the pair of reservoirs—Billings and Guarapiranga—built in the 1920s at the southern end of the city. Later on, Light created a barrier to the normal flow of the Tietê River and diverted this water through the Pinheiros River into the Billings reservoir. Taking advantage of the difference in altitude between the Planalto and the Santos lowlands, the water from Billings was dropped via aboveground piping to the city of Cubatão, supplying the Henry Borden hydroelectric plant (see Figure 6.2, a schematic presentation of this process).

In the late 1940s, its growing population forced São Paulo to use water from the Guarapiranga reservoir to supply the city. The city in turn agreed to return an equivalent quantity of water to Light in the form of sewage. With São Paulo's waste discharged into the Tietê as it flowed through the city, Billings in effect became a sewage stabilization reservoir. Early in the 1970s, when water from Billings was needed to supply the surrounding industrial suburbs to the south of São Paulo (known as ABC, for their main cities Santo André, São Bernardo do Campo, and São Caetano do Sul, but also including Diadema, Rio Grande da Serra, Mauá, and Ribeirão Pires), a dam was built to cut off the area of the Rio Grande facing Rio Grande da Serra. As the city's growth outpaced expectations, São Paulo increasingly needed to secure water from neighboring river basins to meet its water supply and energy needs; the rise in infant mortality in the early 1970s had made the inadequacy of the supply glaringly obvious. By 1980 piped water was reaching 95 percent of the city's population (though not all of the metropolitan area), and the infant mortality rate had been reduced (testimony of Eduardo Riomey Yassuda, in Brasília, Ministério de Minas e Energia, et al. 1983, 37–40).

Administration of water resources was centralized in São Paulo's Department of Water and Electrical Energy (Departamento de Águas e Energia Elétrica, or DAEE), formed in 1951. Decisions about water were made in technocratic state agencies and sometimes were treated as national security issues. State-society interaction was limited to the contractual relationship between the state government and the private firm Light, and eventually, in 1981, even Light was bought up and incorporated into the system of state-owned power companies. With the creation of the Ministry of Mines and Energy (Ministério de Minas e Energia, or MME) in 1960 and the National Department of Water and Electrical Energy (Departamento Nacional de Águas e Energia Elétrica,

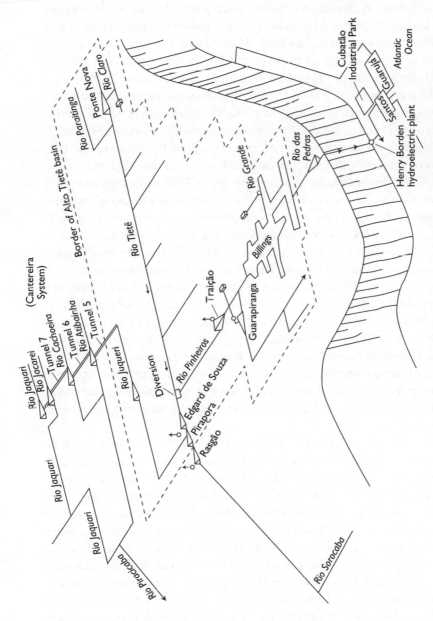

Figure 6.2. The Upper Tietê watershed in relation to neighboring waterways. Adapted from Plano Diretor de Utilização Integrada dos Recursos Hídricos na Região Metropolitana de São Paulo—Plano SANESP—1982. From Ministério das Minas e Energia—CESP—SABESP—ELETROPAULO.

or DNAEE) in 1965, the federal government established a national framework for water policy. DNAEE, a parastatal agency, had authority to intervene in all sectors of water policy; nonetheless, it concentrated on hydroelectricity.[1] Although São Paulo resisted centralization of sanitation services at first (São Paulo [Município] 1992, 21), in 1972 the state government agreed to make the São Paulo Sanitation Company (Cia. de Saneamento Básico do Estado de São Paulo, or SABESP), the state company that was in charge of basic sanitation, responsible for managing resource use and basic sanitation works in municipalities that had already ceded their water and waste authority to state agencies.

Watersheds, of course, do not respect political boundaries. The Tietê River is entirely within the state of São Paulo, and thus by Brazilian law fell under state authority. Because the upper Tietê watershed comprises more than thirty municipalities, however, major coordination problems resulted.[2] Jurisdictional issues were also vertical, between municipal, state, and sometimes federal agencies. The federal government supervised hydroelectric power issues and influenced lending by the National Economic and Social Development Bank or by international financial institutions. At all levels, separate agencies managed water supply and water quality, and there were no mechanisms for coordination with others whose activities affected water (housing, health, industry, and agriculture, for example). New sanitation programs were conceived in isolation from other aspects of water resource management, and indeed sanitation was not even considered *part* of water resource management. Nor, at the federal level, was concern for water pollution: the Secretariat of the Environment, established in 1973, had no authority in this area until the mid-1990s.

In 1975, in response to complaints from local firms in the southern industrial suburbs that pollution of Billings was injuring production, the state government joined the federal Ministry of Mines and Energy to set up the Grupo de Operações Interligadas (Coordinated Operations Group), which proposed to make the Henry Borden hydroelectric plant less dependent upon Billings, thus allowing greater flexibility in determining how to use it (*O Estado de São Paulo* 1975a).[3] At the time, the authorities promised the pollution problem would be resolved within six months (*O Estado de São Paulo* 1975b). A year later, however, newspapers reported large numbers of fish dying in the reservoir because of lack of oxygen. A comprehensive anti-pollution law (Lei 997) was passed in 1976. As the technical capacity to monitor pollution levels grew for the Companhia de Tecnologia de Saneamento Ambiental (Environmental Technology and Improvement Company, or CETESB, the main implementing agency for environmental policy at the state level), industrial effluents began to be more effectively controlled. Organic domestic and other public waste, however, did not, despite ambitious sanitation plans. During the 1970s, the municipal administrations of the cities surrounding Billings, especially Diadema, also began to complain about the reservoir.

By the end of the 1970s, conflict over water use had convinced the federal government that something had to change in the system. At the prodding of DAEE from São Paulo, federal agencies began to discuss integrated river basin management and established Comitês Executivas de Bacia (Watershed Executive Committees) in river basins under federal auspices. Although these committees had only an advisory role, they still influenced the terms of debate. Toward the end of the military regime, in 1983, an international seminar on water resource management in Brasília recommended adoption of an integrated water management program, and in 1985 the Plano Nacional de Recursos Hídricos (National Plan for Water Resources) was published. But the timing was bad: with the changeover from military to civilian rule that year, the reform was put on a back burner, where it stayed for the rest of the decade. The São Paulo state legislature passed a new water resource management law in 1991, followed by many other state governments and, in 1997, by the federal government. The new laws provided for multiple use of water resources, decentralization of water resource management, and participation by users and citizens' groups in management decisions. They also mandated the institution of user fees for water consumption.

Problem Definition and Frame Transformation

Divergent visions of what the "water problem" was about were as central to the conflicts as conflicting interests. Indeed, the two were inseparable. From the early twentieth century to the 1980s, the interests of Light and of state water and energy managers were powerful enough to preclude both discussion of the multiple use of water resources and a conceptual integration of water supply and water quality. As State Secretary of Energy and Sanitation João Oswaldo Leiva said at a 1989 seminar on water resources, "Today, this project [the diversion of Tietê into Billings] is often accused of being one of the causes of pollution in the Metropolitan Region. We can't even say that they forgot to consider basic sanitation when this project was designed. It was not considered at all, because there was a problem to solve. This project had an absolutely single-minded goal, which was to generate electrical energy" (São Paulo [Município] 1992, 5).

The emphasis on energy was consistent with São Paulo's image—and self-image—as the motor driving Brazil's economy. Beginning in the 1950s, the developmentalist vision of rapid economic growth stressed state initiatives in building infrastructure—giving yet more power to the energy sector (Sikkink 1991). This vision shaped the thinking of technical personnel for a long time. The Light system built energy-generating plants, which fueled São Paulo's (and by extension the country's) industrial development. That was seen as such a positive contribution that the University of São Paulo's Escola Politécnica (Engineering School) trained several generations of engineers to see water problems in the upper Tietê watershed from Light's point of view (personal interview, Werner Zulauf, 1991). São Paulo's focus on electrical energy, combined with the metropolitan area's rapid and disorganized growth, meant that by the time policy makers started to worry about the *quality* of water available as well as its quantity, it was late in the day. What changed?

State concern with current and potential conflicts over water-resource use grew during the 1970s. This was a period when urban and regional planning came into vogue, and the first Integrated Metropolitan Development Plan (Plano Metropolitano de Desenvolvimento Integrado, or PMDI) was published in 1971. The 1971 Plano Nacional de Saneamento Básico (National Sanitation Plan, or PLANASA) proposed to meet the needs of more than 80 percent of the urban population for drinking water, in at least 80 percent of the cities and all metropolitan areas of Brazil, by 1980. Nonetheless, the first shift toward a greater emphasis on basic sanitation did not involve significant changes in the prevailing centralized and sectoral vision of the issues. The PLANASA and the state sanitation initiatives it spawned followed an authoritarian and highly technocratic decision-making style. Both water delivery to communities and sewage treatment were viewed as technical problems whose solutions simply required study by qualified personnel, an appropriate plan, and adequate financing.

The interest in planning that produced the metropolitan development plan did not include an interest in civic participation—no one espoused the politicization of technical issues. Press censorship was in force, harsh repression of insurgent student and labor movements a recent memory. Consequently, in the 1970s, opposition to the existing policy process was unlikely to come from popular mobilization; it required an alternative vision with technocratic legitimacy.

Such a vision was supplied, par excellence, by something called, appropriately enough, the Solução Integrada (Integrated Solution). Briefly, the Solução Integrada was the sanitation component of the 1971 metropolitan development plan. It proposed to remove the sewage from the city via a tunnel through the Cantareira mountains and then to treat it in a graduated set of stabilization pools. This system was intuitively attractive because it treated the sewage away from residential populations, and because it was comparatively inexpensive. In addition to its proposal for sewage treatment, the Solução Integrada called for the Tietê to be returned to its natural course, and eventually for Billings to become available to supply water to the metropolitan area.

Although construction was already under way on the Solução Integrada when Paulo Egydio Martins took office in 1971, the new administration canceled it and decided to implement a much more expensive program called SANEGRAN, which involved construction of three large treatment plants to receive inputs through a network of sewers and collectors. Opposition to losing first claim on Billings came from Light, of course; further, Martins is said to have had family members with property in the Vale do Juqueí, where stabilization pools would have been built (personal interview, Fernando Vitor de Araujo Alves, 1991; personal interview, Rodolfo Costa e Silva, 1992). The move to replace the Solução Integrada with SANEGRAN began, as Werner Zulauf put it, a twenty-year battle over sanitation in São Paulo in which the Solução Integrada, often in an idealized form, was held up as the solution that might have been.

Rodolfo Costa e Silva, the architect of the Solução Integrada, brought to the issue of water resource planning a very different perspective from the one propagated at the Escola Politécnica. Prior to being purged from his job by the military for political reasons, he had worked for the Fundação SESP—Serviço Especial de Saúde Pública (Special Service in Public Health), which viewed sanitation as a public health issue. Costa e Silva approached the issue with a vision of the nation characteristic of sectors of the left historically associated with the Brazilian Communist Party:

> I have a national vision, and I am a nationalist. That means I want to see my country, my people, enjoy some of the advantages of civilization. . . . I get satisfaction from saying that I'm not a pure technician (técnico).[4] . . . The

técnico groups are a majority in the state of São Paulo. . . . They are technical
for the sake of being technical. That's what the government wants and that's
what I do. . . . I'm not disparaging this work. But my goal is different. . . .
It's to turn my knowledge into an instrument to help my country free itself
(personal interview, Rodolfo Costa e Silva, 1992).

In speaking of the Solução Integrada, Costa e Silva's passionate dedi-
cation to the ideas of national and public interest were transparent and
became part of the frame created by the juxtaposition of the two plans.
Their different approaches seemed to many actors in both state agencies
and civil society to epitomize the difference between a state dedicated
to the public good and a state that maintained a system of public expenditure marked by state complicity in the predatory, rent-seeking behavior of powerful private interests, especially the large engineering and
construction firms.

Within this perspective, disputes over what substantive policies in fact
represented the public interest became the central motif for contestation.
The Comissão de Defesa da Represa Billings (Billings Dam Defense
Committee) is the best example of this kind of contestation. The origins
of the defense committee lay in the well-off Eldorado neighborhood in
Diadema (see Figure 6.1), an area close enough to where the sewage-
laden river waters entered the reservoir to bear the full brunt of their
impact, and the leadership of Fernando Vitor de Araujo Alves, the community's representative on the municipal council of Diadema. Considered the "Riviera" of São Paulo back in the days when Billings was a
center of elite water recreation, this was a community that could protest
even during the repressive days of the military regime. With the devaluation of their waterfront property, even the least ecologically minded
residents had a powerful motive to do so.

One of the community's resources was one of the oldest neighborhood associations in São Paulo, the Sociedade Amigos de Eldorado,
whose main role was originally to welcome new people to the area. In
1969, the neighborhood association formed the Comissão de Defesa da
Represa Billings. Studying the problem, the members of the commission
decided that its cause was the overcommitment of water resources in
São Paulo to electricity generation.

The commission could count on engineers who collaborated free of
charge, out of frustration with trying to get the authorities to act. It also
tried to organize other constituencies; by 1977, it had succeeded in creating the Comité de Defesa de Billings, which represented more than

forty neighborhood associations near Eldorado and was sending notices repudiating SANEGRAN both to federal authorities and to international financing institutions. The municipal council of Diadema also rejected SANEGRAN unanimously.

In December 1977, Vitor headed a citizen suit against the government of Paulo Egydio Martins for replacing the Solução Integrada with SANEGRAN, using the vehicle of *ação popular* (a public interest lawsuit). Initially, conditions for the suit looked favorable, with considerable support from judicial and legislative committees. But when the suit was adjudicated two years later, Vitor and the others lost, and they suffered severe financial penalties (personal interview, Fernando Vitor, 1991).

An *ação popular* could be brought only on the grounds that a particular action was illegal or harmful (*Revista dos Tribunais* 1981, 57). The plaintiffs pointed to the likelihood of the continued pollution of Billings under SANEGRAN, the lengthy execution and high costs of the project, continued injury to economic and aesthetic values along the reservoir, and an increase in pollution in the Santos lowlands; in addition, they claimed that the SANEGRAN project violated laws, decrees, resolutions, deliberations, and ministerial agreements (76).

The judges ruled that harm would ensue only from faulty management, which could not be attributed to the plan itself. Comparison of SANEGRAN with the Solução Integrada was ruled irrelevant. Claims of harm because of either the cost or the implementation time for the project were rejected on the grounds that the National Housing Bank and the World Bank would not have approved the financial package were it unsound (80). Similarly, because the federal government had a constitutional right to intervene in cases in which water was used to generate electrical energy, the federal government's interest in the case was held to obviate any violation of the Water Capture Area Protection Laws that could be imputed to SANEGRAN (87). Finally, as no merit was found in the plaintiffs' case, they were required to pay the court costs. Vitor also suffered physically from the affair—he had heart surgery in 1977 and again in 1979, preventing him from continuing to play a leadership role. Although he continued to testify at hearings and write opinion pieces for newspapers until his death in the early 1990s, he mistrusted both political parties—such as the leftist Workers' Party (Partido do Trabalhadores, or PT), which won office in many cities in the region in 1988—and the new environmental organizations that began to protest the pollution of Billings and Guarapiranga in the 1980s and 1990s, feeling that they were not serious and were unprepared technically to discuss matters with the technocrats.[5]

The defeat of the suit was by no means the end of the impact of the Solução Integrada. It remains to this day a remarkable example both of the power of ideas and of the symbolic role they can come to play. Because the Solução Integrada existed, it was possible for nontechnical social and political actors to challenge public authority on water policy. Had it not existed, they would have been dismissed much more easily and might not even have tried to intervene. Every critical report or account of sanitation in the upper Tietê watershed mentions the plan; every environmental activist or environmental official in government interviewed in the course of this project mentioned it as well.

It is also significant that the Solução Integrada has adherents (one might almost call them disciples, given how they speak of it) in high positions of government. My personal copy of the plan came from Werner Zulauf, whose inscription to me was from "someone who believed in it." While directing CETESB during the administration of Franco Montoro, a former opposition leader elected governor of São Paulo in 1982 in the first direct gubernatorial election in seventeen years, Zulauf attempted to "rationalize" the implementation of SANEGRAN, most likely influenced by having been involved in the later stages of formulating the Solução Integrada. Like a shadow government existing in counterpoint to sitting ones, the plan has functioned as a shadow sanitation plan for São Paulo for more than a quarter century, making critical action more possible.

The Solução Integrada carried with it political connotations associated with the left, and particularly with the Communist Party, and although not all of its supporters were on the left, polarization around sanitation plans had a political dimension as well. The hegemony of this faction of the *técnico* community in the Montoro administration at the beginning of the 1980s (CETESB more than others at that time) was partially responsible for the relative openness of some of the technical agencies and the willingness of the government to engage in a dialogue with local populations. Even hegemonic inside the bureaucracy, however, they lacked the ability to confront the political power of the large construction lobbies that were the main supporters of SANEGRAN-style solutions. One of the things that undercut them was the lack of democratization.

The Impact of Democratization

If into the 1980s the political frame for contestation of the state's failure to resolve the problems of the Tietê and of Billings was one involving a principled conception of public interest, with democratization came the argument that only public participation in planning could protect that interest. Contestation of the state's failure to resolve the situation of the Tietê and Billings, initially focused on ends, began to center equally on the means by which those ends could be reached. This raised new questions: In what kinds of institutions could organizations from the community participate effectively? What kinds of organizations? In what kinds of decisions?

Many kinds of social movements organized during Brazil's transition to democracy, including an environmental movement (Viola 1987). Neighborhood organizations demanded local infrastructure, and urban squatter movements demanded housing. The Workers' Party formed in 1980 from an alliance among trade unionists, leftist intellectuals, and leaders of social movements emerging from Catholic base communities (Keck 1992). The PT was especially visible in metropolitan São Paulo, where its members were among the most active in a whole range of local movements (Doimo 1995). PT candidates won municipal elections in most of the cities of metropolitan São Paulo in 1988, promising to be responsive to social demands.

At the state level, Montoro promised to find ways to stop releasing sewage from the Tietê into Billings. Environmental organizations credit Montoro with providing space in which they could organize (personal interview, Hermínio Gerônimo Costa, 1991). The State Council for the Environment (CONSEMA), created in 1983, was set up as an organ of the governor's office. The council provided for parity between representatives of state agencies and organizations of civil society (ranging from business and professional associations to environmental groups). CONSEMA participated in formulation of a state environmental and natural resource policy, which endorsed multiple uses of water resources, among other goals.

Other new political instruments became available to activists during the 1980s as well. In 1981, the Política Nacional do Meio Ambiente (National Environmental Policy) included a stipulation that the Ministério Público (District Attorney's Office) could initiate lawsuits on environmental questions. In 1985, Law 7347, known as the Lei da Ação Civil Pública (Law of Public Interest Civil Lawsuits), granted standing to representatives of diffuse interests, including governmental institutions (for example, municipal administrations) and organizations in civil society that had been legally constituted for at least a year and that explicitly included environmental protection among their stated goals. Various municipal administrations in ABC and in Cubatão attempted to use this law to sue the state government for discharging sewage into the Tietê, on to Billings, and thence to Cubatão. All of these suits failed.

In fact, with some notable exceptions, most of the attempts to put pressure on the state government from the outside failed. Inside the state, however, democratization was bringing some fresh air into stale bureaucracies. Radical reformers wanted a major restructuring of state agencies, making them both more participatory internally and more accountable to the constituencies they served. Technical personnel, especially in DAEE, were disturbed by what they perceived as the chaos of this reform process; some farseeing planners among them, notably Flávio Barth, nonetheless recognized an opportunity to modernize water resource management in its wake. Beginning in 1987, Barth began pulling together an alliance of those advocating for participation and accountability and those seeking a new water management model.

For all the new political opportunities that became available in the 1980s, however, a deteriorating economy frustrated most efforts to accomplish substantive changes. The economic slowdown and high inflation of the 1980s worsened living conditions for the poor while compromising state capacity to intervene. SANEGRAN's promise to treat São Paulo's sewage before it reached Billings was stalled for lack of money to finish construction and lack of prior agreement with the municipalities of the region on building the interceptors to take the sewage to the treatment plants. No bank, foreign or national, would finance its continuation. During the Montoro administration, planners decided to scale back the plan and finish one of the treatment plants, which went into operation at a much lower capacity than originally intended. Meanwhile, increasingly, the problem of domestic waste in Billings and Guarapiranga came not just from the Tietê, but from the areas surrounding the reservoirs themselves.

Shortages of low-cost housing, or inability to pay rent at all, pushed poor people in the region to construct housing on illegally occupied land. Organizations concerned with water pollution and those set up to fight for housing, often allies on social issues in general, were at loggerheads over occupation of the water capture area. With democratization, squatters, as well as clandestine developers, could find allies on municipal councils and even in city halls. Cause lawyers were available to work with social movements (Meili 1998), and umbrella organizations of housing groups linked the squatter movements with counterparts elsewhere in the city.

Most of the new settlements violated the Water Capture Area Protection Laws (Laws 889 and 1172 of 1976), which, although they zoned the protected areas for low-intensity use, were neither respected nor enforced. In 1991, EMPLASA, the São Paulo state planning agency, estimated that since the laws' promulgation, more than a million people had moved illegally into the protected area. São Paulo's expansion to the south brought new construction to the banks of the Guarapiranga reservoir. At the same time, in the municipalities of São Bernardo and Santo André, land invasions and irregular real estate developments, as well as trash dumps (both municipal and industrial) proliferated in the protected areas. Real estate developers came up with imaginative new techniques for dodging the minimum lot-size restrictions contained in the laws, for example by selling land not in individual lots but in "ideal fractions" of a larger lot, such that, in condominium style, each owner possessed an unspecified piece of the whole.

Although enforcement of the Water Capture Area Protection Laws was theoretically a state responsibility, land occupation policy and zoning were municipal attributions; the onus of preventing irregular occupations was thus divided, but not always clearly allocated. These occupations posed a serious ecological risk. First, the new developments discharged sewage directly into the reservoirs, and the law prohibited building sanitation infrastructure in this area. Second, deforestation and the removal of vegetation both decreased the amount of water that soaked down into the water table and increased the amount of runoff of soil and other organic material into the reservoirs, adding to eutrophication.[6] The institutional framework for the resolution of these issues was extremely muddled. Municipal governments legislated on land use, CETESB regulated industrial pollution discharges and had to license industrial or commercial establishments in the zoned areas, and EMPLASA had to license residential projects. None intervened effectively in the occupation process. Further, many municipal and state politicians actively promoted occupations, seeking electoral support from new settlers.

This last set of problems posed special dilemmas for the Workers' Party, especially after 1988, when PT candidates were elected mayor in São Paulo and in several industrial suburbs. Thereafter, PT members

composed many of the environmental organizations fighting to protect
the water capture areas, most of the housing organizations fighting for
more flexible policies on their occupation, and the city halls that had to
mediate between these competing interests. The housing movement argued, often with justification, that it had nowhere else to go. The ecological movement argued that the area had to be protected, that "a small
number of people can't be allowed to endanger the water supply of 12
million people," and that other alternatives had to be found for housing.
The municipal administrations were caught in the middle—just how
much so is illustrated by the fact that in lawsuits brought by the São
Bernardo mayor's office against illegal real-estate developers who created fictitious "Community Associations" to occupy the land, many of
the defendants turned out to be Workers' Party members.

Environmental organizations adopted multiple strategies for influ-
encing policy, addressing multiple targets, including public agencies,
particularly CETESB and EMPLASA, and state and municipal legisla-
tors. Members of environmental organizations took positions within
city governments and as legislative aides, and some ran for and won
positions on municipal councils. Many concluded that partisan politics,
reflected in municipal councils, the state legislature, or even municipal
executives, was not likely to attend to the complex tangle of problems
to be resolved. Several, such as the Movimento de Defesa da Vida
(Movement in Defense of Life, or MDV), adopted dramatic attention-
getting tactics to publicize water pollution.

If the Billings Defense Committee was a good example of the kind of
contestation that took place under the military regime, the MDV is a
good example for the postdemocratization period. Interestingly enough,
it also began with residents of the Eldorado region, but this time it was
residents of working-class neighborhoods cut off by high walls from the
more luxurious housing closer to the reservoir. The driving force in the
MDV has been Virgílio Alcides de Farias, a former metalworker who
was laid off because a work-related injury caused him to lose his sight
in one eye.

Farias began to spend time at the Billings reservoir in 1978, when
Luis Inácio Lula da Silva, then president of the São Bernardo metalworkers union, suggested during a strike that workers could supplement
their family's food supply by fishing. Several years later, when he moved
to Eldorado, near where he had fished, Farias realized that the fish were
dying. He sought out people from the environmental movement to try

to understand what was happening. In 1984, he organized a meeting in his neighborhood to try to form a movement with more of an activist orientation than groups like the Billings Defense Committee had. Subsequently, he organized meetings in Diadema, in the municipal council building, and in São Bernardo, at which Rodolfo Costa e Silva (then a consultant to CETESB), other experts from state agencies, and politicians from the region were invited to speak. Out of this process came the MDV, so named because its founders wanted a name that incorporated other concerns besides ecology.

The MDV used creative media-oriented tactics as well as mobilization to attract attention to the problems of the reservoir. Its activists systematically dumped cargoes of dead fish from Billings on the doorsteps of CETESB and EMPLASA and in the halls of the legislative assembly and municipal councils. In 1986 they also blocked highways, talking to drivers of stalled vehicles about the situation, and on several occasions sequestered municipal vehicles that were dumping waste illegally in protected areas.

Farias was a member of the Workers' Party, and many observers saw the MDV as a partisan organization. During the first PT administration in Santo André, Farias worked on the staff of the environment department. Resources from that department were important in helping to organize the signature campaign for a popular amendment that became article 208 of the state constitution, which prohibits discharge of untreated waste into any body of water. Further, a PT legislator introduced an article passed as one of the transitional measures (disposições transitórias) of the state constitution that mandated the end of diverting Tietê waters into Billings.

But although the PT provided important links between the MDV and other organizations (as did Farias's background in the metalworkers' union), it was not central to the movement's identity. The MDV's spectacular direct actions did not spare the PT-led municipal governments either in São Paulo or in the ABC region. Increasingly, Farias and other MDV leaders began to see partisan politics as an impediment to reaching solutions, rather than a path by which programs could be realized. They believed that the movement had to bring together diverse actors around specific goals and stimulate the creation of new institutional spaces in which their issues could be addressed. The MDV was elected to one of the six environmentalist seats in the state environmental council in the early 1990s, gained a seat on the upper Tietê basin committee, and worked closely with state officials during Mario Covas's gubernatorial administration in the mid-1990s to stimulate public involvement in the process of reform.

Participation, according to Farias, must not be limited to consultation on details of plans already drawn up. Instead, it needs to involve the *intervention* of the community in policy formation. This is most likely to happen when prior struggles have built relationships among social actors and a political culture in which contestation from below is expected. The Covas administration brought a marked shift in how state agencies addressed the participation issue. At the beginning of 1996, when organizers of the upper Tietê basin committee approached the MDV, the organization was asked not to approve a project, but to say what needed to be done. This helped to start an organizational process in which civil society was called on to play more than a token role (personal interviews, Virgílio Alcides de Farias, 1991, 1998).

During the 1980s, networks of water activists had been able to do little more than constrain the implementation of traditional water policy, but their persistence laid the groundwork for a more enabling role in the following decade. By the end of the decade, a constellation of committed actors was in place at crucial nodes of the agencies that would be involved in reorganizing water resource management for São Paulo, in community organizations and NGOs, in the press, in international financial institutions, and in transnational advocacy networks monitoring large development and infrastructure projects.

Further, key reform-minded people in technical agencies, especially DAEE, developed and implemented a reform strategy centered on the passage of a new Water Resource Management Law. The reformers worked closely with another network of progressive state employees centered in EMPLASA and the Environmental Secretariat (SEMA), but also included people from CETESB and DAEE. This group stressed the development of links with civil society. Members of this second network were in the main scientifically and technically trained veterans of the student movements of the late 1960s, who had gone to work for the state at the moment in the early 1970s that São Paulo's governors espoused long-term planning and some measure of social reform. They had remained to see that vision lost, had proven themselves professionally, and by the mid-1980s had reached influential positions within their agencies. In the process, many of them had maintained close ties with one another, coordinating when possible to advance their common agendas.

In the 1990s, several relatively autonomous processes converged to produce a new conjuncture or political opportunity for purposive action: a long-delayed redefinition of jurisdiction over water resource management at the federal and state levels; completion of a study by FUNDAP (Fundação de Desenvolvimento Administrativo, or Administrative Development Foundation) for reorganization of water resource management functions in the state; a push to improve the functioning of public agencies in the hope of privatizing them; and the election of a state governor (Covas) in 1994 committed to state reform and to the idea of democratic planning. Under these circumstances, positive state-society synergies began to emerge.

In 1991, most of the municipalities in the region drafted new municipal zoning and development plans. They sought a pragmatic approach to development in the protected areas, calling for relaxation of the existing legal strictures in order to leave current occupants where they were, construct adequate sanitation infrastructure, and institute monitoring and controls to prevent further growth. Although in the case of São Paulo, the plan was shelved when the PT administration left office at the beginning of 1994, its *process* was nonetheless important, opening a dialogue between government officials and housing groups (Villas-Boas 1995; personal interview, Ana Lúcia Ancona, 1991). The pragmatic approach had assumed that new regulations would be implemented more successfully than old ones had been, a dubious proposition. Opponents of revising the Leis de Proteção aos Mananciais (Watershed Protection Laws) argued that installation of infrastructure would only attract more development. Nonetheless, some advances were made.

New Political Opportunities

At the end of 1990, after an episode in which water from Guarapiranga, because of the high concentration of algae, came out of the taps of the Paulista elite smelling and tasting bad, there was more pressure on public organs to do something. Municipal and state authorities formed a monitoring group, SOS Mananciais (Save Our Watersheds), and began to draft a program for the environmental cleanup of the Guarapiranga water capture area, for which the state would seek funding from the federal government and the World Bank. Some increase in monitoring the area and in warnings and fines did occur with SOS Mananciais, mainly in response to tips from environmental organizations active in the area (Villas-Boas 1995, 59–60).

In the early 1990s, the state government once again formulated a project to clean up the Tietê River. Included were many of the same goals that had characterized SANEGRAN, this time with financing from the Inter-American Development Bank. The Tietê project from the outset did count on a considerable amount of participation by environmental organizations. Following the highly publicized travail of an alligator popularly called "Teimoso," or "Stubborn," that had been spotted sunning itself one day on the banks of the Tietê and had subsequently proved impossible to catch, the egregious state of the Tietê became a popular cause. Stories about Teimoso became stories about the state of the river, as reporters speculated on the ability of any living thing to survive in such filth. The El Dorado Radio station (part of the Estado de São Paulo newspaper group) and SOS–Mata Atlantica (Save the Atlantic Forest), one of São Paulo's major environmental groups, ran an extremely successful signature campaign, petitioning the government to clean up the river, and established a coordinating group called SOS–Rio Tietê with financing from São Paulo banking group Unibanco (personal interview, Mario Mantovani, 1996).

In the run-up to the 1992 United Nations Conference on Environment and Development in Rio de Janeiro, funders were seeking environmental projects, and São Paulo's governor, Luiz Antonio Fleury Filho, won backing for the cleanup very quickly. But the usual problems ensued. Recession and hyperinflation eroded counterpart funding; in addition, a major construction firm on the cleanup project went bankrupt in 1994. By the end of the Fleury administration and through the first year of Mario Covas's government, the project was stalled. When it began again in 1995, it did so with more modest goals, and without the pretense that the river would be clean at the project's end. In a sense, the process was a replica of the lofty goals of SANEGRAN and its subsequent modification under the Montoro government in the early 1980s.

The Tietê project was unusual among engineering projects in that it claimed to be responding to strong popular demand, stimulated by a media campaign, and it incorporated SOS–Rio Tietê in the monitoring process as insurance against future trouble. Its design and implementation remained in the purview of engineers. With the inauguration of decentralized watershed management, some of the reformers hoped to make broader citizen participation a central part of building new institutions.

The Basin Committee Process

The new state administrative system for water resource management, established by Law 7.663 in 1991, was the fruit of several years of study and discussion. In 1987, at the prompting of the DAEE reformers, Governor Orestes Quercia had created the Conselho Estadual de Recursos Hídricos (State Water Resource Council), which in turn had set up several study groups with the idea of devising a new statewide administrative plan. Reinforcing this approach, stipulations regarding water use were included in the state constitution that was promulgated August 30, 1989.[7] The council's plan was published in 1990, consistent with its constitutional mandate, and proposed decentralized management of water resources at the level of the watershed, with participation from municipalities, water users, and civil society (São Paulo [Estado] Conselho Estadual de Recursos Hídricos 1990; personal interviews, Flávio Barth, 1999, and Paulo Bezzaril, 1999).

The principles of the new system turned the old, centralized practices on their head. They adopted the river basin (or watershed) as the unit of reference; called for decentralized, participatory, and integrated management; recognized water as a public good to be managed; and mandated that mechanisms be established to charge user fees. Water use for regional development had to be compatible with environmental protection, with priority given to the public water supply. Civil society had to be represented on decision-making bodies. These were to be the state Water Resource Council and regional committees for each river basin, all with tripartite representation of state, municipalities, and civil society. The council was to propose and approve specific actions within the framework of the overall system; a state fund to finance water management projects was also established at this time.

This is the point at which societal actors had to be formally co-opted, in the sense that Philip Selznick used the term fifty years ago, into new forms of state-society collaboration, a process that produces contention both within corporate agencies of the state and within movements and communities. In his classic study of the Tennessee Valley Authority and grassroots organization, Selznick defined co-optation as "the process of absorbing new elements into the leadership or policy-determining structure of an organization as a means of averting threats to its stability or existence" (Selznick [1949] 1966, 13). He went on to distinguish between formal and informal co-optation, the second of which mainly involves powerful outside interest groups and does not immediately concern us.

Formal co-optation, Selznick said, "involves the establishment of openly avowed and formally ordered relationships" and normally results either from a need to reinforce the legitimacy of a governing group by bringing in individuals capable of inspiring confidence in relevant publics, or from the need to establish essentially administrative channels to those publics. He noted as well that formal co-optation rarely involves the transfer of actual power, although it does involve transfer of responsibility; this is normally at the heart of debates within communities over whether or not to participate in such governing organs (Selznick [1949] 1966, 13–14). Nonetheless, for all its inherent difficulties, broadening participation could still have far-reaching consequences for the institution—and "requires an understanding of the possible unanticipated consequences which may ensue when positive social policy is coupled with a commitment to democratic procedure" (Selznick [1949] 1966, 16).

Formation of basin committees that would be viewed broadly as representative was easier said than done and involved a lengthy process of public hearings and meetings that increasingly mobilized local leaders. A great deal depended upon the abilities of initial organizers and their commitment to a broad participatory process and to the existence of a civil society sufficiently prepared to respond to state initiatives. Both of these criteria were met in the case of the upper Tietê basin committee. Some of the work of the committee was further decentralized into basin subcommittees, one of which specifically addressed problems in the region of Billings, and one of which dealt with the area around Guarapiranga.

One of the first issues that had to be addressed was the state of the two reservoirs and the revision of the Lei de Proteção aos Mananciais. In 1996–97 the basin committee sponsored a two-year process of public hearings and debates about both, many of which were jointly sponsored with the Intermunicipal Consortium of Greater ABC (Consórcio Intermunicipal do Grande ABC) and by the Movimento de Defesa da Vida. The new water capture area protection law passed at the end of 1997 drew heavily on this process of discussion, which in the eyes of both state representatives and organizations of civil society was necessary to give legitimacy to actions on a highly controversial issue. In this instance, the natural alliance was between environmental organizations and state agencies; municipalities tended to focus on the need for growth, and for fiscal reasons resisted rezoning any land hitherto designated as urban. The new law established general guidelines for the whole state (the previous law had applied only to the metropolitan region). Each basin committee was made responsible for specific measures tailored for that watershed (personal interview, Gerônico Albuquerque Rocha, 1998).

The new protective legislation would not have satisfied any of the warring parties a decade earlier. It was insufficiently protective for those who argued (correctly) that settlement was undermining the area's role in water capture; it was too protective for those who believed that growth alone would produce the solutions to the "externalities" of the development process. However, the negotiation leading to the new law made it possible to halt new land invasions and to construct social infrastructure in neighborhoods already established. This was, in the end, a significant step for all concerned. Stabilization of the situation had become the sine qua non for any kind of pollution abatement measures to be successful. What changed in the environment or opportunity structure that made the rapid development of state-society synergies possible in this case? Part of the answer lies in the widespread perception among both political and economic actors that the era of huge and expensive development projects is over. Until the mid-1990s, official attitudes toward the system's failures were surprisingly nonchalant, water wastage was rampant, and many expected to resolve water problems by channeling water from distant watersheds by means of fantastically expensive engineering works. It is now clear that no one will finance such enterprises and, further, that global competition rewards effectiveness, not mere size. To fulfill President Cardoso's plan to privatize as much of the public sector as possible, utilities had to be placed on a sound financial footing and made to operate efficiently—otherwise, they were unlikely to interest investors or would be priced too low. Further, the new governor, Mario Covas, made a serious effort to clean up the financial Augean stables left by previous governments enamored of large construction projects. Although construction firms are still major funders of political campaigns, the large Brazilian firms are themselves global actors and must adapt to the new rules of the global marketplace. Thus, while the Covas government actively promoted a change both in democratizing procedures and in reorienting goals, market transition may have helped to neutralize some of the opposition.

This is also a case in which the differences between the Montoro administration in the 1980s and the Covas administration in the 1990s are striking, both in the overall political and economic environment for democratic policy reform, and in the degree to which organizations in civil society were prepared to abandon purely oppositional stances and take on new participatory roles.

The new processes still contain a great many uncertainties. On the plus side, there has been an enormous opening up of channels of information, communication, and joint action between state agencies and organizations within civil society, together with the increasing commitment of particular individuals within some state technical agencies to this process. Nonetheless, others within those same technical agencies still think that participatory decision-making processes needlessly politicize essentially technical issues and slow down the implementation of effective solutions.

Other important procedural impediments remain as well. Successful implementation of the law to protect the water capture areas requires some kind of compensation to the municipalities most affected by this designation of their territory. A legislative act to establish this compensatory fund was passed in 1993, and as of May 1998 it was still languishing on the governor's desk, awaiting signature. The elaboration of the Billings cleanup project has also been quite slow, bringing it into the end of Covas's four years in office and an electoral period. Suspicions about electoral uses of components of the project worry environmental organizations (personal interview, Virgílio Alcides de Farias, 1998).

Until the basin committees have a sufficiently long history of activity, their effective centrality to the process remains highly dependent upon the political will of the governor. Further, their power will depend on effective implementation of the basin agencies that will collect and manage user fees—a still-contested process. The long preparatory period, the density of relations within and among state agencies and civil society organizations, and the relative abundance of technical expertise give São Paulo a special advantage over other Brazilian states, where these characteristics are less likely to be united. Even in São Paulo, experience has shown that relatively small shifts could still render the basin committees' interventions more formal than real. Basin committees are not a panacea, but they are a good example of the kind of institutional experimentation that is necessary if cities like São Paulo hope to construct viable solutions to their water problems.

Conclusions

Until the 1990s, the likelihood that social capital would create syner-gistic relationships around integrated and rational use of water resources in São Paulo appeared quite small. Consider the notions of complemen-tarity and embeddedness that Evans deems essential to synergy (see chapter 1; Evans 1997b). If complementarity implies mutually suppor-tive relations between public and private actors in which there is a "clear division of labor based on the contrasting properties of public and pri-vate institutions" (1997b, 179), and embeddedness implies "ties that connect citizens and public officials across the public-private divide" (1997b, 180) and that build norms and loyalties, then for a long time, we were dealing with a case of "dyssynergy." The story I have told here appears to contain precious few elements of successful public-private interactions. There are a great many roads half traveled and hopes that ended in disappointment. The results appear more likely to produce greater public-private mistrust than anything else.

And yet, despite this rather pessimistic picture, when presented with the opportunity to develop meaningful alternatives to existing institu-tions and processes, there appeared to be a reservoir of social trust on which to draw that was much deeper than the history would have sug-gested. How can we explain this puzzle?

Many highly committed activists continued through good times and bad to seek ways to influence political outcomes, maintaining contact with allies in the state apparatus or taking on state employment them-selves. In this study, I found the boundary between activists within and outside of the state to be extremely thin and constantly shifting. This continuing relationship can contribute to diverse outcomes: in good times, innovation, "complementarity," and institutional reform, and in bad times, the mobilization of protest or collaborative efforts to block policies through strategic leakage of information, lawsuits, creation of splashy media events, foot dragging and delaying tactics, demands by credible outsiders for more studies, or in some instances mobilization of international advocacy campaigns (Keck and Sikkink 1998a).

Networks capable of erecting roadblocks to harmful policies often result from the construction of an enabling network during some earlier, more favorable, conjuncture. The network of those with some relation to the Solução Integrada is a good example (personal interview, Nelson Nucci, 1999). It is certainly not an automatic outcome; here the schol-arly desire to build models falls victim to a high level of voluntarism and accident in real life. Networks usually depend for their maintenance on a few committed individuals. If one moves away, another gets a better job in another agency, or another is immobilized in a car accident, a blocking network can easily collapse; leaders are harder to replace in hard times than they are when there is progress to be made. Nonetheless, where networks continue to exist, they can jump-start a process of positive state-society interaction when the political conjuncture opens up.

Thus we might infer that initiating positive state-society synergies requires the presence of dedicated activists within and outside of the state, who have or quickly build a relationship of trust in a political environment in which, at the very least, powerful opponents of desired policy changes are neutralized and, at best, opportunities exist to build broad alliances around them.

However, to build policy change into the institutional practices of government agencies and social actors, the voluntary moment has to give way quickly to designing other kinds of incentives for collaboration of both state and societal agents. This dilemma has not been resolved in the fifty years since Selznick wrote about the TVA; if anything, increasing distances between technical personnel and publics have made it worse. Water engineers in São Paulo fear that too much civic participation in decision-making bodies on water issues may undermine effective program designs. But the argument here highlights the possibility that well-developed interactive networks between state and societal agents can mitigate some of the fears both of the community organizations and of the water engineers. The process by which the basin committees were established suggests a second hypothesis: When "co-optation" of community leaders into programs or planning initiatives designed under state auspices takes place on the basis of already functioning networks, the level of social trust should be higher, and the ability to address diverse publics greater. Further, when preexisting networks have built interpersonal loyalties over time between state and societal actors, these may be a foundation on which meaningful citizen participation can be built.

Whether or not the development of such networks can become the basis for the eventual "embeddedness" of social capital is a historically specific question. There is no guarantee, even with the development of new institutions in São Paulo, that this process will not be reversed. Further, there is no guarantee that the creation of sectoral councils will not simply reproduce, in different institutional form, corporatist relationships, or that interbureaucratic competition will not simply be supplanted by intercouncil contests. Where preexisting social capital is not as strong as it was in São Paulo, these new institutional relationships are likely to be easily manipulated. Nonetheless, by feeding a continuing exchange among intellectuals, activists, technical personnel, and policy makers, they keep the conversation alive and create the possibility of subsequent network development.

Notes

The title of this article is from Samuel Taylor Coleridge, The Rime of the Ancient Mariner, *part II, stanza 9 (1798).*

The following institutions supported the research on which this article is based: The Howard Heinz Endowment / Center for Latin American Studies, University of Pittsburgh, Research Grant on Current Latin American Issues; the Joint Committee on Latin American Studies and the Advanced Fellowship in Foreign Policy Studies of the Social Science Research Council and the American Council of Learned Societies, with funds provided by the Ford Foundation; the John D. and Catherine T. MacArthur Foundation; and the Johns Hopkins University. I also thank Denise Capelo for research assistance. I have benefited from previous comments from the participants in this volume at the December 1997 workshop on livable cities sponsored by the Social Capital and Public Affairs Project; from participants in the Environmental Politics Seminar of the International Studies Center at the University of California at Berkeley; and especially from Ramachandra Guha, from numerous conversations with Jonathan Fox, and of course from Peter Evans, who continues to be, as always, an inspiration.

1. There were exceptions. In São Paulo, a special program was developed for the Vale de Paraíba in the 1960s in response to serious conflict among users; the program aimed to use hydroelectric potential within a broader vision of regional development, based on the model of basin management pioneered by the Tennessee Valley Authority in the 1930s United States (Fundação do Desenvolvimento Administrativo 1989, 30–31).

2. Ownership of water resources in Brazil was assigned as follows: Surface water, lakes, or rivers touching more than one state or another nation were the property of the nation. Water that is wholly contained in one state and is not on federal land was owned by that state. Only water on private land that was not otherwise classified as public or common was considered private. Groundwater was considered a mineral and thus was owned by the federal government. Groundwater contributing to the navigability of rivers was also federal property. Spring water was the property of the owner of the land on which it rose (United Nations Food and Agriculture Organization 1983, 43–44). This system was revised by the 1987 constitution, but confusion between state and federal attributions remained.

3. The idea was to make alternative sources of hydroelectric power Cubatão's primary energy supplier, with the Light plant used only during peak periods.

4. Strictly speaking, "technician" is not an adequate translation for *técnico*, which really refers to a professional in a technical field with a technical vision of problems. Nor is "technocrat," for which an equivalent exists in Portuguese. I will therefore use the Portuguese word *técnico* in the text hereafter.

5. Fernando Vitor's death was related neither to his heart condition nor to his activism. He fancied himself somewhat of a ladies' man and died from a shot fired by a jealous husband.

6. Eutrophication, or the enrichment of a body of water with plant nutrients, leads to accelerated growth of aquatic plants, especially algae, which in turn reduces light intensity and can produce toxins that kill fish. A useful terminological reference for nonscientists is Allaby 1989.

7. Articles 205 to 213.

:: 7 ::

Sustainability, Livelihood, and Community Mobilization in the Ajusco "Ecological Reserve"

KEITH PEZZOLI

The "irregular" settlements that have grown up in the Ajusco greenbelt of Mexico City pose the contradictions of livelihood and sustainability in a stark and dramatic way. They have also been the site of intensively creative efforts to reconcile the livelihood needs of poor communities with the larger urban area's requirements of ecological sustainability. For three decades, poor communities struggled on the slopes of the Ajusco reserve to secure the land, housing, and services that they needed without destroying the area's value as an ecological reserve. At its height, this effort was embodied in the concept of "ecologically productive settlements" (*colonias ecológicas productivas,* or CEPs), which seemed to offer the basis of a resolution.

If, in the end, the CEP concept did not prove to be a viable solution, it remains a creative response that left a cultural legacy for Mexico City's quest for livability. Even more important, the fight to bring CEPs into being, and its aftermath, contains invaluable lessons for anyone trying to understand the dynamics of community-based environmental action. This chapter attempts to dissect these lessons and their implications for general theories of political ecology and livability. It grows out of fifteen years of study, analysis, and participant observation among the communities of the Ajusco region.[1]

Ajusco is a rapidly urbanizing miniregion at Mexico City's southwestern edge. Its forestland, high rainfall and aquifer recharge capacity, and agricultural as well as recreational value have made it one of Mexico

City's most prized natural assets. At the same time, it is a place where the viability of public-sector control over land use, self-help housing provision, and the politics of planning for ecological sustainability find their most serious testing ground. Ajusco is an archetypal case for illustrating the politics of sustainability, degradation, and livelihood in urban Mexico and elsewhere in the developing world.

The urban edge of Mexico City's ecological reserve is, to use Foucault's (1983) phrase, a frontier for the relationship of power—"the line at which, instead of manipulating and inducing actions in a calculated manner, one must be content with reacting to them after the event" (p. 225). Urban expansion into Ajusco has involved fraudulent schemes by real estate developers, illegal sales of communal and *ejidal* property,[2] land invasions and violence, mass eradication of incipient low-income settlements, popular resistance and opposition movements, widespread corruption, and deepening ecological disruption. There is a high degree of quasi-institutionalized violence at these frontiers, violence manifested as an "industry of destruction"—a self-contradictory form of low-income housing production in which irregular settlement is followed by eradication in an iterative process until the poor people eventually stick to the landscape. Even the most cursory analysis of Ajusco will quickly reveal that the status quo is unsustainable.

Urban encroachment into the Ajusco greenbelt, starting in the late 1970s and continuing to this day, has been driven by contradictory forces and clashing values in an ongoing process of creative destruction. The process is creative insofar as it has indeed produced some much needed popular-sector housing. But the growth is ecologically destructive. Notwithstanding official discourse that has long trumpeted the high value of Ajusco's environmental services (for example, as a forested "sink" for atmospheric pollution, and as an important site for recharging the city's aquifer), the area's ecosystems continue to be seriously degraded. Over the past two decades, Ajusco has been the site of an outwardly shifting urban-ecological frontier at which pressing issues of sustainability and livelihood are played out through a tense and ambivalent set of state-society relations.

The government's past reaction to irregular settlement and community-based environmental action in Ajusco (during the 1980s and early 1990s) was generally reactive and contradictory. Such a disposition may change. The political restructuring taking place in Mexico and, more specifically, in Mexico City's Federal District may enable a more proactive and environmentally constructive role for the state. But such an outcome is certainly not preordained. The victory of the PRD (Partido Revolucionario Democratico) in the Federal District in 1997 put issues of social justice and equity higher up on the political agenda, but it certainly did not wipe out the deep historical, material, and cultural barriers to more environmentally sustainable forms of development.

There is now a substantial body of literature claiming that the conjoining of community and state initiatives (that is, state-society synergy) embodies a powerful but still unrealized potential for moving development onto a more sustainable path.[3] This paper examines these claims in light of the specific experience of the Ajusco region, using a political-ecology perspective. As an analytic framework, political ecology argues that creating sustainable human settlements depends upon the type and degree of access that community groups have to means of production, administration, communication, and innovation. The holism of this analytic approach posits state-society synergy as a catalyst, not as an end unto itself. There is a broader constellation of forces (what Peter Evans calls an "ecology of agents") to take into account. Even so, state-society synergy is crucial; it is essential to spurring the kind of collaborative innovation, social experimentation, and social learning necessary to move development onto a more sustainable path.

My analysis of events in Ajusco begins with a brief description of the area's biogeography. Following that, the story unfolds in chronological order. First, attention is drawn to the late 1970s. This is when the first fifty families got a foothold in the Ajusco greenbelt. Just a few years later, by the early 1980s, there were more than twenty thousand people in a cluster of thirteen irregular settlements (colonias populares)—collectively know as Los Belvederes. During the first few years of this process, there were a number of small-scale evictions (desalojos). By 1983, a large-scale eviction seemed imminent. Citing the need to halt environmental degradation, the government announced plans to relocate most of Los Belvederes to another part of the city.

At this point, the events that constitute the most instructive part of the story, and the heart of this chapter, began. A group of popular organizations launched an innovative counteroffensive with help from external agents. People from Bosques del Pedregal, one of the most active colonias in Los Belvederes, led the movement. The grassroots campaign mobilized hundreds of families under the banner of promoting "ecologically productive settlements" and sustainable land use (that is, land use incorporating ecological and conservationist principles). Strategies used to build support for the CEP movement included an effective use of the mass media, cross-sectoral coalition building, and transnational net-working for solidarity and financial support. This paper's focus on the CEP movement sheds light on the political dynamics of community struggles for life space and livelihood and the challenges involved in trying to integrate these struggles with strategies that enhance sustainability.

The Ajusco "Ecological Reserve"

The zone of Ajusco gets its name from one of the peaks within its bounds, the snowcapped Ajusco volcano. It is a verdant mountainous and wooded area covering roughly eighty square kilometers on the southwestern fringe of Mexico City. The rugged terrain—rising from two thousand to four thousand meters—is part of a volcanic mountain range called the Sierra del Ajusco. This range forms the southern limit of the Central Mexican Basin. Most of Ajusco is designated as an ecological conservation area, a natural reserve, or a park.

Much of the official discourse about the region expresses concern about the degradation of Ajusco's natural capital. For instance, in terms of "environmental services," the zone is valued for its abundant winter rainfall. Given its permeable volcanic subsoil, much of Ajusco's rainfall used to be absorbed, thereby helping to recharge the city's aquifers (Quadri de la Torre 1993). The conversion of land use in the zone from nonurban to urban uses has had a significant negative impact on hydrological patterns. Wilk's 1991 study of Tlalpan's northern subwatershed (which includes that part of Ajusco examined in this paper) calculates that there has been a geometric increase in runoff. Over the period from 1959 to 1985, runoff increased from 14.5 to 20.5 percent of the total rainfall. By 1989, runoff had reached an estimated 23 percent of the total rainfall (Wilk 1991, 8). Runoff, along with domestic and industrial wastewater, finds its way into the storm-water collection system, most of which is ultimately pumped out of the basin to the north. This is especially problematic given that groundwater supplies more than 70 percent of Mexico City's water. Increased runoff, coupled with the over-exploitation of groundwater supplies, has caused large-scale land subsidence (an average of 7.5 meters in downtown Mexico City). Subsidence, in turn, has damaged the city's infrastructure and led to increased flooding.[4]

Besides playing an important role in hydrological functions, Ajusco is valued for its rural uses, including farming, forestry, and ranching

(Rapoport and López-Moreno 1987; Mexico DDF 1989a, 1989b). It is also valued for its majestic open space and wealth of biodiversity, including a cover of trees and vegetation believed to be significant for sustaining favorable microclimatic conditions (Wilk 1991; Soberón 1990). Ajusco is actually considered the richest biotic zone in the Valley of Mexico (Quadri de la Torre 1991, 44); more than a thousand species of plants have been counted there. Biologists, ecologists, and social scientists have drawn attention to the zone of Ajusco from diverse perspectives. Yet a certain level of consensus exists among them. As one environmental scientist puts it: "Ajusco painfully illustrates how the ecological crisis in Mexico involves interlocking relations among the economy, ecology, and politics, and that our lifestyle over the medium and long term is not viable."[5]

Critics and supporters alike refer to the Ajusco greenbelt as the government's environmental litmus test. It is a highly contested terrain subject to intense pressures of urban expansion, where interests of the state, popular groups, *ejidatarios,* and developers clash. The urban poor are not the only ones who have staked out claims for land in Ajusco. The zone's abundant green space, clean air, and panoramic vistas have attracted real estate developers and higher-income groups interested in upper-class development. Historically, economically better-off groups have concentrated in the southwestern part of the city, and in the case of Ajusco the competition for land is especially intense (Schteingart 1987). Within the same ecological reserve, one finds well-protected enclaves of luxury villas not far from sprawling squatter settlements (Schteingart 1989; Figuereo Osnaya 1992).

The government claims that Ajusco is a proving ground—a place to demonstrate how growth can be controlled, how social protest can be mollified, and how the ecology can be protected and sustained. The first set of plans to limit urban growth in Ajusco was drawn up in 1976. On paper, Ajusco was designated as a buffer zone intended to be a natural barrier against urban expansion. In practice, it has not worked that way. Between 1980 and 1986, the government extended the legally designated urban limit line three times to accommodate urban encroachment inside Ajusco. From 1986 to 1996, the urban-ecological boundary was moved again several times to accommodate growth. Planners and officials that I interviewed at the highest levels of the Department of the Federal District held the view that the sharp intensity of social and political turmoil in the illegally urbanizing parts of Ajusco, coupled with the area's increasingly serious ecological problems, has confronted the city administration with its most serious and difficult challenges regarding land use and environmental planning.

My first extended stay in Ajusco was during 1983, at which time I spent roughly eight months living in Bosques del Pedregal, one of the thirteen contiguous settlements that make up Los Belvederes. My most recent visit to Los Belvederes was during late 1997. Over this fourteen-year period I accumulated nearly two years of experience living and doing research in the field. More important, by maintaining close relations with select families over the long run, I have been able to follow the careers of local grassroots activists. One of them—Hipólito Bravo López—began his activist career as a poor but charismatic leader of several popular movements and community organizations in Ajusco during the 1980s. Now he is a *diputado,* an elected government representative in Mexico City's new Legislative Assembly of the Federal District (Asemblea Legislativa del Distrito Federal).

My repeat visits to Ajusco have enabled me to witness firsthand the zone's rapid rural-to-urban transformation. By periodically climbing to the top of a thirty-meter-high metal tower (constructed for the transmission of television signals), I have literally watched urban sprawl encroach deeper and deeper into the region's so-called ecological reserve. The sprawl has continued despite formidable barriers both physical (stone walls, police blockades) and symbolic (signs delimiting the outer limits of the urban area). Bosques del Pedregal was the first irregular settlement to get a foothold in Ajusco.[6]

The Formation of Bosques del Pedregal (Late 1970s): The Social Bases of the Initial Struggle for Land

How is it that Bosques del Pedregal was able to gain a foothold in the greenbelt zone of Ajusco despite land use designations prohibiting it? Was the process a chaotic and unruly one? To what degree did the production of this irregular settlement involve state-society synergy? Such questions call attention to the urban housing problem writ large, not only in Mexico, but also in most other urban areas of the developing world.

It has been impossible for most of Mexico's urban families to purchase a housing unit in the formal (that is, legally sanctioned) real estate market. Reasons for this include Mexico's widely skewed distribution of income, the rapid rate of urban and demographic growth, the lack of mechanisms for low-income housing finance, and the inability of the economy to generate enough well-paying jobs. For the most part, only the middle and upper classes have been able to access formal sector housing, either in subsidized middle-class public housing or in private developments. Lacking viable alternatives, millions of Mexico City's inhabitants have occupied land that is unsuitable for urban development. Such settlements occupy the barren, desiccated lakebed of Texcoco, hills that are unstable from mining, sites next to railway lines or factories that emit toxic waste, and, as in the case of Ajusco, zones designated for ecological conservation.[7]

Most of the popular housing in Mexico City has been built by the occupants themselves, or through informal sector contracting. Perhaps as much as 65 percent of the city's total existing stock was produced with some form of "self-help" (Pezzoli 1995). Must housing produced in this way starts out with an "irregular" status (that is, illegal or semilegal); the residents do not possess legal title to the land they occupy. Although this may give the impression that such settlements develop *outside of the law,* such an impression is misleading. As Antonio Azuela (1987) points out, despite such settlements being in some way illegal, or rather because they are, "the law becomes a real issue which influences the strategies of the social agents involved, thus shaping social relations and in some cases, the very structure of urban space" (p. 523). At the same time, the development of irregular settlements is not an entirely oppositional process that pits society against state. Indeed, the built environment of such human settlements (including roads, schools, water and sanitation systems) is typically "coproduced" by community groups in conjunction with state agencies. Community groups provide labor, while the state provides materials or technical services.[8]

Given how entrenched irregular settlement processes are as a form of housing production, and how law and legitimacy play a key role in so-called illegal and semilegal processes of access to land, it is not hard to demonstrate that the origin of Bosques del Pedregal followed a predictable pattern. Like many other irregular settlements, the development of Bosques del Pedregal involved a great deal of self-help, combined with the coproduction of public goods and services.

The history of Bosques del Pedregal begins in 1977. It was around this time that a critical mass of families had begun to consolidate their position in an agricultural and forested area on the south side of the railroad tracks. Said railroad tracks designated the beginning of the so-called ecological buffer zone.[9] Crossing the tracks in the late 1970s marked a turning point. It initiated the rapid spread of irregular settle-

ment into the up-sloping hills of Ajusco. It is beyond the scope of this
paper to detail the complicated juridical and land tenure aspects of subdivision in this transition zone (see Pezzoli 1998). Suffice it to say, many
of the people who first entered the transition zone paid *ejidatarios* (members of a legally recognized farming community) for the land—often
making a deposit followed by monthly payments. The demand for land
intensified, and soon more and more people took lots without paying
anything. In this way the origin of Bosques del Pedregal is best characterized as a mix of illegal sales and small-scale "invasions."[10]

People staked their claims for land in Bosques del Pedregal by erecting
small dwellings made of rocks, branches, and cardboard. Most people
settling there came from other parts of the Federal District, but some
came directly from rural areas. In one of few demographic studies of
this area, survey data shows that 62 percent of the families earned less
than the minimum salary, 15 percent earned the minimum salary, and
15 percent earned between one and one and one-half times the minimum
salary (Schteingart 1986, 22).

On three occasions during early 1977, *ejidatarios* initiated police action against the so-called invaders. Hundreds of dwelling units were torn
down and burned. After each *desalojo*, some people dropped out, never
to return. Others returned again and again—consolidating themselves
as a group with common interests. A fourth attempt to eradicate the
settlement on June 6, 1977, was successfully resisted. The *colonos* knew
the eviction was coming, so they had mobilized a defense. They organized brigades to solicit support from students of UNAM (the Universidad Autonoma Nacional de México—the local campus of the National
University) and from trade unions. University students helped the *colonos* make banners with painted messages declaring UNAM-Bosques
solidarity. Other experienced popular groups that were active in citywide grassroots movements (notably, Campamento Dos de Octubre—
Bloque Urbano de Colonias Populares) also contributed banners. And
the grassroots organizers sent letters and telegrams to Mexico City's
mayor *(regente)* and the president. When the police tried to evict them,
the *colonos* had their defensive strategy in place: they argued that they
would not vacate the premises until they received a response to their
letters, they hung the banners showing the support they had from the
students and unions, and they gave signals—holding "sticks, machetes,
and rocks"—that made clear their willingness to defend their claims
(*UnoMásUno,* n.d. 1982).

Warding off this eviction bought some time. And the *colonos* used it to consolidate their organization. They formed a "Mesa Directiva" (Executive Committee), a group of five or six activists whose self-declared task was to organize four commissions: planning and subdivision, press and propaganda, security and vigilance, and land allocation. Members of the mesa were not elected; they were self-appointed working-class leaders, and their power was based in their capacity to allocate land.[11] One of them was affiliated with the PRI (Partido Revolucionario Institucional) and thus had some influence with local government officials. Two other members, both semiskilled construction workers, had prior experience as grassroots organizers in the nearby popular settlement of Tlalpan.

The first major decision of the mesa was to define what would be the boundaries of Bosques del Pedregal. The space was defined strategically; it was not merely filled in some chaotic or anarchic fashion. Once the territory to be occupied was delineated, the leaders set aside land for streets, services, and open space. With some help from students studying architecture, they marked off street lanes with lime and branches, following the trajectory of the streets downhill.[12] At the same time, they marked off neighborhood blocks and allocated lots. Initially, each lot was approximately 500 square meters, but they decided to divide the lots into two approximately 250-square-meter lots so that more people could be brought in right away. The political organization of the *colonia* depended in part on the accomplishment of this territorial division.

At first, the objective was to populate the settlement as quickly as possible. Yet land was not allocated indiscriminately; there were two basic conditions—set by the mesa. First, each incoming family had to set up a dwelling unit right away and occupy it. This meant that they had to bring all their belongings and begin living in the *colonia,* despite the considerable risks and hardships involved. If someone set up a dwelling unit but did not occupy it full time, the mesa would reallocate the land. Brigades actually checked on occupancy. The idea was that if a family was really needy, they would be willing to set up their homestead immediately despite the insecurity. Until the settlement had a significant number of full-time resident families, the risk of eviction would be high.

The second condition that had to be met if a family wanted land was financial. Families had to pay a weekly fee to cover the mesa's expenses: to support the leaders to work as activists, to file an *amparo* (a court injunction to stay the pending eviction), and to construct an elementary school. The construction of the school offers telling insight into the contradictory nature of the state and the dynamics of coproduction.

The establishment of an elementary school is one of the first and most crucial tasks in the consolidation of an irregular settlement. The requirement that people had to establish roots and live in Bosques del Pedregal full time meant that families had to take their kids out of school. There was no public transportation linking the nascent settlement to the rest of the city. Thus, ferrying children back and forth to their old schools was practically impossible. This presented the first families of Bosques del Pedregal with a major problem. To establish an elementary school, they needed to register a plan that would be officially sanctioned. The plan had to include a duly designated site (federal land) for a building. And the site had to have access to sewer lines so that the school could be equipped with toilets. At first glance, these would seem to be intractable problems. Not only was the settlement considered illegal, it was under active threat of eradication. The local government agency *(delegación)* responsible for land use and urban development was adamant about its position not to supply any services to Bosques del Pedregal. So what did the *colonos* do?

To get their school, they first drew up a list of all the children in, and soon to be in, the settlement. This was necessary to demonstrate need. With this list, and with a provisional building in place that was constructed with their own money and labor, the *colonos* were able to get the support of a government official in the federal department of education. This official was not concerned about the illegal status of the settlement; it was his mandate to attend to the needs of schoolchildren. From him, the *colonos* were able to get a report endorsing the need for establishing an elementary school. And this report enabled them to get a teacher. Once the school was up and running, the *colonos* broke the news to the local *delegación* that the school was "official." Thus they were able to use the school as a shield—local government agencies are typically less inclined to eradicate a place filled with schoolchildren.

The Consolidation of Social Capital in Los Belvederes and the Rising Threat of a Mass Eviction (Early 1980s)

As was the case with the school, efforts to consolidate the settlement's social capital also embodied legal tactics. Social capital includes "the norms of trust and reciprocity and the networks of repeated interaction that sustain them" (Evans 1997b, 2).[13] In less than a year, the Mesa Directiva developed serious problems of accountability. According to oral testimony from two leaders who defected from the mesa and started an alternative group, the mesa became exploitative; it no longer served the best interests of the *colonos*. Apparently, leaders of the mesa had taken advantage of the situation in a way that primarily benefited themselves. For instance, one leader reportedly took over the commission of land allocation by arguing that he had "pull" within the *delegación*. He sold land and charged fees to *colonos*, but the benefits of the proceeds did not reach the community. In a community newsletter, it was argued that "political manipulation was common—they brought us like sheep to the acts of the PRI" (Boletín de Colonos 1986, 11). This prompted dissension from the mesa, and an alternative group was formed—a group that quickly gained widespread support.

The group was called the General Council of Representatives, Civil Association (Consejo General de Representantes, hereafter referred to as the council). In a meeting on June 24, 1979, thirty community leaders voted to approve the bylaws and articles of incorporation of the council. At the same time, they elected the representatives that would serve in the council. Shortly after this, during a general assembly of the entire community, the decisions were ratified, and after filing proof of the events with a notary public, the council became a legal entity.

The organizational structure of the council was modeled after a workers' union based at UNAM, where some of the grassroots activists in Bosques del Pedregal had gained experience. The council's objective was to create a form of legal representation that would encourage the greatest possible community participation in settlement affairs. Around the same time, several other incipient settlements of Los Belvederes (notably Dos de Octubre and Belvedere) constituted their own independent organizations. As a form of legitimation, the community leaders in all three settlements sought juridical status for their grassroots organizations. Forms of legitimation arising from popular social practices substitute for state law as far as they fulfill the role of a legal system in "normal" situations (Azuela 1984, 524). Popular groups often solicit juridical recognition for their organizations in order to convince settlers and authorities that their control over land is legitimate. Here we see an inherent contradiction: *colonos* organize to challenge dominant social and political relations of power, but in so doing they take on an identity defined by the very system they oppose.

By the early 1980s, around twenty thousand people occupied the greenbelt zone of Ajusco. The thirteen contiguous settlements, which had come to be called Los Belvederes, covered 171 hectares (431 acres) divided into 219 blocks containing five thousand lots approximately two hundred square meters each. During 1983, federal and local government officials began to repeatedly announce that the illegal settlements in Ajusco would be eradicated.

Also in 1983, the General Directorate of Urban Restructuring and Ecological Protection (Dirección General de Reordinación Urbana y Protección Ecológica) was created. This new top-level office within Mexico City's Federal District Department (DDF) was created to deal with the capital's urban planning and environmental problems. The official policy line coming out of the DDF at this time was that the irregular settlements of Ajusco were destroying the environment. Hidalgo Cortes, head of the Directorate of Areas and Territorial Resources (Dirección de Areas y Recuros Territoriales; DART), argued that "the industry of invasion" must be stopped and that in the extreme case, upward of ten thousand families would have to be relocated (*El Día,* October 2, 1983).

Official opinion regarding Ajusco was recorded in a legal document (dated August 1983) called a Dictamen Pericial (Expert Judgment), which was part of a complex legal proceeding known as a Juicio de Amparo (Court Injunction Trial). It was elaborated by a branch office within the Ministry of Urban Development and Ecology in response to complaints formally registered by a grassroots leader from one of the threatened settlements in Los Belvederes that the government was unfairly targeting the area's lower-income settlements for eviction when the upper-income settlements in the same so-called ecological reserve were not under such threat. The judgment found, however, that the inhabitants of Los Belvederes disturbed the ecology of the zone and that they should not be permitted to remain. This "judgment," as well as pronounced threats by various levels of government, served as a rallying point around which grassroots groups articulated countervailing arguments.

Community groups in Los Belvederes mobilized to resist the forced relocation. Herein lies the most instructive part of the story—the innovative organized resistance. Besides well-worn strategies of marches and demonstrations, the grassroots movement generated bottom-up, proactive environmental action.[14] Aided by technical assistance from external agents, grassroots activists in Los Belvederes began to promote innovative productive ecology projects as a countervailing strategy to secure the presence of the families in the zone.

Community-Based Environmental Action as a Countervailing Force: The CEP Movement (Mid-1980s)

Community activists in Los Belvederes argued that they could point the way to a new development for Mexico City: far from being a blight on nature—which was the general view—each settlement would be transformed into a CEP, a *colonia ecológica productiva,* suggesting a productive, sustainable future. Participants in the productive ecology movement argued that the demand for land in the area makes it impossible to maintain the entire zone as a greenbelt for "consumption" in the form of a national park or ecological reserve. Yet it is possible to develop a greenbelt for production, a place wherein grassroots social experimentation may be promoted to generate new forms of development that use resources sustainably and minimize ecological disruption.[15]

The CEP advocates did not argue that the entire ecological reserve should be abandoned in favor of productive ecology. What they proposed was admittedly only a partial solution. It was generally understood by the movement leaders that larger-scale issues figured into the challenge of sustainability (for example, the political economy of urban-rural development at the national and international levels). The CEP initiative was conceptualized as a drive for social justice and equity as much as it was a drive for environmental improvement. There was an understanding that empowerment of community groups was an essential starting point, a necessary step in a larger struggle to eventually enable the adjustment and scaling-up of local initiatives such that they make sense in the broader scheme of things.

The grassroots activists argued that their call for an experimental greenbelt for production sharply contrasted with the government's approach to planning, which treated housing, economic, and ecological problems as separate issues. The activists argued that these problems couldn't be solved separately. Faced with chronic scarcities of income and resources, participants in the grassroots ecology movement saw no alternatives outside of promoting self-reliant forms of urbanization. Their proposal centered on the concept of productive ecology, which calls for the development of appropriate technology that can reduce the cost of generating employment and recover capital investment through the rational use and reuse of resources.

In many ways, the main arguments and the working hypotheses outlined by the CEP advocates were consistent with Habitat II's 1996 program for poverty reduction.[16] These arguments and hypotheses were as follows:

1. The current population of Bosques del Pedregal is not marginal; it is productive and can be an active agent in technological development. Furthermore, it is possible and necessary to conjoin productive development with ecological equilibrium, and in this way to generate a mode of urban development that does not provoke antagonism between these two factors.

2. The conservationist focus that the Tlalpan Ward has maintained conceives of Ajusco as a national park. But this conception disassociates the necessity of reforestation from the possibility of production. Given the demands on this space, it will be impossible to maintain it as a greenbelt for consumption. Instead, it should be developed as a greenbelt for production.

3. Through community pilot projects—involving the operation and maintenance of appropriate technologies as well as the generation and distribution of resources—the auto-administrative capacity of the community can be elevated; so can its productive capacity. In terms of production, it is estimated that with an initial investment of 100 million pesos (approximately U.S. $140,000), 340 jobs can be created.[17]

4. Promoting social experimentation in Bosques del Pedregal to ameliorate the problems in Ajusco is in the national interest. If the *colonia ecológica productiva* model is successful, it could benefit others by way of example.

5. The project coincides with the political intent of the Mexican Constitution and the government of the Federal District. It fits within the guidelines of the Development Plan for the Metropolitan Zone of Mexico City and the Central Region.

Such initiatives are promising, but as the subsequent evolution of this case demonstrates, it is often difficult to mobilize the financial and technical capital—not to mention the social capital—necessary to implement such strategies. It is a classic problem of inadequate access to the means of production (both material and sociocultural). For successful project development and maintenance, there must be an adequate supply of money, technical expertise, state support, and social capital. In the case of the CEP movement, access to each of these means of production was limited.

The efforts to get an alternative sewage system called SIRDO up and running provide a specific illustration of the general problem. SIRDO is an acronym for the Sistema Integrado de Reciclamiento de Desechos Organicos (Integrated System for Organic Waste Recycling). This term was coined by Josefina Mena Abraham, an architect and the director of the Grupo de Tecnología Alternativa (GTA), which was responsible for promoting the technology. The terms *seco* (dry) and *húmedo* (wet) differentiate the two basic types of SIRDOs (Mena 1987). The SIRDO-seco, a closed system that resembles an outhouse, is the simpler of the two models. In 1985 three SIRDO-secos were put into operation in Bosques del Pedregal, several families using each one simultaneously. Inputs included urine, fecal matter, and organic matter of all sorts, such as vegetable husks and peelings, discarded food, weeds, and paper products. When properly tended to—which was not always the case—the waste inputs into these eco-outhouses ended up as a brown granular fertilizer.

The SIRDO-húmedo is a more complex system, involving a decentralization of urban infrastructure. It is supposed to perform the same functions as a SIRDO-seco, but it is also meant to treat and recycle *aguas negras* (sewage effluent) and *agua gris* (soapy dish, bath, and laundry water), and it is designed on a larger scale: it can serve from twenty to a thousand families. In 1985, the construction of a SIRDO-húmedo to serve 120 families was begun in Bosques with funding from an Austrian solidarity group (a group of professionals sympathetic to the ecology movement).[18] Although it never happened, each housing unit was supposed to be linked to the SIRDO-húmedo system via two tubes: one for *agua gris* and one for *aguas negras*.[19] The SIRDO technology was at the centerpiece of a plan to create local jobs and to bolster community solidarity through collective ownership of the means of production, not just for generating exchange value but also for systematically supporting production for use value.

Several factors worked against the SIRDO-húmedo from the very start: it was difficult to raise funds for it, the state did not support it, and while the community did support it as a technical argument to ward off eviction, the level of comprehension of the technology outside the immediate circle of advocates was actually very low. The scarcity of funding forced the *colonos* to try to raise money from clothing drives

and other community-based fund-raising events. Some funds were also
raised from two outside groups: the Austrian solidarity group already
mentioned, and the MISEROR Foundation, a Catholic philanthropic
agency brought into the *colonia* by the GTA. Because of galloping inflation during the late 1980s, the funds raised were enough to cover the
cost of only four eco-outhouses. Enough was raised to begin, but not to
complete, the SIRDO-húmedo system. Consequently, after absorbing a
great deal of community effort and resources, the SIRDO-húmedo technology sat idle for a long time, creating the appearance that all the effort
had been for nothing.

Ironically, the deathblow to the project came when the state eventually began to install regular sewage infrastructure. This was a contradictory move on the state's part, since the government had said all along
(from 1983 to 1993) that the steep incline and rocky, volcanic terrain
would make the installation of "normal" infrastructure in Ajusco impossible. Apparently, the wealthy residents who live in the same general
vicinity persuaded the state to proceed with the extremely costly "normal" service. In addition, the new Programa Nacional de Solidaridad
(National Solidarity Program) made new infrastructure funds available.
While the installation of normal infrastructure might seem at first like a
superlative solution, in practice, "regular" sewer systems on this sort of
terrain may not be superior to alternative technologies. First of all, they
are indeed very costly to construct and put a serious drain on the government's budget. Besides that, once in place, they can be plagued with
problems. Indeed, in many parts of Los Belvederes the system functions
fewer than four days per week.

As if the funding problems and lack of support for the alternative
technology were not enough, there were technical problems as well.
With reference to the case of El Molino, also in Mexico City, Coulomb
(1991) argues that the GTA's approach disempowers community groups.
He notes that external technical agents such as the GTA sometimes use
colonias as experimental testing grounds without full disclosure, and
without the consent of the *colonias* involved. In the case of the SIRDO's
failure to work in El Molino, Coulomb argues that it was not yet a
proven technology, and certain factors associated with its function
clashed with social norms and expectations. This played a role in the
demise of the project in Bosques del Pedregal as well.

The CEP proposal may have been overambitious, but it was not without grounding in realism. As researchers have begun to point out, popular groups have an important role to play in the design, development,

and management of urban services. As a study carried out by an interdisciplinary group at Mexico City's Universidad Autónoma Metropolitana (UAM) describes it, "access to urban services now forms part of
an ensemble of specific demands that interrelate diverse facets of social,
economic, and urban life. To acquire services is an urban demand, this
is certain, but it is intimately related with the necessity for employment,
conditions of transportation, education, health, and environmental conditions" (Hiernaux 1991, 283).[20] The key, as was argued in the CEP
proposal, is to link the provision or coproduction of urban services with
economic development that is socially necessary and ecologically sustainable.

At its zenith, the CEP movement had hundreds of families rallying
under its "productive ecology" banner. At the same time, the movement
had networked across the urban-rural divide and had successfully articulated multiclass alliances with independent researchers, university students, newspaper columnists, international agencies, and campesinos
both locally and from the northern part of the country. For instance,
the movement gained the support of a middle-class group of professionals in an architectural firm called AL-CE, Sistemas en Imagin. This group
helped the movement produce a slide show, which was used by the
movement in public forums to explain their concept of productive
ecology.

Another example of a multiclass alliance is the relationship the movement developed with faculty in the biology department at the National
University (UNAM). The biologists did a study that documented other
major sources of pollution in the zone (such as automobiles, paper production, furniture manufacture, and a government-sanctioned garbage
dump). Working with the scientists, the movement was able to use this
information to take some of the focus off the *colonias* as sources of
environmental degradation (Schteingart 1986, 27).

Notoriety from all of the publicity bolstered the stock of social capital
used to drive the project in the first place. In other words, an effective
use of the "means of communication" (especially the news media) was
an important factor driving the project. The leaders felt empowered by
the recognition that they were engaged in something unique, innovative,
and important. Some of this recognition came from prestigious institutions. For instance, professor Martha Schteingart of the Colegio de México acknowledged that the CEP project "is an example of creativity
and of the search for alternatives to improve the community, demonstrating at the same time, the importance of the independent organiza-

tion of settlers and of their urban struggle to offer new solutions to the urban and ecological problematic" (1986, 30).

The CEP movement proved to be an effective countervailing force insofar as it stayed the state's hand from dislodging the *colonos*. To the extent that state-society synergy existed in this instance, it arose out of oppositional dynamics. The *colonos* presented their case to the local government (for example, by showing their documentary) in a fashion designed to win an argument. But in so doing, they sharpened their argument. In the end, the community won. The government agreed to incorporate the threatened settlements into the legally designated urban area.

Los Belvederes in Transition to Legal Status (1990s)

When the legal status of Los Belvederes changed, so did the terms of collective social struggle. Winning the right to have these settlements incorporated into the legally designated urban area highlighted problems outside the realm of ecological discourse—thereby prioritizing other strategies. New battles had to be waged to secure the best terms for regularization and to resolve litigation regarding fraudulent land transactions and boundary disputes.[21]

Ironically, the ecologically oriented CEP movement resulted in victory in terms of community members' individual livelihood agendas but removed much of the impetus for further mobilization around the environmental agenda. At the same time, the "victory" reduced motivation to maintain the solidarity that had made it possible to begin with. This pattern is typical and presents a major dilemma for community mobilization. As one grassroots organization describes it: "Periods of strong mobilization correspond to the struggle to satisfy permanent needs (access to legally secure land for housing, piped water supply, a school) or to unexpected crises such as transportation fare increases or compensation for grave accidents, but as soon as the critical juncture is passed, demands resume on general terms and organization disappears" (Movimiento Revolucionario del Pueblo 1983, 6).

In an effort to ward off this type of drain on social capital, leaders of the CEP initiative headed up a barrio-wide opposition movement called the Coalición Popular y Independiente (the Popular and Independent Coalition). The coalition opposed the government's approach to land tenure regularization, fearing that it would undermine their community solidarity, which was based, in part, on collective control over the land. The coalition believed that the legalization of the zone—by way of institutionalizing private property on an individual basis—would undermine the strength of popular organizations and thereby erode the potential for collective approaches to the zone's problems. Those in opposition to privatization sought instead to have the land expropriated and granted to the community for collective stewardship in the form of a cooperative land bank. It didn't happen.

The groups in opposition to the state's approach to land tenure regularization were in the minority. Most of the families simply wanted to get security of tenure. They wanted an official deed. The sale of the deeds was coordinated by state officials (some of whom reaped illicit benefits). Many of the supposed landowners recognized by the state had no legitimate claim to the land at all. Although there were disputes, some violent, most families were willing to pay for the land yet again—and at prices that reflected the value they had added to the land by developing it. This dynamic certainly presents another complicating factor. On the one hand, there was the element of corruption; on the other, there was the fact that the families themselves shared in prevailing ideological beliefs that, if available, individual solutions to the land tenure question were more likely to be effective than collective ones.

Innovative community-based environmental action like that of the CEP movement may successfully oppose injustices and, in the process, shake up the government's dominant political party apparatus. However, as Marris (1982) points out, the power to disrupt social and political relationships is not symmetrical with the power to establish new relationships and new social meaning. People have certain expectations forged over time about politics, politicians, and the institutions of society and how they function. Popular groups with new environmental and democratic agendas must oppose not only the state's coercive apparatus and judicial system, but also the fragmenting and depoliticizing ideologies of consumerism and possessive individualism, as well as more traditional codes of behavior, including clientelism, paternalism, and caciquism, all of which are deeply embedded in civil society. It is not enough to argue that community-based development requires continuity and cohesion in terms of social organization and that it needs the support of the state. It appears that "sustainability" also demands a restructuring of governance and of the value systems that shape political community and civil society.

Sustainability, Livelihood, and State-Society Synergy (Late 1990s)

The rigidity of the Mexican political system, which has been characterized by its enormous capacity to control opposition and popular discontent through corporatist and populist mechanisms, can no longer be
taken for granted. The crises of the 1990s have reduced the government's
resources and legitimacy—thereby eroding its capacity to maintain traditional populist policies and to continue disciplining corporatist organizations. In a manner of speaking, the process of political restructuring
taking place in Mexico has thrust Ajusco from its position at the ecological frontier in relationships of power into the halls of mainstream
power. Hipólito Bravo López, one of the principal grassroots leaders of
the CEP and of the Coalición Popular y Independiente (which had been
vilified by the local government), is now a pivotal government figure
himself: as already mentioned, he is a *diputado* in the new Legislative
Assembly of the Federal District. This assembly represents an important
advance in the structure of democratic governance in Mexico City. Historically, the president of Mexico appointed Federal District officials.
Now all major political positions are slated to be filled by free elections.
The July 6, 1997, elections are said to have been the most competitive
and transparent in Mexico's modern history. For the first time ever,
citizens of Mexico City directly elected a governor. The winner was the
PRD candidate, Cuauhtémoc Cárdenas.[22]

The case of Hipólito Bravo López, a member of the PRD, is not unusual. Many of those elected to the new legislative body were catapulted
there from their bases in popular organizations. In Ajusco, Diputado
Bravo López has a local government office in his home base of Bosques
del Pedregal. I met with him there in October 1997, and on the chalk-
board at the front of the community meeting hall he listed his top priorities for outreach, which he characterized to me as requiring effective state-society synergy. The priorities for action concerned regulariz-
ing land tenure, building urban infrastructure, creating employment
(through cooperatives and microindustry development), and ensuring
public security, education, public health, and ecological conservation.
The agenda and approach of Bravo López fits with the platform spelled
out by the PRD party leader, Cárdenas. In an open letter to the citizens
of the Federal District prior to the elections, Cárdenas outlined his proposal for the capital (Cárdenas 1997). In it he spelled out a program for
the "Dignification of Public Management" (Dignificación de la Gestión

Pública), which included capacity-building measures for government personnel, an emphasis on promoting a culture of collaboration, and respect for public service.

If they could be implemented, the measures called for in Cárdenas's Dignification of Public Management program could go a long way toward enabling effective state-society synergy. However, the struggle for social transformation is constrained by the general level of organization and consciousness in the broader process of political conflict. It depends not only on changes that may occur within the arena of electoral politics, but also on the ongoing politicization of popular groups that are coalescing within civil society.

The economic factors and quasi-institutionalized politics that have driven irregular settlement over the past several decades are not going to vanish overnight. Indeed, one month after Cárdenas was sworn in, police evicted six hundred squatters who had invaded yet another section of the ecological reserve. And during April 1998, a blaze blackened a thousand acres of a wooded section of the ecological reserve on the western edge of the city. It is believed to have been deliberately set to clear the way for the encroachment of illegal subdivisions.[23] In another part of the city, dump trucks have been unloading tons of construction rubble near a protected lake, filling in marshy soil, possibly to pave the way for an illegal subdivision.

In view of this ongoing crisis, it is obvious that the status quo is reaching its limits. A concerted effort needs to be made to advance systems of innovation through networking, collaboration, and education. The objective, as characterized by the opposition party now in control of the Federal District, is a moving target: the continuous improvement of state-society synergy through social experimentation and social learning. This constitutes perhaps the most fundamental difference between the outreach strategy of PRD *diputado* Bravo López and previous "community development" initiatives spearheaded by the PRI. Bravo López is explicit about engendering positive state-society synergies through strategic coproduction.

The Community Development Program for Ajusco that was implemented by local PRI officials during the mid-1980s had dramatically different goals. The PRI program had two elements: the Program of Community Organization for Social Integration and the Program of Social and Cultural Action. The second element amounted to very little; its highlight was an occasional state-sponsored basketball game or beauty pageant. The first was more significant. At its core were strategies of surveillance and social control. When questioned as to whether his office actually engaged in strategies aimed to repress or "disintegrate" certain popular groups, the director of the Community Development Program responded:

> We are an administrative institution, but we also have a political nature, one hundred percent. So we have friends and we have enemies; the coalition is our enemy because they are not with the PRI. As I was telling you, the coalition is disorganized—in part our institution contributes to this. It is not a mere accident that I don't take it upon myself to always hand out documents to the same person in the coalition. I give out a copy here and a copy there. This gives us the advantage. It is one of our methods, a form of *contra-politica*. . . . In this way we selectively support some groups and push others down; this is our business here.[24]

The contrast between Hipólito Bravo López's vision and the traditional clientelism that was embodied in the PRI apparatus does not, of course, ensure that livelihood and sustainability will be reconciled, or even that state-society synergies aimed at pursuing improved livelihood for his constituents will be built. Nonetheless, Bravo López's journey from community activist to full-fledged participant in district politics demonstrates the renewed vitality of a political system that seemed hopelessly sclerotic in the 1980s, when the communities of Los Belvederes were proposing the CEP strategy. It raises the possibility that the next time a group of local communities proposes an innovative way to reconcile livelihood and sustainability, the response of politicians and the state may be more supportive and imaginative.

Conclusion

It has now been a full decade since the Brundtland Report, also known as *Our Common Future* (World Commission on Environment and Development 1987), first injected sustainable development into mainstream discourse, and it has been more than five years since the drafting of *Agenda 21* at the 1992 Earth Summit (the United Nations Conference on the Environment and Development, or UNCED).[25] Interest in the promise of sustainability as an environmentally integrative and transformative praxis has never been higher. The importance of local-level action is underscored in *Agenda 21;* Adrian Atkinson's 1994 content analysis of the document found that more than two-thirds of all actions identified as necessary to engender sustainable development will have to be taken at the local level (p. 98). Such theoretical appreciation of the strategic importance of local-level grassroots initiatives provides a counterweight to the pessimism of structural analysis, but it must be joined with careful analysis of the actual dynamics of concrete local actions.

The story of the communities of Los Belvederes and the changing human geography of the Ajusco reserve illuminate both the potential and the contradictions of local-level actions in pursuit of livability. Los Belvederes can be analyzed as a victorious struggle by a poor community that possessed little in the way of obvious resources yet still transformed a precarious existence into a much more secure one for thousands of families. It should also be celebrated for having added an intriguing, innovative vision—the ecologically productive settlement—to existing ideas about how movements for sustainability and livelihood might be integrated, and for having made a serious effort to implement this vision. It must also, however, be acknowledged that in the end, the new vision did not prevail, and sustainability was sacrificed for livelihood. In this crucial sense, the story of Los Belvederes is one of defeat. The outcome of the story shows how prevailing attitudes, beliefs, and expectations, based on a consumerist and possessive individualist culture, can make it difficult to keep people focused on alternative strategies aimed at engendering sustainable habitats.

On the livelihood side, the results are impressive. The families of Ajusco basically built their settlements themselves and managed to build a coalition that would sustain the settlements politically. This feat depended on the active involvement of extralocal NGOs. Curiously, given the oppositional relationship between these communities and the state, and the state's general reliance on an ineffectual strategy of reactive management by crisis, the community's victory on the livelihood front was also made possible by a kind of state-society synergy. Inputs from the government, including materials for building such things as milk stores, schools, roadways, and sewer lines, and—most crucially—for achieving legal recognition, were essential to transforming Los Belvederes from a set of threatened shanties into a community of viable, secure homes.

On the sustainability side, the results are more discouraging. In the end, the larger goal of sustainability was subordinated by a more traditional quest for security and livelihood on the part of individual families. The synergy that enabled the coproduction of the built environment did not strategically target "sustainable development"—even though doing so was reportedly the official policy of the Mexican government.

The CEP movement suggested programs and strategies for approaching
sustainability, but its proponents did not get the support they needed
from the state. Even at the community level, individual "consumerist"
strategies began to predominate over collective concerns once individual
legal titles had been secured. Nonetheless, the defeat on the sustainability side is not as bleak as it might appear.

Even though the idea of the CEP was not coupled with a subsequent
ability to implement the vision, the story illustrates how an environmental vision for alternative development can be a powerful political
tool for communities involved in life space and livelihood struggles. Such
ideas and visions constitute important "means of innovation." They are
essential grist for the mill of crafting goals (or what Evans refers to as
"imaginaries" in chapter 1). Furthermore, the revitalization of the political process in the Federal District—as exemplified by the story of
Hipólito Bravo López—opens up the possibility that future forays into
the realm of alternative development may benefit from a more synergistic response from the state and, if they get one, may have a higher prob-
ability of success.

Examining the twists and turns that mark the struggles of the families
of Los Belvederes to combine livelihood and sustainability in Ajusco
generates a new appreciation for the need for an interdisciplinary approach to planning that builds into itself a strategic emphasis on social
experimentation, feedback loops, social learning, and continuous improvement. The overarching challenge is to build on concrete experiences like that of Ajusco in a way that allows us to articulate and promote the kind of collaborative innovation necessary to move development onto a more socially just, equitable, and sustainable path.

Notes

*I would like to acknowledge Martha Schteingart for her valuable comments on
the first draft of this chapter. I am especially grateful to Peter Evans. His insight
into the interactive nature of state-society relations and ecologies of political
agents provides us with a powerful systems view of the livable cities challenge.*

1. Pezzoli 1998 offers the most complete description of my work in the
Ajusco region. See also Pezzoli 1995.

2. *Ejidal* land refers to property that was distributed to landless peasants
(ejidatarios) through agrarian reform after the Mexican Revolution.

3. In addition to chapter 1 in this volume, see Evans 1997b, Tendler 1997,
Watson 1992, Watson and Jagannathan 1995, and Douglass 1996.

4. An excellent and comprehensive study titled "Mexico City's Water Sup-

ply: Improving the Outlook for Sustainability" puts the meaning of such figures in context. The study was completed in 1995 by the Joint Academies on the Mexico City Water Supply: the Mexico Academy of Science (Academia de la Investigación Científica, A.C.) and the National Research Council of the U.S. National Academy of Sciences and U.S. National Academy of Engineering. It is available from the National Academy Press (1-800-624-6242).

5. Gabriel Quadri de la Torre, cited in the newspaper *UnoMásUno*, February 2, 1984.

6. The part of Ajusco containing Bosques del Pedregal and the rest of Los Belvederes is commonly referred to as Ajusco Medio. For simplicity's sake, I'll refer to this area as simply Ajusco.

7. To meet current demand for housing in the Federal District, there is a need to construct at least sixty-five thousand housing units every year into the foreseeable future (Méndez 1995). Yet during 1995, only forty-five thousand housing units were produced. The backlog—estimated to be four hundred thousand units—has continued to grow. To begin closing the gap, the government promises to promote sites and service projects. Yet very little land has actually been set aside for such projects (Elizondro, cited in Méndez 1995).

8. Ostrom (1997, 86) notes how positive state-society synergies can result from "coproduction" of this sort—a process wherein citizens play "an active role in producing public goods and services of consequence to them."

9. Later this ambiguous "buffer zone" designation would be dropped in favor of a hard division (an urban limit line) separating the urban area and the ecological conservation area.

10. Until recently, *ejidal* land was inalienable; it could not be sold even by the *ejidatarios*, who held a legitimate historical claim to it as their communal property.

11. The rise and fall of the Mesa Directiva, which occurred in less than a year, marked the beginning of ten years of struggle during which five major transformations in the composition of the popular organizations would take place.

12. Certain activists insisted on a street pattern that inclined the steep grade in switchback fashion, but the more conventional method of extending the existing layout prevailed. As a result, the streets in Bosques del Pedregal are so steep that vehicular access into the *colonia* is limited.

13. For an excellent discussion of social capital, see Woolcock 1997. Also see the Web site at http://www.jsri.msu.edu/soccap.

14. Friedmann and Rangan (1993, 4) define environmental action as "the efforts and struggles by rural and urban communities to gain access to and to gain control over the natural resources upon which their lives and livelihoods depend."

15. The close parallels between the CEP concept and the idea of "extractive reserves," which was being developed in a very different context (the Brazilian Amazon) by very different groups (rubber tappers and their NGO allies) is indicative of the universal appeal of such efforts to meld livelihood and sustainability (see Keck 1995; Keck and Sikkink 1998b).

16. Strategies spelled out in the Habitat II program include generating and

supporting livelihood opportunities at the neighborhood and community level through formal- and informal-sector economic development; environmental infrastructure reticulation—networking water, sanitation, drainage, solid waste recycling and disposal—via community contracting; and community management involving action planning, formation of cooperatives, advocacy and participation, security of tenure, and access to credit (United Nations 1997).

17. This calculation includes job creation from investments in the SIRDO technology as well as in urban agriculture, horticulture, fish farming, the raising of rabbits, and the establishment of community workshops (see Grupo de Tecnología Alternativa 1992b).

18. Peter Baumgartner, a sociologist from Austria whom I had introduced to leaders of Bosques del Pedregal in 1984, informally constituted this group. Although some of its members were in the Green Party, the group did not have an official Green Party status. Baumgartner put together an audio-visual project that described the situation in Ajusco, and he showed it in Austria as a means of raising money for grassroots projects in Bosques del Pedregal.

19. The tube for *agua gris* conducts fluid away from each house to a filtering device that enables 70 percent of the fluid to be recycled for irrigation. The *aguas negras* are conducted to a sedimentation tank in which anaerobic digestion takes place. The sludge from this initial process is then passed into another holding tank, where it is mixed with other solid organic household wastes, deposited on a daily basis. There, the contents undergo aerobiotic decomposition. The final product is a solid organic fertilizer.

20. Three aspects of peripheral urban expansion were analyzed in the UAM study: socioeconomic formation, spatial structure, and environmental conditions. The study focused on the extension of urban services to the city's periphery, the relation of this process to social dynamics (in particular, state-society relations), and how all this affects the environment. The UAM research team found that "the periphery is not only a form of settlement, rather it signifies a form of subsistence. The proliferation of small businesses (family owned or not) is a phenomenon parallel to the consolidation of the settlement" (Hiernaux 1991, 286). The businesses were of three basic types: services (e.g., food vendors), material depots (e.g., cement, bricks, lumber), and workshops (e.g., equipment repair).

21. See Pezzoli 1998.

22. Cárdenas won the election with 48 percent of the popular vote. In the legislative assembly the PRD received 45 percent of the vote and now occupies thirty-eight seats out of a total of sixty-six. The PRI won twelve seats, with 24 percent of the vote, and the Partido Acción Nacional (PAN) ten, with 18 percent. The remaining 13 percent of the vote was divided among the Partido Verde Ecologista Méxicano (PVEM), which will hold four seats, and the Partido del Trabajo (PT) and the Partido Cardenista (PC), each of which will occupy one seat. (Cited in the document entitled "1997 Mid-Term Elections Consolidate Nation's Democracy, September 1997, at http://www.presidencia.gob.mx/welcome/lib_od.htm.)

23. In an Associated Press news story, Mark Stevenson quotes the assistant environmental secretary of Mexico City's Federal District as saying the blaze

"was intentional and presumably aimed at changing the use" of parkland where construction is prohibited (Associated Press, AP Worldstream, April 28, 1998, http://web.lexis-nexis.com). The other information in this paragraph derives from Stevenson's story as well.

24. Interview with the director of the Community Development Program, Sub-Directorate of Ajusco, Tlalpan, Federal District, September 23, 1987.

25. *Agenda 21* is a forty-chapter document endorsed by nearly all of the world's heads of state. It spells out "a set of integrated strategies and detailed programmes to halt and reverse the effects of environmental degradation" (Robinson 1993).

:: 8 ::

Political Strategies for More Livable Cities

Lessons from Six Cases of Development and Political Transition

PETER EVANS

What has looking at Bangkok, Budapest, Hanoi, Ho Chi Minh City, Mexico City, São Paulo, Seoul, and Taipei told us about the politics of urban livelihood and sustainability? We began our comparative analysis with two general propositions: first, that any analysis of livability should begin by looking at communities, NGOs, political parties, and "the variegated collection of organizations that constitute the state"; second, that all of these were likely to be imperfect agents of livability and therefore it was necessary to think of agents of livability in terms of "ecologies of agents" rather than single actors. Both propositions were vindicated by the specifics of the cases.

Across this highly diverse range of cities, community action in pursuit of livability is ubiquitous. Communities consistently appear as the motivating force in struggles for livability. They take on problems and powerful adversaries with remarkable tenacity. NGOs enter as invaluable allies, providing ideological resources, new "imaginaries," and linkages to broader arenas and potentially powerful allies. Political parties play a more equivocal role but are sometimes crucial allies as well. States emerge as disaggregated actors, simultaneously part of the problem and part of the solution. Some set of state agencies must be part of the mix if greater livability is to be achieved.

The imperfections of all these actors were as evident as their centrality. Local communities often had difficulty coming together internally around common projects. Their parochialism divided them from other

communities, and their tendency to abandon ecological goals for livelihood when the two came into conflict made them undependable as
agents of sustainability. NGOs were less present than we expected they
would be, operating as auxiliaries to communities that had begun mo-
bilizing on their own more often than as independent agents of livability.
The imperfections of political parties and state bureaucracies were obvious from the beginning.

Given the imperfections of each type of actor, progress toward livability could be envisaged only by thinking in terms of ecologies of agents,
in which synergies compensated for imperfections and the overall effects
transcended the capabilities of individual actors. Each case offered examples of synergistic interactions among different actors (accompanied,
of course, by examples of conflicts, cross-purposes, and undercutting).
It was also evident, as Keck emphasized in her analysis, that the operation of ecologies of agents depends fundamentally on networks of individuals, situated in different organizational settings, whose connections across these settings create the possibility of synergistic action.

This concluding chapter will try to build on these basic insights by
doing three things. First, it will try to present an integrated picture of
the findings of the six studies with respect to communities, NGOs, political parties, and states as actors in pursuit of livability. Then it will
evaluate the impact of the global context of the "twin transitions" to
market orientation and electoral democracy on the pursuit of livability
in this set of cities. Finally, it will elaborate the overall implications of
this research for the feasibility of generating ecologies of agents that will
in fact contribute to livability.

Communities

The initial intuition that communities are the place to start is thoroughly
reinforced by these studies. In each one, communities come to the fore
as agents of livability both in the sense of trying to secure livelihood and
in the sense of defending the urban environment against degradation.
Wat Chonglom takes livability into its own hands, turning its thoroughly
degraded location into a livable community. Los Belvederes wrests a
foundation for livelihood from a hostile state and tries (albeit unsuc-
cessfully) to do it in a way that will not prejudice the sustainability of
the larger urban region. O'Rourke finds that community pressure is the
most important check on industrial pollution in Vietnam. In Taiwan,
communities are the key political force in the fight against industrial

pollution and the most important political counterweights to over-development. In São Paulo, it is a local community—Eldorado—that spearheads the fight to protect the Billings reservoir from the "accumulationist" strategy of degradation promoted by the state and private industry. In Gille's case, it is the political impotence of the local communities that makes dumping toxic industrial wastes a "rational" economic strategy for the Budapest Chemical Works.

Given this fundamental role, the question of community empowerment comes immediately to the fore. What gives communities the capacity to act? What gives them the capacity to prevail in the face of what Douglass calls the "manifold, seemingly unrelenting forces [that] challenge the viability of low-income communities"? Is there evidence that communities' capacity for collective action is likely to be robust over time? Or is community action an anachronism, left over from a more place-based world, likely to wither in the face of the social dislocations and concentration of power that are the hallmark of the information age (cf. Castells 1997)?

The social and political assets of communities as revealed in these studies are consistent with a "social capital" perspective and suggest important extensions to that perspective. As would be expected, shared longevity of residence and common cultural ties are associated with the ability to act collectively. The residents of Wat Chonglom, who epitomize effective collective action, have for the most part been living together in the same slum community for a quarter of a century, share the same religion (Buddhism), and in many cases come from the same province of origin. O'Rourke's most successful community, Dona Bochang, is similar. A shared history going back almost fifty years and a shared, actively practiced, minority identity (Catholic) underlie its ability to act cohesively.

Likewise, again consistent with a social capital perspective, the existence of an associational life helps. Churches, like Dona Bochang's (or Wolgoksa-dong's), are one source of associational life, but there are others. Keck shows how Eldorado's long-established neighborhood association helped nurture and make effective a strong sense of identification with the locale. The residents of Wat Chonglom are actively involved in a multiplicity of neighborhood committees. In Hsiao and Liu's study, the membership of the Chihshan Yen community's housewives in the Homemakers' Union Environmental Protection Foundation help knit the community together.

While the long-standing social ties and associational life emphasized by a social capital perspective produce the expected positive effects, other dynamics are also at work. On the one hand, one of the communities that would seem most socially "traditional"—Gille's Garé—is also one of the most powerless (at least pre-1989). On the other hand, there are examples in which cohesion and the capacity for collective action seem to be "bootstrapped" rather than based on a long-standing endowment of social capital. In Pezzoli's analysis of Los Belvederes, community is created out of the struggle for land. To be sure, a number of community members had previous experience with organizations and collective action, but in Los Belvederes social capital is less a heritage and more a consequence of the experience (and necessity) of working together.

Even when a community has the advantage of initial endowments of social capital, the positive effects of collective action are important. In Wat Chonglom, Douglass and his collaborators emphasize, the sense of efficacy gained through the successful execution of projects was central to enhancing community cohesion and capacity for future collective action. These studies argue for a reciprocal relation between social capital and collective action. Social capital helps make collective action possible, but collective action is an important source of social capital.

These studies do not suggest that the demise of "traditional" communities will mark the end of communities as important political actors. They suggest that contemporary urban communities can construct the capacity for collective action and that the experience of engaging in struggles for livability is a good way to construct it. They also suggest that the capacity for collective action may emerge, even in unlikely communities, once the achievement of some common end seems like a feasible possibility. The transformation that Gille reports in Garé is the nicest example. Freed from repressive central political control after 1989 and stimulated by the arrival of new leadership, a community that had appeared socially and politically dead began an active pursuit of its collective interests.

Just as these studies caution us against overemphasizing the extent to which the capacity for collective action is a historical endowment, they also underline inescapable differences across communities depending on the social and the human resources that they can command. Throughout these studies, the danger of talking about "communities" without specifying their socioeconomic status is clear. Urban middle-class communities are privileged—privileged in the human resources that they can draw on internally and privileged in their linkages to elites and elite organizations. While all communities share place-based interests in preserving the city as habitat, poor communities have only a precarious claim on the right to livelihood, and this separates them from their more privileged middle-class counterparts.

The contrasting positions of poor and middle-class communities come through most clearly in Hsiao and Liu's analysis of Taipei. Here middle-class communities fight to maintain the quality of life in their neighborhoods, while the poor must struggle to maintain any foothold in the city at all. In the most vivid case—the eviction of the poor from the cemetery-slum in Kang-Le—the green space to improve quality of life comes directly out of the poor's living space. An analogous kind of conflict occurs in relation to pollution as illustrated by Gille's tale of how better-connected communities are likely to export degradation to sociopolitically isolated "wasteland" communities like Garé. Given the political advantages of more affluent, educated communities, conflicting community interests are likely to be resolved at the expense of poorer communities, exacerbating their marginalization.

Even when the interests of poor and middle-class communities are not so directly in conflict, poor communities have a harder time defending themselves against degradation. The problem is as much lack of linkages as a lack of economic resources per se. O'Rourke's contrast of the poor and slightly better-off communities affected by the pollution of the Lam Thao fertilizer plant illustrates the point nicely. The poorer, more distant community lacks the education and sophistication necessary to make its claim in a legally effective way and, more important, is bereft of effective ties to higher levels of the political apparatus.

While recognizing the magnitude of the obstacles that poor communities face in realizing their interests, it is important not to underestimate their political capacity. With little in the way of resources beyond determination and some prior organizing experience, the residents of Los Belvederes started from "homes" of rocks and cardboard, survived repeated evictions, created a community of permanent homes, and eventually secured schools, sewers, and a legally recognized right to their land. Poverty did not stop Wat Chonglom from remaking itself in a more livable vein. Even the persistently oppressed squatters of Wolgoksa-dong managed to defend themselves against eviction and force the delivery of a variety of city services.[1] Poor communities are political actors, and often very effective ones, despite the odds stacked against them.

The most complex and interesting consequences of the differences between poor and middle-class communities revolve around the relations of these communities to issues of environmental sustainability. Poor and middle-class communities both play important roles acting on behalf of sustainability, but poor communities relate to sustainability in particularly complex and ambivalent ways.

These studies provide a variety of compelling illustrations of how poverty puts poor communities on the front lines of battles for sustainability. Affluent communities don't live at the back walls of polluting factories; toxic wastes are not dumped in their backyards. Nor do affluent communities have to worry about forcing city administrations to provide them with water or to extend sewers into their neighborhoods. Being forced to confront degradation directly puts poor communities in the position of fighting battles that are essential to their immediate interests but simultaneously on behalf of the general interests of society in sustainability.

When the community next to Viet Tri Chemicals arrives at the factory gates to complain that the factory's effluents have killed their fish, they are protecting their immediate livelihood interests, but they are also creating pressure for the factory to reduce its emissions, and in that way they benefit the entire city and its hinterland. When the favelas of São Paulo fight to have SABESP extend water and sewer lines into their neighborhoods, they are fighting for their immediate interests, but they are also fighting to reduce the chance of cholera and other public health risks that affect the entire city. No less than rural communities defending forests and rivers, urban communities can be simultaneously self-interested political actors and agents of a universal interest in greater sustainability.

If the immediate interests of poor communities always paralleled universal interests in sustainability, the political analysis of urban livability would be more straightforward (and more optimistic). Unfortunately, the limited livelihood options available to poor communities often put them in the position of having to pursue interests that are in direct contradiction to larger interests in sustainability. Keck's story of the poor communities that have occupied the ecologically sensitive area surround São Paulo's Guarapiranga dam is a prime example. In this case, there is a clear contradiction between the only strategy left open to these communities to gain affordable housing and the ecological sustainability of the city's watershed. As members of the Paulista environmental movement put it trenchantly: "A small number of people can't be allowed to endanger the water supply of 12 million people" (chapter 6). The communities of Los Belvederes are part of a similar contradiction. As Pezzoli explains, their successful efforts to carve out possibilities for livelihood in the face of the hostile socioeconomic environment of Mexico City also make them contributors to the potentially disastrous depletion of the aquifers on which the entire city depends for its water supply.

The relation of middle-class communities to sustainability issues is different. Middle-class residents pursuing their livelihoods as individuals may have equally (or greater) negative effects on sustainability—given their greater propensity to consume energy and generate waste, especially once they become enmeshed in "car culture." Nonetheless, the collective mobilization of middle-class communities is rarely focused on anti-sustainability projects. To the contrary, when middle-class communities act collectively, it is more likely to be on the side of sustainability. As Hsiao and Liu point out, middle-class people may be attached to their cars, but they demonstrate against parking lots.

When sustainability issues do capture the attention of middle-class communities—which is generally when their accustomed "quality of life" is threatened—their privileged position gives them extra leverage. Keck's description of the role of the community of Eldorado is an archetypal example. When São Paulo's Billings reservoir began to smell, the well-to-do residents of Eldorado were in a good position to spearhead the campaign not just to clean up the reservoir but to reverse the approach to water management that sent the pollution to Billings in the first place. Their mobilization was less likely to evoke the wrath of the military regime's security apparatus than similar activities on the part of a working-class community. Eldorado could draw on sophisticated community members such as Fernando Vitor, who understood the media and the legal system and were themselves part of the local political system. It could also count on a variety of useful linkages—as, for example, with engineers who provided free technical advice (chapter 6).

An important commonality cuts across poor and middle-class communities. In both, issues related to sustainability stimulate public, collective involvement. This is true of middle-class communities from Hungary (chapter 5) to Taiwan (chapter 3). It is also true of poor communities from Vietnam (chapter 4) to Mexico (chapter 7). This mutually reinforcing relation between collective action and sustainability is one of the hopeful threads that runs through all six studies. Sustainability issues lend themselves to collective action, and collective organization is likely to direct community attention toward sustainability issues.

Fully realizing the potential for mobilization around issues of sustainability is a greater challenge in the case of poor communities. Their position on the front lines of struggles against degradation gives them special importance as agents of livability. At the same time, the frequency with which they are put in the position of sacrificing sustainability in order to secure livelihood undercuts this potential. Finding ways to resolve the latter contradiction is one of the principal challenges to the politics of livability. This is what makes Pezzoli's study of Los Belvederes such a fascinating case. The vision of the *colonia ecológica productiva* (CEP) opened the possibility of resolving livelihood problems without threatening the ecological resources of the Ajusco preserve. Even though implementation proved inviable in the end, it remains one of the most imaginative attempts at reorienting a quest for livelihood in an ecological direction.

The example of Los Belvederes also demonstrates how politically powerful ecological claims can be for poor communities. The idea of the CEP enabled Los Belvederes to attract extralocal allies and project its demands onto a citywide political stage. If it had not so quickly proved infeasible, the CEP might have proved an urban analogy to the idea of rural "extractive reserves," which enabled disempowered Brazilian peasants to build quite an effective set of transnational alliances with First World NGOs around the same time (see Keck 1995; Keck and Sikkink 1998a). When poor communities succeed in linking livelihood struggles to the universalistic goal of ecological sustainability, the political balance shifts in their favor.

Convincing connections between livelihood struggles and sustainability goals are a key to making poor communities effective agents of livability. The challenge of making such connections also underscores the implausibility of achieving livability on the basis of community empowerment alone. Communities supply the fundamental energy for change and hold environmental strategies to the fundamental test of improved well-being at the level of day-to-day experience, but their energy and experiential grounding must be complemented by broader sets of ideas and organization.

Intermediary Organizations: NGOs and Political Parties

Many kinds of intermediaries serve to connect the struggles of individual communities with the surrounding political and social milieu in these studies: universities, churches, social movement organizations,[2] NGOs (in the strict sense of formal, translocal organizations with some professional staff and independent fund-raising capabilities), and political parties. All of them are important, but two will be the principal focus of the analysis here: NGOs and political parties.

Formally organized, translocal NGOs are not nearly as ubiquitous in these studies as one might expect from their salience in the general literature on environmental activism. In some cases, such as Vietnam, Korea, and Hungary pre-1989, the relative absence of NGOs reflects effective state efforts to restrict their activities. In other contexts, such as Bangkok and São Paulo, NGOs are widely active, but for some reason they don't emerge as central actors in our cases. When they do appear, however, they play a crucial role in magnifying the ability of communities to realize livelihood goals and, even more important, in connecting livelihood and sustainability issues.

Pezzoli's analysis of Los Belvederes again provides the most striking example. Without the local NGO, Grupo de Tecnología Alternativa (GTA), community activists in Los Belvederes would never have been able to credibly project the conceptualization of the CEP. Once formulated, the CEP idea drew Los Belvederes to the attention of Austrian environmentalists and gave the community the political clout that goes with access to the media. This combination of providing access to a broader range of ideas and supplying connections to a network of other potentially supportive organizations is the archetypal NGO contribution.

O'Rourke's Tae Kwang shoe factory provided an even more powerful "NGO effect." In this case, the community of workers was completely outmatched in its local environment by the power of the Nike subcontractor that employed them. Once their situation came to the attention of a transnational network of NGOs, one of the key sources of the local company's power—its ties to transnational capital—became an Achilles' heel. Once transnational connections were made, the core of Nike's economic power—its universally known brand name—could be leveraged against it. As in the case of Los Belvederes, NGOs were able to transform immediate local struggles over the working environment into a specific instance of universal issues, in this case human rights and social justice.

Environmental NGOs were also central to the quest for livability in Taiwan, but in this case, Hsiao and Liu's analysis reveals weaknesses as well as strengths. Unlike the NGOs involved with Los Belvederes or in the Nike case, environmental NGOs in Taiwan have, according to Hsiao and Liu, "remained silent on issues relating to the urban poor." Middle-class concerns with quality of life are extended to the countryside, but Taiwanese NGOs seem blind to the idea that livelihood and sustainability issues must be joined together in order to generate a viable politics of livability. The Taipei case implies that if overcoming the potential contradictions between livelihood struggles and sustainability issues is a central problem in making poor communities better agents of livability, then overcoming the tendency to privilege sustainability issues at the expense of questions of the livelihood and the well-being of poor communities is the central issue for environmental NGOs.

The role of political parties is both more ubiquitous and more complex than that of NGOs. These six studies contain examples of all of the negative effects on independent community mobilization traditionally attributed to political parties—co-opting community leaders, constructing "clientelistic" networks that demobilize both leaders and their constituents, dividing and distracting communities by involving them in self-interested partisan conflicts, and so on. At the same time, there are a significant number of instances in which political parties, especially opposition parties, support communities' pursuit of greater livability.

Dominant parties are more likely to be part of the problem than part of the solution. In Korea and Hungary, for example, the positive functions of dominant parties for communities in pursuit of livability are hard to find. In at least one surprising case, however, the dominant party seems to provide useful alternative ways of getting to state agencies. In O'Rourke's description, certain local organizations of the Vietnamese Communist Party deliver community grievances upward in an unexpectedly capillary fashion. Obviously, representation is combined with control, with the balance depending on particular local circumstances, but the possibility of positive linkages via even a dominant party cannot be dismissed out of hand.

One important traditional role for party politicians is to act as intermediary between communities and the state agencies that supply infrastructure and services to communities. This relationship can bring with it the divisive and demobilizing side effects (as Pezzoli argues in relation to the PRI's "Community Development Program" for Ajusco), but the negative political effects must be balanced against the positive effects of the infrastructure itself. In both the Mexico City and São Paulo cases, the extent to which even "illegal" communities were able to negotiate the provision of services from the state is impressive. Political parties played a central role in these negotiations.

Opposition parties may be less effective at providing traditional services, but they deliver more positive political side effects. When opposition parties become strong enough to win local or state-level elections, they do two important things. First, when they grow out of a base in social and community movements, opposition parties support increased participation by communities and social movement groups. Second, they challenge the exclusive emphasis on accumulation that generally characterizes the discourse of dominant parties (and the economic elites that support them). These effects can be seen both in Asia (Taiwan) and in Latin America (Mexico and Brazil).

In Taipei, the emergence of political competition and opposition parties made challenging the degrading strategies of economic accumulation politically feasible. Given the KMT's unremitting pursuit of accumulation at any cost and its tightly constructed alliances with dominant economic elites, the opposition Democratic Progressive Party (DPP) really had little choice other than to include more emphasis on livability in its definition of development. The DPP's historic ties to the environmental movement made it a natural to bring environmental politics more to the fore, giving community groups and social movements a powerful ally in their fights for parks and preservation. (Of course, as more DPP leaders got into office, their ties with the environmental movement sometimes had the negative effect of dampening the movement's enthusiasm for protesting these officials' own infringements on sustainability.)

Despite the PRI's traditional rhetorical emphasis on welfare, the PRD (Partido Revolucionario Democratico) in Mexico City found itself in a position not unlike the DPP's: the party had to find an alternative base to counter the formidable alliance of ruling party and private capital. Greater openness to unaffiliated community and social movement groups made political sense. In São Paulo, although there was no real dominant party to contend with at the end of military rule, the election of an opposition governor in 1982 had a similarly invigorating effect on the politics of livability. The new Montoro government was willing to think about new forms of watershed management. In addition, according to Keck, "environmental organizations credit Montoro with providing space in which they could organize."

This is not to say that the rise of opposition parties is inevitably linked to greater ideological emphasis on livability. Despite the high hopes surrounding the return to civilian rule in Korea in 1987, the politicians of the former opposition have proved almost as thoroughly (if less repressively) attached to the old politics of accumulation as their military predecessors were. Likewise, despite the important role played by the environmental movement in undermining the Communist Party's hegemony in Hungary, the new parties that emerged after the transition seem to have little interest in an agenda of livability. Even in the case of Taiwan's DPP, as Hsiao and Liu point out, opposition politicians have proved themselves far from immune to the lure of overdevelopment in pursuit of world city status.

Likewise, even when opposition parties are willing to raise the banner of livability, their sponsorship may be flawed by their political roots. The DPP in Taipei and the Workers' Party (Partido dos Trabalhadores, or PT) in São Paulo illustrate contrasting ways in which parties can go astray. In the case of the DPP, Hsiao and Liu make it clear that the party carries with it the flaws of the environmentalist NGOs that were its early allies. Like them, the party is strong on parks and preservation but relatively indifferent to the livelihood of poor communities. Similarly, the PT ended up mirroring the contradictions of the working-class communities that are its principal base. In theory, the PT should have been exceptionally effective in helping community groups to find strategies that would integrate livelihood struggles with sustainability issues. The PT has a much longer history of working with the poor and marginalized communities than the DPP and PRD. In addition, the PT could count a number of activists from the environmental movement among its membership. In practice, however, the PT was unable to formulate a strategy that would reconcile these two constituencies. While its environmentalist constituency was condemning the invasions of reservoir areas, its community-based militants were prominent among the leadership of the invaders (chapter 6). Rather than the party becoming a vehicle for resolution of the contradictions between livelihood and sustainability issues, the contradictions became an organizational problem for the party itself.

If parties are not the uniformly nefarious actors that they were sometimes portrayed to be in the literature on urban community struggles, they are, even under the best of circumstances, imperfect intermediaries, certainly not solutions in themselves. Parties (particularly opposition parties) can, however, provide two kinds of support. At the macro level, they can open political space for communities and other social movement groups to participate in debates over rules and policies. They also create discursive space enabling imaginaries to extend beyond the standard monolithic emphasis on development and accumulation. At the micro level, they can provide organizational niches that give innovative community leaders extra leverage. In São Paulo, Virgílio Farias used his position in the environment department of the local PT administration to organize one of the Movimento de Defesa da Vida's important early campaigns. The PRD victory in Mexico City gave Ajusco's Hipólito Bravo López a chance to develop his leadership skills and experiment with new ways of building his community's external linkages.

Suggesting that parties are the solution to communities' needs for external linkages would be foolish. Control, clientelism and co-optation, and the quest for partisan advantage play much too large a role in the repertoires of even progressive parties. Nonetheless, it would be equally foolish for activists and community leaders to ignore the possibilities that party structures afford and the ways that oppositional parties can open up the larger political environment for new discourses and new forms of participation.

Overall, the external connections that intermediaries provide play an essential role in enabling communities to become effective agents of livability. Romantic visions in which individual communities can somehow resolve problems of livelihood and sustainability on their own are analytically misguided and a political disservice.

Douglass's analysis of the case of Wat Chonglom and its implications for other slum communities in Bangkok makes the point best. Wat Chonglom is the best example among all of the six studies of the successful self-reliant pursuit of livability. Yet Douglass and his collaborators are clear that external connections—primarily in the form of two university professors and the outside loan that they helped the community arrange—played a catalytic role in moving the community onto a trajectory of enhanced livability. Furthermore, they are equally clear that even in Bangkok, where the state encourages self-reliance, Wat Chonglom is the exception that proves the rule, and "attempts to follow the self-reliant model in other slum communities revealed the model's limitations."

Self-reliant internal organization gives poor communities the capacity to make effective use of external linkages, but intermediary organizations still have an essential role to play. They bring new ideas and strategic inputs that magnify the returns of internal efforts. They help communities find ways to reconcile their limited livelihood options with sustainability. They improve the odds in uneven conflicts between urban communities and those who see the city as a place to accumulate money and power rather than as a place to live. They are likely to be a crucial component in any assemblage of actors capable of producing greater livability.

Allies and Enemies in the State

Even in a globalized world, the predilections and capacities of states have a powerful effect on the prospects of communities looking for livability. Yet if political parties are ambiguous organizations, states are ambiguous actors in even more complicated ways. These six studies reveal states as congregations of agencies, filled with both opponents and allies of projects of livability. The internal mix of agencies varies across states and over time.

While there is much variation among these states, there is also an important commonality. The one thing that this variegated set of developing and transitional states—capitalist and state socialist, democratic and authoritarian—shares most clearly is an "accumulationist" bias. From pretransition state socialist Hungary to transitional Vietnam to developmentalist Taiwan to corporatist Mexico to "savage capitalist" Brazil, all of these states appear to be dominated by a surprisingly similar focus on the accumulation of wealth and productive capacity within their borders. The KMT happily allies with developers destroying Taipei's hillsides in hopes that new luxury housing will help turn the city into a world city. Potential damage to industrial production is the only viable "environmentalist" argument in Budapest. The core of São Paulo's water policy from the 1940s to the 1960s was trying to ensure that utility companies could generate enough power to fuel industrial growth, even if it meant pumping sewage into the city's reservoir. The domination of the state's imaginary by this "accumulationist" project makes it that much clearer why communities must be the driving forces behind livability goals.

In other dimensions, variation outweighs commonality. In Douglass's portrayal the Korean and Thai states have contrasting defects. The Korean state is oppressive to an extent that makes it next to impossible for self-initiated community-level organizations to thrive. Communities rise in self-defense—as for example under the threat of eviction—but the kind of rich associational life that would foster capacity for collective action on behalf of livability is stifled. At the same time, the Korean state is quite efficient in delivering public infrastructure and even amenities to poor communities like Wolgoksa-dong. The Thai state, while allowing local initiatives to flourish where they can (as in Wat Chonglom), is ineffectual in providing the kind of support and infrastructure that poor communities need to transform local living situations.

Gille replicates a similar contrast in her comparison of the Hungarian state during the state socialist period with the state in its post-1989 incarnation. By eliminating all possibilities for voice on the part of disadvantaged local communities in the pre-1989 period, the state paved the way for ecological disasters like the toxic waste dump in Garé. By withdrawing from active participation in livability issues in the post-1989 period, the state left these same communities without the organizational, political, and material resources that they needed to resolve their problems.

Communities can't do without states. There is no dearth of examples in these studies of how the power of the state is used to impose degradation on communities and to smother community-based projects of livability. Yet communities suffer as much from the incapacity of the state to implement its own projects of livability as they do from its excessive capacity to facilitate projects of accumulation at the expense of livelihood and sustainability.

Communities need capable public institutions desperately, but, unfortunately, they need states quite different from the ones that currently confront them. The question is how that difference might be reduced. The apparent inability of existing states to combine capacity for effective public action with openness to grassroots initiatives and responsiveness to community needs defines what is lacking in existing public institutions. Political efforts to restructure existing state apparatuses at the national level are admirable endeavors, worth pursuing but unlikely to produce the desired combination of capacity and openness in the foreseeable future. Efforts to transform city administrations are more promising, but local governments will still sit in the shadow of national rules and power. Less ambitious, but more likely to produce concrete results, are what might be called "jujitsu tactics"—efforts to leverage the conflicts and contradictions that already exist within state apparatuses to shift the balance of state action toward livability.

Jujitsu tactics are based on the premise that most public institutions are both collections of organizations, some of which actually have a vested interest in promoting livability, and aggregations of individual incumbents, some of whom are potential allies. Even state apparatuses with relatively effective forms of hierarchical coordination are fraught with conflicts among competing projects and organizations. The balance of power among these competing interests within the state depends in part on the effectiveness of their allies in society. If communities, NGOs, and other institutions can make more effective use of potential allies and find ways to strengthen the position of these allies in their conflicts within the state, prospects for livability increase substantially.

As would be expected, those parts of the state apparatus that have the most direct relations to the task of accumulation tend to be the best developed and most powerful. Those concerned with livability are weaker and less developed. O'Rourke characterizes Vietnam's environmental agencies as "very young and very weak," "underfunded and understaffed." He observes, not surprisingly, that "in internal government battles, environmental agencies generally lose." He illustrates the point by noting the consistent inability of the Hanoi Department of Science, Technology, and Environment (DOSTE) to make any headway against the power of the Department of Industry (DOI), having failed to shut down a single one of the DOI's two hundred factories, despite clear environmental violations (as in the case of Ba Nhat). Hsiao and Liu paint a similar picture of the Taiwanese Environmental Protection Agency's unequal battle against the accumulationist thrust of the mainstream ministries. Any effort to boost the state's contribution to livability must start by recognizing this discouraging differential.

Despite their relative weakness, allies within the state are still crucial resources for communities and other social groups working to secure livelihood and sustainability. This is especially the case when communities mobilize against powerful private interests. Their success ultimately depends on their ability to gain allies within the state. Again this is laid out most clearly in O'Rourke's cases. None of his communities can win by simply confronting the polluting firms themselves. Only when direct community pressure is combined with some kind of support from the state does victory become a possibility.

State agencies vary by level as well as by function. Confronted with an accumulationist government at the national level, communities are often able to find allies at the local level. In Taiwan, when alliance with the national KMT regime was hopeless, the municipal-level DPP government of Taipei was an ally on at least some issues. In Vietnam, communities' environmental concerns are a nuisance from the point of view of the national Ministry of Industry but a priority for local officials in Viet Tri City. The point is not that all local administrations are arrayed on the side of livability; they may well turn out to be the creatures of local contractors and developers. The point is that splits between the interests of local and central administrations are another point of potential leverage for communities.

The contribution of allies within the state apparatus may not be in terms of the direct exercise of political power. State agencies, or networks of individuals within state agencies, may, like NGOs, become sources of new ideas or imaginaries. The best example is the Solução Integrada, which plays a role in Keck's story of São Paulo's watershed almost as important as the role of the CEP in Pezzoli's account of Los Belvederes. The Solução Integrada, devised in the mid-1970s by a state technocrat who saw himself as a nationalist working in the service of society rather than as a technician, was still invoked by community activists fifteen years later as proof that the pollution of Billings reservoir was not an inevitable consequence of the city's growth.

The middle-level "whistle-blowers" in Gille's description of Hungary are a different sort of example of how individuals and networks within the state apparatus can offer intangible resources in livability struggles. Gille points out that when the Hungarian state did allow environmental considerations to deflect its accumulationist agenda, it was because middle-level technocrats with sustainability concerns managed to get the ear of officials in more powerful parts of the state apparatus. Likewise, in the rare cases when community mobilization around environmental issues emerged in pre-1989 Hungary, information from allies working within local government played a crucial role in getting things started.

Those inside the state who are trying to make cities more livable depend on the existence of mobilized communities just as much as communities and social movements depend on allies within the state. As O'Rourke points out, the ability of environmental agencies to overcome the resistance of their opponents within the state depends on the political vitality of community demands. Without active communities, agencies and individuals within the state have no political case to counter the primacy of accumulation.

Keck's analysis of the Solução Integrada is a nice illustration of how much generators of ideas within the state apparatus need mobilized communities if they hope to turn their ideas into realities. However technically compelling and compatible with the long-run general interests of the city Rodolfo Costa e Silva's plan might have been, the interests of the electrical utilities and the governor's relatives easily checkmated it in the absence of community pressure. Even during the Montoro administration in São Paulo, when, according to Keck, technocrats favorable to the Solução Integrada were hegemonic within the bureaucracy, they were unable to prevail.

The complementarity between what is possible from within the state apparatus and what can be done from outside is evident. Those working inside the state apparatus command technical expertise and the legitimacy that goes with it. They lack the political legitimacy that communities can command, as well as the determination that comes from being forced to endure the day-to-day effects of degradation.

"State-society synergy" is not just an abstract concept. It is shorthand for the myriad concrete relationships of mutual support that connect communities, NGOs, and social movements with individuals and organizations inside the state who put a priority on livelihood and sustainability. Keck's description of São Paulo's "water networks" offers a vivid picture of state-society synergy made concrete: "Activists within and outside the state have formed ties and shared ideas in community groups, environmental organizations, universities, and technical agencies, their loose linkages sustaining a vision of water policy centered on preserving the quality of the water supply and the contribution of local water sources to the metropolitan area's quality of life."

State-society synergy does not, however, mean an absence of conflict between communities and state agencies. Paradoxically, conflict is likely to be first and foremost with agencies that are supposed to be part of the solutions. Communities and NGOs are more likely to find themselves attacking environmental agencies and social service organizations for "not doing their jobs" than they are to try to mobilize against the Ministry of Industry for doing its job in an effective but tunnel-vision way. This makes good political sense. Potential allies are both more vulnerable and more likely to change their ways than agencies with opposing agendas and constituencies. Dramatic and aggressive actions to force environmental or state sanitation agencies to do their job—actions such as dumping dead fish on the agencies' front steps—may not seem "synergistic" on the surface, but they are as important to the process as quieter, more obviously collaborative relations.

Unlike markets, states—even relatively undemocratic states—can be held accountable. You can fight with them. Having somewhere to direct demands, someone to hold responsible who is supposed to be able to deliver redress, is a key ingredient in making mobilization seem worthwhile. Thus, even when they play an adversarial role, states can be important catalysts to the mobilization of communities. For Vietnamese communities fighting against industrial pollution, the passage of the 1994 environmental law and the creation of state agencies with environmental responsibilities was important, not so much because the agencies were able to enforce the regulations but because the communities now had a legitimate target at which to direct their grievances. For Garé, in would-be neoliberal Hungary, the withdrawal of the state left them with no one against whom their claims could be pressed.

Once the evolution of people's living circumstances appears to depend only on "market forces," no one is responsible and collective mobilization seems nonsensical. Los Belvederes illustrates the point. As long as the community's demands were directed primarily against the state, collective mobilization made sense. Solidarity was essential to the struggle for legalization. Mobilization also made sense as a means of securing collective goods from the state, such as the materials to build milk stores and schools. Once legalization was achieved, the residents began to relate to the housing market as individuals, and internal conflicts dissipated the social capital built up over years of collective action.

The web of relations that tie state and society together around issues of livability is intricate and convoluted. Livability depends on the extent to which communities and other groups in civil society that are trying to make cities livable can build ties with people and agencies within the state who share the same agenda. How likely this is to occur depends, in turn, on the effects of the shifting global context, more specifically on the consequences of the twin transitions to market orientation and electoral democracy.

Effects of the Twin Transitions

The introductory chapter to this volume juxtaposed two pictures of the changing global context. On the one hand, there was the triumphalist vision in which the twin transitions were in themselves the solution. On the other, there was Castells's daunting vision of the global networks that compose the "space of flows" and seem to ensure the dominance of interests inimical to livability. Both visions agreed on the increasing structural dominance of global markets. Neither left much room for agency on the part of groups fighting for urban livability. After looking at these six studies, a different picture emerges.

Nothing in these studies negates the idea that global markets are having a fundamental impact on how Third World cities work, but they hardly support that triumphalist view that markets are in themselves answers to problems of livelihood and sustainability. Certainly the two cases that witnessed the most dramatic moves in the direction of market orientation—Vietnam and Hungary—offer little in support of the triumphalists. In Hungary, where hopes were highest that market orientation would bring reductions in degradation, Gille shows that degradation was intimately connected to market-conforming economic strategies; she suggests that it was a lack of political accountability more than a lack of market orientation that led to communist degradation. Nor does O'Rourke find evidence that increased market orientation is driving "ecological modernization" in Vietnam.

None of this is to say that the contemporary mode of accumulation is qualitatively more threatening to sustainability than its predecessors were. The current quest for world-city status is no more environmentally destructive than the strategies of import-substituting industrialization that were in vogue a half century ago, or the reliance on extractive exports that dominated Third World economic strategies in the nineteenth century. If current economic expansion is more ecologically threatening than past growth, it is because populations several times as dense and cities hundreds of times larger make the achievement of ecological sustainability correspondingly more pressing, but there is no evidence in these studies that current accumulation strategies themselves are inherently more degrading.

The negative impact of the global economy in these studies is more political than it is economic. The desire to construct policies that will advantage cities in global markets leads those in power to ignore problems of livability and sustainability. This is most obvious in the case of Taiwan's desire to make Taipei a regional winner in the contest for global city status. Hungarian officials' failure to anticipate the toxic by-products of the Budapest Chemical Works' economic success represents an earlier version of the same problem. Because BCW was singularly effective (relative to other local firms) in relating to global markets, the toxic impact of its strategy was ignored.

After looking at these studies, the paramount question is not whether global markets are the solution. They are not. The question is whether the second of the twin transitions—electoral democracy—can compensate for the tendency of global markets to divert policy makers from questions of livability. The immediate answer is probably not, but the evolution of the political context does seem to be moving in a positive direction.

The institutionalization of electoral politics as the dominant mode of determining political succession has expanded the space for political mobilization at the community level in almost all of the countries examined here. Even though party competition and the leaders it produces do not usually focus on livability, they are less likely to disrupt and repress self-initiated local efforts at making cities more livable. The space for community-level mobilization created by democratization is made easier to use by other, complementary institutional changes.

Complementing new space for mobilization, there have been important additions to the state-level institutional instruments available to those interested in sustainability. We can lament the relative weakness of environmental agencies, but it is important to remember that most of these agencies didn't exist at all two or three decades ago. The same is true of laws constraining accumulation in the name of sustainability. The authors of these studies comment on the panoply of sweeping new laws that have been put in place from Brazil to Taiwan to Vietnam. If these laws were actually enforced, there would be a monumental improvement on the sustainability front. Of course, they are not, and outrage is an appropriate response. Yet, as in the case of the still ineffectual state agencies, these legal rules must be seen as potentially powerful tools, whose utilization depends on building the political foundations that will make them real.

There is also one less tangible but unquestionably positive change in the global context. The ubiquity with which environmental discourse has become part of politics, even in cities where degradation continues apace, is impressive. The political efficacy of the CEP idea in Mexico City, the popularity of the campaign to clean up the Tietê in São Paulo, and the convictions of Vietnamese peasants that they have a right to a cleaner environment all reflect a positive change in the global ideological context.

Two cautionary notes should be raised before coming to positive conclusions. First, it is important to note what might be called the "transition effect." These cases suggest an association between transitions to electoral democracy and the effervescence of environmental organizations. Authoritarian regimes under fire seemed to find environmental movements the least threatening among the possible oppositional movements and therefore allowed them to gain a vanguard position during the transition. Hungary and Taiwan are the best examples.

Hsiao and Liu underline the fact that environmental movements played an important pioneering role in providing opportunities for civic mobilization during Taiwan's transition to electoral democracy. Gille observes that in Hungary, "from about 1987 to 1990, the state showed an unprecedented openness to environmental initiatives," and because of that, more general democratic demands were expressed indirectly, through environmental protests. What is disturbing about the "transition effect," especially in the Hungarian case, is that once environmentalism "lost its potential for filling in for other political issues," activists and their technocratic allies abandoned the movement, in some cases disavowing sustainability concerns altogether.

The fact that sustainability retains its political charisma in cases where the transition to elections is well past (Brazil) and where the transitions to electoral rule is not yet in sight (Vietnam) is reassuring. Nonetheless, it is important not to confuse a temporary transition effect with a long-term, secular trend in the direction of increasing the political impact for movements focused on environmental issues.

The second cautionary note involves a problem that transcends transitional regimes and is therefore more serious. If the openness of otherwise authoritarian regimes to environmental demands is striking, middle-class indifference to social justice arguments as a basis for livelihood demands is equally so. The Taiwanese case has already been underlined as a prime example. Hsiao and Liu see middle-class movements focused on "quality of life" kinds of sustainability demands as likely to treat the livelihood demands of poorer communities with callous disregard rather than as part of a general movement for more livable cities.

If the global ideological context has become more favorable to the introduction of sustainability issues, it may well have become less permeable to the interjection of the social justice concerns that are essential to the pursuit of livability. It is hard to find evidence for a burgeoning of social movements and NGOs on the livelihood side comparable to their blossoming on the environmental side. This is a serious problem and underlines again the potential benefits of uniting immediate livelihood struggles with broader sustainability issues. Demonstrating that local fights to improve living conditions are simultaneously in service of universal sustainability goals is the best way to endow them with ideological clout.

Despite these two cautionary notes, there is no overall evidence that states are becoming more rapaciously committed to accumulation than they have been in the past, or that the political-legal matrices within which struggles over livability must be fought are less favorable today than they were a generation ago. If neither the macrolevel political-legal context nor the general thrust of economic policies has regressed, and if space for political action on behalf of livability has, if anything, expanded in recent decades, the question must be: How can this space best be exploited?

Ecologies of Actors and the Pursuit of Livability

The persistent resilience of community efforts to make their own corners of the city more livable is as impressive as the obstacles they confront. It is impossible to read the stories of Los Belvederes, Wat Chonglom, Dona Bochang, or even the thoroughly oppressed Wolgoksa-dong and the "wasteland" Garé, and conclude that the political battle for livability is over. Place-based agency turns out to be hard to kill. At the same time, it is clear from these studies that calls for community empowerment will not, in themselves, produce the kind of progress toward livability that is needed. Mobilized communities are not enough.

The concept of an "ecology of agents" that was put forward in the introductory chapter can now be given more content. Like Castells's vision of the "network society," the idea of ecologies of local political agents focuses on the power of connections rather than the capacities of individual actors. Though it does not negate the existence of Castells's space of flows, this imagery focuses on a more modest set of networks, with very different aims, rooted in the "space of places." While more modest, the constellations of actors that are the focus of these studies still have the potential to collectively effect change, if only they can figure out how to better exploit the social and ideological resources at their disposal.

Each type of actor—communities, intermediary organizations, and state agencies—has a complementary contribution to make to the fight for livability. The capacity of each depends on its internal coherence as well as the aggregated experience and ability of its individual members, but the power of each to effect change also depends fundamentally on its relations to the others. State agencies depend on political pressure from communities. NGOs without a community base lack legitimacy. Communities without external ties are politically weak and parochial. Only when this constellation of actors functions in an interconnected, complementary way does it have a chance of making cities more livable.

Interconnection can take two forms. Formal linkages and alliances officially connect groups, organizations, agencies, or other social entities. Networks of individuals operate within organizations and agencies and, more important, trespass the boundaries of groups and formal organizations and thereby make it easier to bring disparate entities together. The key is nurturing those networks and alliances that are particularly oriented toward pursuing livability.

The process of building these networks and alliances is already under way, as these six studies make clear. But too many opportunities for building ties, making connections, and exploiting potential synergies are being overlooked. They are overlooked because categorical divisions and lack of a shared cultural framework blind actors to complementary possibilities. Technocrats underestimate the extent to which they need communities; community leaders dismiss those working in the state as bureaucrats; NGOs dismiss both ordinary citizens and technocrats as pedestrian and shortsighted. Communities and NGOs are suspicious of supporting plans to increase the capacity of state agencies as long as construction firms and real estate developers appear to be the state's dominant interlocutors. Those working in state agencies are reluctant to jeopardize the privileged status of technocratic qualification by granting legitimacy to community inputs.

For cities to become more livable, groups and individuals inside and outside of the state must become more conscious of the necessity of looking for complementarities, forging alliances, and bridging differences that separate the multiple agendas that are part of livability. Bureaucrats must be open to direct democratic demands, regardless of how inconvenient and unreasonable they might be. Communities must be willing to provide political backing for increasing the capacity of state agencies, despite the risk that the capacity might be misused or captured. NGOs must use their greater political and institutional flexibility to build ties in both directions. Perhaps most important, actors both inside and outside of the state must be on the lookout for new institutional forms—such as Keck's basin committees—that hold the promise of transcending old impasses.

The vision of agency that emerges here is not revolutionary. It is built on the accretion of small changes—filling a gap in a network so that it becomes more robust; using a network to give activists a head start on a contested issue by sharing crucial information; discovering which public agency is likely to be vulnerable to pressure and taking advantage of that vulnerability; finding new ways to think about the governance of key collective goods, such as drinking water. The battles won through this kind of accretive process are important not just because of their contribution to livability but also because winning them simultaneously builds both institutional infrastructure and capacity for collective action.

Is this strategic vision of communities, organizations, and individuals, interconnected in synergistic ways, playing complementary roles that cumulate, sufficient to trump the admittedly weighty forces undermining the quest for livability? Perhaps not, but they are certainly strategies worth exploring, especially for those with a "passion for the possible."[3]

Notes

The acknowledgment in the introductory chapter applies even more thoroughly to this one. The ideas presented in this chapter are derived from those developed by my collaborators in the previous chapters, as well as from our discussions, both in person and in countless e-mails over the course of three years.

1. Conversely, it is important not to exaggerate the extent of middle-class privilege. The educated middle-class community around Ba Nhat Chemicals was less successful in securing redress than the poor agriculturalists around the Lam Thao plant (although not less successful than the agriculturalists' even poorer cousins across the river).

2. Social movement organizations (sometimes referred to as SMOs) are more local and less professionalized than NGOs. They may expand out from a base in particular communities to make connections to other communities, or they may start as issue-based groups. The Billings Defense Committee and the Movimento de Defesa da Vida (chapter 6) are good examples of social movement organizations.

3. See the discussion of Hirschman's "possibilism" at the end of chapter 1.

References

Abers, Rebecca. 1996. "From Ideas to Practice: The Partido dos Trabalhadores and Participatory Governance in Brazil." *Latin American Perspectives* 23 (4): 35–53.

———. 1997. "Inventing Local Democracy: Neighborhood Organizing and Participatory Policy-Making in Porto Alegre, Brazil." Ph.D. dissertation, Department of Urban Planning, University of California, Los Angeles.

Afsah, Shakeb, Benoit Laplante, and David Wheeler. 1996. "Controlling Industrial Pollution: A New Paradigm." Washington, D.C.: World Bank.

Allaby, Michael. 1989. *Dictionary of the Environment.* New York: New York University Press.

Ames, Barry. 1995. "Electoral Strategy under Open List Proportional Representation." *American Journal of Political Science* 29 (2): 406–33 (May).

Amsden, Alice. 1989. *Asia's Next Giant: South Korea and Late Industrialization.* New York: Oxford University Press.

Andrews, Richard N. L. 1993. "Environmental Policy in the Czech and Slovak Republic." In *Environment and Democratic Transition: Policy and Politics in Central and Eastern Europe.* Ed. A. Vári and P. Tamás, 5–48. Boston: Kluwer Academic Publishers.

Archives of Baranya County. 1979a. Minutes from Meeting of the Council of Baranya County on April 10, p. 5.

———. 1979b. Chronicle of the Village of Bosta.

———. 1981. Chronicle of the Village of Garé.

Archives of the Budapest Chemical Works. 1968. Letter by the president of the BCW.

Archives of the Council of Baranya County. Agricultural and Food Department of the Executive Committee of the Council of Pécs. 1976. Letter, p. 1.

———. 1978. Minutes from Meeting of County Officials and Representatives of the Pécs Tannery, June 25.

Ard-am, Orathai. 1998. "Community-Based Environmental Management in Bangkok." Bangkok: Mahidol University Institute for Population and Social Research. Draft.

Ard-am, Orathai, and Roger Chical. 1993. *Research and Development on Basic Minimum Needs in Low-Income Urban Communities: The Case of Wat Chonglom*. Nakornpathom: Institute for Population and Social Research, Mahidol University.

Ard-am, Orathai, and Kusol Soonthorndhada. 1994. "Household Economy and Environmental Management in Bangkok: The Cases of Wat Chonglom and Yen-ar-kard." *Asian Journal of Environmental Management* 2 (1): 37–48.

———. 1997. "Household Economy and Environmental Management in Bangkok: The Cases of Wat Chonglom and Yen-ar-kard (II)." Bangkok: Mahidol University. Draft.

Ashford, Nicholas A., and George Heaton. 1983. "Regulation and Technological Innovation in the Chemicals Industry." *Law and Contemporary Problems* 46 (3): 109–57.

Asian Journal of Environmental Management (AJEM). 1994. Special issue on community-based urban environmental management in Asia, ed. M. Douglass, Y. S. Lee, and K. Lowry, 2 (1).

Atkinson, Adrian. 1994. "The Contribution of Cities to Sustainability." *Third World Planning Review* 16 (2): 97–101.

Azuela de la Cueva, Antonio. 1987. "Low-Income Settlements and the Law in Mexico City." *International Journal of Urban and Regional Research* 11 (4): 523–42.

Baiocchi, Gianpaolo. 2000. "Synergizing Civil Society: The Politics of Democratic Decentralization in Porto Alegre, Brazil." Paper prepared for the International Conference on Democratic Decentralization, May 24–28, Trivandam, Kerala, India.

Balogh, István. 1982. *Egy korty halál* (A sip of death). Budapest: RTV-Minerva.

Beck, Ulrich. 1995. *Ecological Politics in an Age of Risk*. Cambridge, England: Polity Press.

Benjamin, Medea. 1999. "Nike: What's It All About?" Position paper available on the Internet at www.globalexchange.com.

Berki, Sándor. 1992. "Trójai falovak, szent tehenek és más állatfajok" (Trojan horses, sacred cows and other animal species). In *Leltár*, 113–21. Budapest: MTA Társadalmi Konfliktusok Kutató Központja.

Berner, Erhard, and Rudiger Korff. 1995. "Globalization and Local Resistance: The Creation of Localities in Manila and Bangkok." *International Journal of Urban and Regional Research* 19:208–22.

Bissell, Trim. 1999. "Nike, Reebok Compete to Set Labor Rights Pace." Position paper available on the Internet at www.compugraph.com/clr.

Boonyabancha, S., P. Niym, S. Patpui, K. Suksumake, and S. Maier. 1988. "Struggle to Stay: A Case Study of People in Slum Kong Toey Fighting for Their Home." Bangkok: Duang Prateep Foundation.

Borja, Jordi, and Manuel Castells. 1997. *Local and Global: Management of Cities in the Information Age*. London: Earthscan Publications, Ltd.

Bosques del Pedregal. 1984. "Colonia Ecologica Productiva." Bosques del Pedregal, Ajusco, México D.F. Mimeograph.

Brasília, Ministério de Minas e Energia, Departamento Nacional de Águas e Energia Elétrica, and Divisão de Controle de Recursos Hídricos. 1985. *Plano Nacional de Recursos Hídricos*, Documento preliminar, consolidando informações já disponiveis, Janeiro 1985, Brasília.

Brasília, Ministério de Minas e Energia, Departamento Nacional de Águas e Energia Elétrica, Ministério de Interior, Secretaria do Meio Ambiente, Secretario de Planejamento, and Conselho Nacional de Pesquisas. CEEIBH. 1983. *Seminario Internacional de Gestão de Recursos Hídricos, Anais*. Vol. 2. Brasília: Ministerio de Minas e Energia.

Brehm, John, and Wendy Rahn. 1997. "Individual-Level Evidence for the Causes and Consequences of Social Capital." *American Journal of Political Science* 41 (3): 999–1023.

Burawoy, Michael. 1985. *The Politics of Production*. London: Verso.

Buttel, Fred. 1992. "Environmentalization: Origins, Processes and Implications for Rural Change." *Rural Sociology* 57 (1): 1–27.

———. 1998. "Some Observations on State-Society Synergy and Urban Sustainability." Unpublished ms., University of Wisconsin, Madison.

Cairncross, Sandy, Jorge Hardoy, and David Satterthwaite. 1990. "New Partnerships for Healthy Cities." In *The Poor Die Young: Housing and Health in Third World Cities*. Ed. Jorge E. Hardoy, Sandy Cairncross, and David Satterthwaite, 245–65. London: Earthscan Publications, Ltd.

Canter, Larry W. 1996. *Environmental Impact Assessment*. 2nd ed. New York: McGraw-Hill.

Cárdenas, Cuauhtémoc. 1997. "La economía de la capital: Propuesta económica de Cuauhtémoc Cárdenas." *Economía Informa* 259 (Julio–Agosto): 6–9.

Castells, Manuel. 1977. *The Urban Question*. Cambridge: MIT Press.

———. 1983. *The City and the Grassroots: A Cross-Cultural Theory of Urban Social Movements*. Berkeley: University of California Press.

———. 1989. *The Informational City: Information Technology, Economic Restructuring, and the Urban-Regional Process*. Oxford: Blackwell.

———. 1996. *The Rise of the Network Society*. Vol. 1 of *The Information Age: Economy, Society, and Culture*. Oxford: Blackwell.

———. 1997. *The Power of Identity*. Vol. 2 of *The Information Age: Economy, Society, and Culture*. Oxford: Blackwell.

———. 1998. *End of Millennium*. Vol. 3 of *The Information Age: Economy, Society, and Culture*. Oxford: Blackwell.

Chai Doksok and Won Bae Kim. 1998. "Regional Development Policies in Korea: Policy Responses to Recent Issues." *Regional Development Dialogue* 19 (2): 32–44.

Chambers, Robert. 1987. "Sustainable Rural Livelihoods: A Strategy for People, Environment, and Development." Paper presented at conference on sustainable development, Only One Earth, April 28–30, at Regents College, London.

Chan, Cecilia. 1986. "The Process Intervention Model in Neighbourhood Work: The Mount Davis Community Development Project." Ed. Social Welfare and

Training Committee, *Casebook 1988,* 98–117. Hong Kong: Hong Kong Council of Social Sciences.

Chan, Cecilia, Fiona Chang, and Regina Cheung. 1994. "Dynamics of Community Participation in Environmental Management in Low-Income Communities in Hong Kong." *Asian Journal of Environmental Management* 2 (1): 11–16.

Chang, Shih-chiao. 1993. "The Experience of and Outlook for Taiwan's Urban Environment and Development" (in Chinese). In *Chinese Cities and Regional Development: Prospect for the Twenty-first Century.* Ed. Yue-man Yeung, 425–52. Hong Kong: Hong Kong Institute of Asia-Pacific Studies, the Chinese University of Hong Kong.

Chen, Cheng-Tzeng, and Chun-Kuang Chen. 1997. "The Minister and County Magistrate Call a Stop of Hillside Development" (in Chinese). *China Times,* August 19.

Chen, Chun-Hsiung. 1998. "Heavy Sentences for County Officials and Developers: The Case of Lincoln Hillside Development" (in Chinese). *China Times,* September 30.

Chen, Dung-Sheng. 1995. *The City of Money and Power: A Sociological Analysis of Local Factions, Conglomerates, and Urban Development in Metropolitan Taipei* (in Chinese). Taipei: Ju-Liu Publishing Co.

Chi, Chih-ko. 1997. "Urban Planning: We Should Listen to the Voice of the People" (in Chinese). *China Times,* July 21.

Chi, Chun-Chieh, H. H. Michael Hsiao, and Juju Chin-Shou Wang. 1996. "Evolution and Conflict of Environmental Discourse in Taiwan." Paper presented at the Association of Asian Studies Annual Meeting, Honolulu, Hawaii.

Chiang, Nora Huang, and Hsin-Huang Michael Hsiao. 1985. "Taibei: History and Problems of Development." In *Chinese Cities: The Growth of the Metropolis since 1949.* Ed. Victor F. S. Sit, 188–209. New York: Oxford University Press.

Chin, Fu-chen, An-wei Dai, and Pei-chun Hsieh. 1997. "Families Evicted Because of Park: Rootless Old People, Stroke Victims, Recluses, Alcoholics" (in Chinese). *United Evening News,* July 23.

Chu, Yun-han. 1989. "The Oligarchic Economy and the Authoritative Political System" (in Chinese). In *Monopoly and Exploitation: The Political Economic Analysis of Authoritarianism.* Ed. Hsin-Huang Michael Hsiao et al., 139–60. Taipei: Taiwan Research Fund.

Clifford, Mark. 1988. "Too Many People Looking for Too Few Houses." *Far Eastern Economic Review,* September 8, 84–85.

Coalition against the City Government Bulldozers. 1997. *My Home Is at Kang-Le District: The Documents of the Movement against Bulldozers of the City Government* (in Chinese). Taipei: Coalition against the City Government Bulldozers.

Cohen, Michael. 1996. "HABITAT II and the Challenge of the Urban Environment: Bringing Together the Two Definitions of Habitat." *International Social Science Journal* 48 (1): 95–101.

Colby, Michael E. 1991. "Environmental Management in Development: The Evolution of Paradigms." *Ecological Economics* 3:193–214.

Comité da Bacia Hidrográfica do Alto Tietê, Consórcio Intermunicipal do Grande ABC, and MDV—Movimento de Defesa da Vida. 1996. *Anais: Jornada de Debates Billings.* São Paulo. Unpublished document.

Contreras Salcedo, Jaime. 1996. "Arranca Hoy la Avi; Vivienda Digna y Seguridad en la Tenencia a las Familias." *Excelsior,* May 16.

Coulomb, René. 1991. "La Participación de los Servicios Urbanos: ¿Estrategias de Sobrevivencia o Prácticas Autogestionarias?" In *Servicios Urbanos, Gestion Local, y Medio Ambiente.* Ed. Martha Schteingart and Luciano d'Andrea, 265–80. México D.F.: El Colegio de México and CE.R.FE.

Cronon, William. 1991. *Nature's Metropolis: Chicago and the Great West.* New York: W. W. Norton.

DANCED (Danish Cooperation of Environment and Development). 1996. *Urban Environmental Management in Thailand—A Strategic Planning Process.* Bangkok: NESDB/DANCED.

Davalos, Renato. 1996. "Condiciones Inadecuadas en Una de Cada 4 Viviendas, Admite un Plan de Gobierno." *Excelsior,* May 17.

Davis, Mike. 1998. *Ecology of Fear: Los Angeles and the Imagination of Disaster.* New York: Henry Holt and Co.

DeBardeleben, Joan. 1985. *The Environment and Marxism-Leninism: The Soviet and East German Experience.* Boulder, Colo.: Westview Press.

Department of Budget, Accounting, and Statistics. 1997. *The Statistical Abstract of Taipei City, 1997.* Taipei: Department of Budget, Accounting, and Statistics, Taipei City Government, Republic of China.

Desai, Uday, ed. 1998. *Ecological Policy and Politics in Developing Countries.* Albany: State University of New York Press.

Diani, Mario. 1995. *Green Networks: A Structural Analysis of the Italian Environmental Movement.* Edinburgh: Edinburgh University Press.

Doimo, Ana Maria. 1995. *A Vez e a Voz do Popular: Movimentos Sociais e Participação Política no Brasil pós-70.* Rio de Janeiro: Relume-Dumará / ANPOCS.

Douglass, Mike. 1992. "The Political Economy of Urban Poverty and Environmental Management in Asia: Access, Empowerment, and Community Based Alternatives." *Environment and Urbanization* 4 (2): 9–32.

———. 1993. "Urban Poverty and Policy Alternatives in Asia." Chap. 4 in *UNESCAP, State of Urbanization in Asia.* Bangkok: UNESCAP.

———. 1994. "The 'Developmental State' and the Asian Newly Industrialized Economies." *Environment and Planning* A 26:543–66.

———. 1996. "City and Community: Toward Environmental Sustainability." In *World Resources, 1996–97.* Ed. World Resources Institute, 125–48. Washington, D.C.: World Resources Institute.

———. 1997. "Urban Poverty and Environmental Management: A Comparative Analysis of Community Activation in Asian Cities." In *Community Mobilization and the Environment in Hong Kong.* Ed. Peter Hills and Cecilia Chan, 53–95. Hong Kong: Hong Kong University Centre of Urban Planning and Environmental Management.

———. 1998a. "World City Formation on the Asia Pacific Rim: Poverty, 'Everyday' Forms of Civil Society, and Environmental Management." In *Cities*

for Citizens: Planning and the Rise of Civil Society in a Global Age. Ed.
Mike Douglass and John Friedmann, 107–37. New York: John Wiley and
Sons.

————. 1998b. "East Asian Urbanization—Patterns, Problems, and Prospects."
Discussion paper, Institute for International Studies, Asia / Pacific Research
Center, Stanford University.

Douglass, Mike, and Yok-shiu F. Lee. 1996. "Urban Priorities for Action" and
"City and Community: Toward Environmental Sustainability." In *World
Resources, 1996–97.* Ed. World Resources Institute, 103–24, 125–48. Wash-
ington, D.C.: World Resources Institute.

Douglass, Mike, Yok-shiu F. Lee, and Kem Lowry. 1994. Introduction to the
special issue on community-based urban environmental management in Asia.
Asian Journal of Environmental Management 2 (1): vii–xiv.

Douglass, Mike, and Malia Zoghlin. 1994. "Sustainable Cities from the Grassroots: Livelihood, Habitat, and Social Networks in Suan Phlu, Bangkok."
Third World Planning Review 16 (2): 171–200.

Dourojeanni, A., and M. Nelson. 1987. "Integrated Water Resource Management in Latin America and the Caribbean: Opportunities and Constraints."
Water Science and Technology 19 (9): 201–10.

Drakakis-Smith, David. 1995. "Third World Cities: Sustainable Urban Development." *Urban Studies* 32 (4–5): 659–77.

Eckstein, Susan. 1990a. "Poor People vs. the State and Capital: Anatomy of a
Successful Community Mobilization for Housing in Mexico City." *International Journal of Urban and Regional Research* 14 (2): 274–96.

————. 1990b. "Urbanization Revisited: Inner-City Slum of Hope and Squatter
Settlement of Despair." *World Development* 18 (2): 165–81.

Economist Intelligence Unit (EIU, a part of the *Economist* magazine). 1997 and
1998. Vietnam Country Profile, London.

————. 2000. Vietnam Country Report, London.

Eden, Sally. 1996. *Environmental Issues and Business: Implications of a Changing Agenda.* Chichester, England: John Wiley and Sons.

Evans, Peter. 1995. *Embedded Autonomy: States and Industrial Transformation.* Princeton: Princeton University Press.

————. 1996a. "Development Strategies across the Public-Private Divide." Introduction to Special Section "Government Action, Social Capital, and Development: Creating Synergy across the Public-Private Divide." *World Development* 24 (6): 1033–37.

————. 1996b. "Government Action, Social Capital, and Development: Reviewing the Evidence on Synergy." *World Development* 24 (6): 1119–32.

————. 1997a. "The Eclipse of the State? Reflections on Stateness in an Era of
Globalization." *World Politics* 50:62–87.

————. 2000. "Fighting Marginalization with Transnational Networks:
Counter-Hegemonic Globalization." *Contemporary Sociology* 29 (1): 230–
41.

————, ed. 1997b. *State-Society Synergy: Government and Social Capital in
Development.* Berkeley: University of California, International and Area
Studies.

Fei, Kuo-Jen. 1998. "Seventy Percent of Taipei Residents Urge a Complete Prohibition of Hillside Development" (in Chinese). *China Times,* October 27.

Ferguson, James. 1998. "Transnational Topographies of Power: Beyond 'the State' and 'Civil Society'." In "The Study of African Politics," unpublished manuscript presented at the Institute for International Studies, April 24 at the University of California, Berkeley.

Ferreira, Lúcia da Costa. 1993. *Os Fantasmas do Vale: Qualidade Ambiental e Cidadania.* Campinas: Editora da UNICAMP.

Fforde, Adam, and Stefan de Vylder. 1996. *From Plan to Market—The Economic Transition in Vietnam.* Boulder, Colo.: Westview Press.

Figueiredo, Rubens, and Bolivar Lamounier. 1996. *As Cidades que Dão Certo: Experiências Inovadores na Administração Pública Brasileira.* Brasília: M. H. Comunicação.

Figuereo Osnaya, Luis. 1992. "Venta de Residencias en Zonas Ecológicas de Cuajimalpa." *UnoMásUno,* July 18.

Fiorini, Daniel J. 1995. *Making Environmental Policy.* Berkeley: University of California Press.

Fligstein, Neil. 1996. "Markets as Politics: A Political-Cultural Approach to Market Institutions." *American Sociological Review* 61 (August): 656–73.

Foucault, Michel. 1983. "The Subject and Power." In *Michel Foucault: Beyond Structuralism and Hermeneutics.* Ed. Hubert L. Dreyfus and Paul Rabinow, 208–26. Chicago: University of Chicago Press.

Fox, Jonathan. 1996. "How Does Civil Society Thicken?: The Political Construction of Social Capital in Rural Mexico." *World Development* 24 (6): 1089–1104.

Friedmann, John. 1986. "The World City Hypothesis." *Development and Change* 17:69–83.

———. 1992. *Empowerment: The Politics of Alternative Development.* Cambridge, Mass., and Oxford: Blackwell.

———. 1997. *World City Futures: The Role of Urban and Regional Policies in the Asia-Pacific Region.* Occasional paper no. 56. Hong Kong: Hong Kong Institute of Asia-Pacific Studies, the Chinese University of Hong Kong.

Friedmann, John, and Haripriya Rangan, eds. 1993. *In Defense of Livelihood: Comparative Studies on Environmental Action.* West Hartford, Conn.: UNRISD and Kumarian Press.

Friedmann, John, and Mauricio Salguero. 1988. "The Barrio Economy and Collective Self-Empowerment in Latin America: A Framework and Agenda for Research." In *Comparative Urban and Community Research.* Vol. 1. Ed. Michael P. Smith, 3–37. New Brunswick, N.J.: Transaction Books.

Fundação do Desenvolvimento Administrativo (FUNDAP). 1989. *Sistema Estadual de Gestão de Recursos Hídricos, Relatório Base, Volume 3–Anexo 1: Análises Historico-Institucionais em Nível da União e do Estado de São Paulo. Levantamento de Decisões Relevantes para Gestão de Recursos Hídricos no Estado de São Paulo e Atribuições Institucionais.* São Paulo: GTS / FUNDAP.

Gans, Herbert J. 1962. *The Urban Villagers: Group and Class in the Life of Italian-Americans.* New York: The Free Press.

Gaventa, John. 1980. *Power and Powerlessness: Quiescence and Rebellion in an Appalachian Valley.* Urbana and Chicago: University of Illinois Press.

Gereffi, Gary. 1990. "Paths of Industrialization: An Overview." In *Manufacturing Miracles: Paths of Industrialization in Latin America and East Asia.* Ed. Gary Gereffi and Donald L. Wyman, 3–31. Princeton: Princeton University Press.

Giddens, Anthony. 1994. *Beyond the Left and Right: The Future of Radical Politics.* Stanford: Stanford University Press.

Gille, Zsuzsa. 1997. "Two Pairs of Women's Boots for a Hectare of Land: Nature and the Construction of the Environmental Problem in State Socialism." *Capitalism, Nature, Socialism* 8 (4): 1–21.

———. 1998. "Conceptions of Waste and the Production of Wastelands: Hungary since 1948." In *Environmental Issues and World-System Analysis.* Ed. W. Goldfrank, D. Goodman, and A. Szasz. Westport, Conn.: Greenwood Press.

Gitlin, Todd. 1980. *The Whole World Is Watching.* Berkeley: University of California Press.

Gohn, Maria da Glória. 1991. *Movimentos Sociais e Luta pela Moradia.* São Paulo: Loyola.

Goldman, Marshall I. 1972. *The Spoils of Progress: Environmental Pollution in the Soviet Union.* Cambridge: MIT Press.

Gottlieb, Robert, ed. 1995. *Reducing Toxics: A New Approach to Policy and Industrial Decision Making.* Washington, D.C.: Island Press.

Greenhouse, Steven. 1997. "Nike Shoe Plant in Vietnam Is Called Unsafe for Workers." *New York Times,* November 8.

Grupo de Tecnología Alternativa [GTA]. 1992a. "Reporte Final Programa de Investigación IDRC/GTA/SIRDO." Report prepared for the International Center for Development Research, Project no. 3–P–88–0104. México D.F.

———. 1992b. *The SIRDO Integral System for Recycling Organic Waste from México.* México D.F.: GTA, S.C.

Gugler, Josef. 1993. "Third World Urbanization Re-Examined." *International Journal of Comtemporary Sociology* 30 (1): 21–38.

Gustafson, Thane. 1981. *Reform in Soviet Politics: Lessons of Recent Policies on Land and Water.* Cambridge: Cambridge University Press.

Haggard, Stephan. 1990. *Pathways from the Periphery: The Politics of Growth in the Newly Industrializing Countries.* Ithaca, N.Y.: Cornell University Press.

Hagopian, Frances. 1996. *Traditional Politics and Regime Change in Brazil.* Cambridge: Cambridge University Press.

Hajba, Eva. 1995. "The Rise and Fall of the Hungarian Greens." In *Hungary: The Politics of Transition.* Ed. Terry Cox and Andy Furlong, 180–191. London: Frank Cass.

Hardoy, Jorge, D. Mitlin, and D. Satterthwaite. 1992. *Environmental Problems in Third World Cities.* London: Earthscan Publications, Ltd.

Hardoy, Jorge, and David Satterthwaite. 1989. *Squatter Citizen: Life in the Urban Third World.* London: Earthscan Publications, Ltd.

Harvey, David. 1973. *Social Justice and the City.* London: Edward Arnold.

————. 1992. "Social Justice, Postmodernism, and the City." *International Journal of Urban and Regional Research* 16 (4): 589–601.

————. 1996. *Justice, Nature, and the Geography of Difference.* Malden, Mass.: Blackwell Publishers Inc.

————. 1997. "Contested Cities: Social Process and Spatial Form." In *Transforming Cities: Contested Governance and New Spatial Divisions.* Ed. N. Jewson and S. MacGregor, 19–27. London: Routledge.

Hiernaux, Daniel. 1991. "Servicios Urbanos, Grupos Populares, y Medio Ambiente en Chalco, México." In *Servicios Urbanos, Gestion Local, y Medio Ambiente.* Ed. Martha Schteingart and Luciano d'Andrea, 281–304. México D.F.: El Colegio de México and CE.R.FE.

Hirschman, Albert. 1971. *A Bias toward Hope.* New Haven: Yale University Press.

————. 1984. *Getting Ahead Collectively: Grassroots Experiences in Latin America.* New York: Pergamon Press.

Hsiao, Hsin-Huang Michael. 1988. *Anti-Pollution Protest Movements in Taiwan in the 1980s: A Structural Analysis* (in Chinese). Taipei: Environmental Protection Administration.

————. 1994. "The Character and Changes of Taiwan's Local Environmental Protest Movements: 1981–1991" (in Chinese). In *Environmental Protection and Industrial Policies.* Ed. Taiwan Research Fund, 550–73. Taipei: Vanguard Publication Co.

————. 1997a. *A Symbiotic Relationship with Tension: The Relationship Between EPA and Local Environmental Groups* (in Chinese). Taipei: Environmental Protection Administration.

————. 1997b. *Taiwan's Local Environmental Protest Movements: 1991–1996* (in Chinese). Taipei: Environmental Protection Administration.

Hsiao, Hsin-Huang Michael, and Hwa-Jen Liu. 1997. "Land-Housing Problems and the Limits of the Non-Homeowners Movement in Taiwan." *Chinese Sociology and Anthropology* 29:42–65.

Hsiao, Hsin-Huang Michael, et al. 1997. *Re-creating the New Functions of Urban Development: An Analysis on the Eviction Case of the Nos. 14–15 Park in Taipei* (in Chinese). Unpublished report sponsored by the Department of Social Affairs, Taipei Municipal Government.

Hsu, K'ung-Jung. 1988. "A Sociological Analysis of the Housing Market in Peripheral Taipei" (in Chinese). *Taiwan: A Radical Quarterly in Social Studies* 1 (2–3): 149–210.

Huang, U-An. 1983. *The History of Taipei's Development* (in Chinese). Taipei: Taipei Archive Committee.

Jacobs, Jane. 1961. *The Death and Life of Great American Cities.* New York: Vintage Books.

Jancar-Webster, Barbara. 1991. "Environmental Politics in Eastern Europe in the 1980s." In *To Breathe Free: Eastern Europe's Environmental Crisis.* Ed. Joan DeBardeleben, 25–56. Baltimore: Johns Hopkins University Press.

The Joint Academies on the Mexico City Water Supply, National Research Council. 1995. *Mexico City's Water Supply: Improving the Outlook for Sustainability.* Washington, D.C.: National Academy Press.

Jornal da Tarde. 1971. "Estas fotos não mostram tudo: Faltam as 400 toneladas diárias de esgôto," October 20.

Juhász, Judit, Anna Vári, and János Tölgyesi. 1993. "Environmental Conflict and Political Change: Public Perception on [*sic*] Low-Level Radioactive Waste Management in Hungary." In *Environment and Democratic Transition: Policy and Politics in Central and Eastern Europe.* Ed. A. Vári and P. Tamás, 227–48. Boston: Kluwer Academic Publishers.

Kaderják, Péter, and Ágnes Csermely. 1997. "Direct Impacts of Industrial Restructuring on Air Pollutant and Hazardous Waste Emissions in Hungary." In *Economics for Environmental Policy in Transition Economies: An Analysis of the Hungarian Experience.* Ed. P. Kaderják and J. Powell, 15–38. Cheltenham, U.K.: Edward Elgar.

Kaothien, Utis. 1994. "Urban Poverty Alleviation Programs in Thailand." Paper delivered at the Regional Workshop on Community-Based Programmes for Urban Poverty Alleviation, May 9–13 in Kuala Lumpur.

Kaothien, Utis, and Witit Rachatatanun. 1991. *Urban Poverty in Thailand: Review of Past Trends and Policy Formation.* Bangkok: Government of Thailand, National Economic and Social Development Board, Urban Planning Division.

Keck, Margaret E. 1992. *The Workers' Party and Democratization in Brazil.* New Haven: Yale University Press.

———. 1995. "Social Equity and Environmental Politics in Brazil: Lessons from the Rubber Tappers of Acre." *Comparative Politics* 27 (4): 409–24.

Keck, Margaret, and Kathryn Sikkink. 1998a. *Activists beyond Borders: Advocacy Networks in International Politics.* Ithaca, N.Y.: Cornell University Press.

———. 1998b. "Transnational Advocacy Networks in the Movement Society." In *The Social Movement Society: Contentious Politics for a New Century.* Ed. David S. Meyer and Sidney Tarrow, 217–38. Lanham, Md.: Rowman and Littlefield.

Kim, Ik Ki. 1991. "The Environmental Problems of Poor Communities in Seoul." Paper presented at the International Meeting and Workshop on Community-Based Environmental Management in Asia, October 22–25 at Mahidol University, Bangkok.

———. 1994. "The Environmental Problems in Urban Communities and the Protection of the Environment in Korea." *Korea Journal of Population and Development* 23 (1): 63–76.

Kim, Ik Ki, and Jun Kwang Hee. 1994. "The Urban Poor and Environmental Management in Korea: A Case Study for Wolgoksa-dong, Seoul." *Asian Journal of Environmental Management* 2 (1): 1–10.

———. 1996. "The Urban Poor and Environmental Management in Korea: A Case Study for Wolgoksa-dong, Seoul (II)." Seoul: Dongguk University. Unpublished paper.

Kim, Yong-Woong. 1995. "Spatial Changes and Regional Development." In *Cities and Nation: Planning Issues and Policies of Korea.* Ed. Gun Young Lee and Hyun Sik Kim, 53–78. Seoul: KRIHS.

KNCFH (Korean NGOs and CBOs Forum for Habitat II). 1996. "Voices of the

Korean NGOs and CBOs to Habitat II." Paper presented at the Habitat II conference, May 30, Istanbul.

Knight, Richard V. 1993. "Sustainable Development—Sustainable Cities." *International Social Science Journal* 45 (1): 35–54.

Konrad, Gyorgy, and Ivan Szelényi. 1979. *The Intellectuals on the Road to Class Power*. New York: Harcourt Brace Jovanovich.

Kowarick, Lúcio, and Clara Ant. 1994. "One Hundred Years of Overcrowding: Slum Tenements in the City." In *Social Struggles and the City: The Case of São Paulo*. Ed. Lúcio Kowarick, 60–76. New York: Monthly Review Press.

Kowarick, Lúcio, and Nabil G. Bonduki. 1994. "Urban Space and Political Space: From Populism to Redemocratization." In *Social Struggles and the City: The Case of São Paulo*. Ed. Lúcio Kowarick, 121–47. New York: Monthly Review Press.

Kraft, M. E., and N. J. Vig, eds. 1990. *Environmental Policy in the 1990s*. Washington, D.C.: Congressional Quarterly.

Lawrence, Anne T., and David Morell. 1995. "Leading-Edge Environmental Management: Motivation, Opportunity, Resources, and Processes." *Research in Corporate Social Performance and Policy*. Supplement 1: 99–126.

Lee, Boon Thong. 1998. "Globalization, Tele-revolution and the Urban Space." Paper presented at the Workshop on Southeast Asia under Globalization, the Program for Southeast Asian Area Studies (PROSEA), Academia Sinica, Taipei.

Lee, Kathleen. 1993. *Poverty, Community Mobilization, and the Built Environment in a Newly Industrializing Economy: A Case of the Urban Poor in Seoul*. Master's thesis, Department of Urban and Regional Planning, University of Hawaii.

Lee, Su-Hoon. 1995. "Environmental Movements in South Korea." Paper presented at the First Workshop on Asia's Environmental Movements in Comparative Perspective, November 29–December 1, Honolulu.

Lee, Terence R. 1990. *Water Resources Management in Latin America and the Caribbean*. Boulder, Colo.: Westview Press.

Lee, Yok-shiu F. 1992. "Urban Community-Based Environmental Management: The Role of Nongovernmental Organizations." Paper presented at the Supercities International Conference on the Environment, October 26–30 at San Francisco State University.

———. 1998. "Intermediary Institutions, Community Organizations, and Urban Environmental Management: The Case of Three Bangkok Slums." *World Development* 26 (6): 993–1011.

Lee Ki-baik. 1984. *A New History of Korea*. Cambridge: Harvard University Press.

LePoer, Barbara L., ed. 1987. *Thailand: A Country Study*. Washington, D.C.: Federal Research Division, Library of Congress.

Lipschutz, Ronnie D., and Judith Mayer. 1996. *Global Civil Society and Global Environmental Governance: The Politics of Nature from Place to Planet*. Albany: State University of New York Press.

Logan, John, and Harvey Molotch. 1987. *Urban Fortunes: The Political Economy of Place*. Berkeley: University of California Press.

Logan, John, Rachel Bridges Whaley, and Kyle Crowder. 1997. "The Character and Consequences of Growth Regimes: An Assessment of Twenty Years of Research." *Urban Affairs Review* 32 (5): 603–30.

Long, Norton. 1958. "The Local Community as an Ecology of Games." *American Journal of Sociology* 64 (3): 251–61.

Machimura, Takashi. 1992. "The Urban Restructuring Process in Tokyo in the 1980s: Transforming Tokyo into a World City." *International Journal of Urban and Regional Research* 16:114–28.

Manser, Roger. 1993. *The Squandered Dividend: The Free Market and the Environment in Eastern Europe.* London: Earthscan Publications Ltd.

Marris, Peter. 1982. *Community Planning and Conceptions of Change.* Boston: Routledge and Kegan Paul.

McAdam, Doug. 1988. *Freedom Summer.* New York: Oxford University Press.

———. 1999. *Political Process and the Development of Black Insurgency, 1930–1970.* 2nd ed. Chicago: University of Chicago Press.

McAdam, Doug, John McCarthy, and Mayer Zald. 1996. *Comparative Perspectives on Social Movements.* New York: Cambridge University Press.

McConnell, Grant. 1966. *Private Power and American Democracy.* New York: Knopf.

McCubbins, Mathew D., and Thomas Schwartz. 1984. "Congressional Oversight Overlooked: Police Patrols versus Fire Alarms." *American Journal of Political Science* 28:165–79.

McGee, T. G., and Ira Robinson, eds. 1995. *The New Southeast Asia: Managing the Mega-Urban Regions.* Vancouver: University of British Columbia Press.

Mega-Cities Project. 1996. *Environmental Innovations for Sustainable Mega-Cities: Sharing Approaches to Work.* New York: Mega-Cities Project, Inc.

Meili, Stephen. 1998. "Cause Lawyers and Social Movements: A Comparative Perspective on Democratic Change in Argentina and Brazil." In *Cause Lawyering: Political Commitments and Professional Responsibilities.* Ed. Austin Sarat and Stuart Scheingold. New York: Oxford University Press.

Melucci, Alberto. 1989. *Nomads of the Present: Social Movements and Individual Needs in Contemporary Society.* London: Hutchinson / Radius.

Mena Abraham, Josefina. 1987. "Technologia alternativa, transformación de desechos y desarrollo urbano." *Estudios Demograficos y Urbanos* 2 (3).

Méndez, Rosa María. 1995. "Explica Gobierno programa de vivienda: Se agota la reserva territorial—Elizondo." *Reforma,* Ciudad y Metrópoli section, February 3.

Mexico, DDF. 1989a. "Decreto pro el que se Establece como Zona Prioritaria de Preservación del Equilibrio Ecológico y se Declara Zona Sujeta a Conservación Ecológica, como Area Natural Protegida, la Superficie de 727-61-42 Hectáreas." *Diario Official,* June 28.

———. 1989b. "Programa de Manejo de la Zona Sujeta a Conservación Ecologica." *Gaceta Oficial del Departamento del Distrito Federal,* no. 26:5–10.

Meyer, John, et al. 1997. "The Structuring of a World Environmental Regime, 1870–1990," *International Organization* 51 (4): 623–51.

Mi, Fu-Kuo. 1988. "Public Housing Policy in Taiwan" (in Chinese). *Taiwan: A Radical Quarterly in Social Studies* 1 (2–3): 97–147.

Migdal, Joel, Atul Kohli, and Vivienne Shue, eds. 1994. *State Power and Social Forces: Domination and Transformation in the Third World.* Cambridge: Cambridge University Press.

Minhoto Júnior, Alcebíades da Silva. 1981. "Ação Popular—Proteção ambiental—Projeto SANEGRAN . . ." *Revista dos Tribunais* 548:57–89.

Mol, Arthur P. J. 1995. *The Refinement of Production: Ecological Modernization Theory and the Chemical Industry.* Utrecht: Van Arkel.

Mol, Arthur P. J., and David A. Sonnenfeld, eds. 2000. *Ecological Modernization around the World: Debates and Critical Perspectives.* London: Frank Cass and Co.

Moldova, György. 1995. *Magyarország szennybemenetele.* (Hungary's ascension to the heaven of dirt.) Budapest: Dunkakanyar 2000 Könyvkiadó.

Mollenkopf, John H. 1983. *The Contested City.* Princeton: Princeton University Press.

Molotch, Harvey. 1976. "The City as a Growth Machine: Toward a Political Economy of Place." *The American Journal of Sociology* 82:209–30.

Molotch, Harvey, and John Logan. 1984. "Tensions in the Growth Machine: Overcoming Resistance to Value-Free Development." *Social Problems* 31 (5): 483–99.

Momsen, Janet. 1991. *Women and Development in the Third World.* New York: Routledge.

Movimiento Revolucionario del Pueblo (MRP). 1983. "Elementos de Lina Politica para el Movimiento Urbano Popular." México, D.F. Mimeograph.

Mueller, Charles C. 1995. "Environmental Problems Inherent to a Development Style: Degradation and Poverty in Brazil." *Environment and Urbanization* 7 (2): 67–84.

Mumford, Lewis. 1989. *The City in History: Its Origins, Its Transformations, and Its Prospects.* New York: MJF Books.

Nguyen Duc Khien. 1996. "Report on the Environmental Management Practices of Hanoi's DOSTE." Paper presented at the VCEP Seminar on Environmental Management, August 20–23 in Hanoi.

Nguyen Hai. 1993. "Ministry Alarmed over Surging Chemical Pollution." *Vietnam Investment Review* 100 (September 13).

O'Connor, James. 1988. "Capitalism, Nature, Socialism: A Theoretical Introduction." *Capitalism, Nature, Socialism* 1 (1): 11–38.

O'Connor, Martin, ed. 1994. *Is Capitalism Sustainable? Political Economy and the Politics of Ecology.* New York: Guilford Press.

O Estado de São Paulo. 1975a. "Convênio da Billings será assinado amanhã," February 5.

———. 1975b. "Em 180 dias, a regularização da represa Billings," March 4.

———. 1977. "Emplasa promete Billings sem poluição em dois anos," July 5.

Office of Technology Assessment (OTA). 1994. *Industry, Technology, and the Environment: Competitive Challenges and Business Opportunities.* Washington, D.C.: Government Printing Office.

Oliveira, Carlos Thadeu C. de, and Oscar Adolfo Sanchez. 1996. "Decentralização e saneamento básico no Estado de São Paulo." *Debates Sócio-Ambentais* (CEDEC) 1 (3): 4–5.

Organization for Economic Cooperation and Development (OECD). 1994. *Input-Based Pollution Estimates for Environmental Assessment in Developing Countries*. Paris: OECD Working Papers.

O'Rourke, Dara. 1997. "Smoke from a Hired Gun: A Critique of Nike's Labor and Environmental Auditing in Vietnam as Performed by Ernst and Young." Published on the Internet at www.corpwatch.org/trac/nike/ernst/.

O'Rourke, Dara, and Garrett Brown. 1999. "Beginning to Just Do It: Current Workplace and Environmental Conditions at the Tae Kwang Vina Nike Shoe Factory in Vietnam." Published on the Internet at www.globalexchange.org/economy/corporations/nike/vt.html, March 14.

Ostrom, Elinor. 1997. "Crossing the Great Divide: Coproduction, Synergy, and Development." In *State-Society Synergy: Government and Social Capital in Development*. Ed. Peter Evans, 85–118. Berkeley: University of California Press.

Padco-LIF. 1990. *Bangkok Land Market Assessment*. Bangkok: National Economic and Social Development Board / Thailand Development Research Institute.

Peet, Richard, and Michael Watts. 1996. "Liberation Ecology: Development, Sustainability, and Environment in an Age of Market Triumphalism." In *Liberation Ecologies: Environment, Development, and Social Movements*. Ed. Richard Peet and Michael Watts, 1–45. London and New York: Routledge.

Peluso, Nancy. 1992. *Rich Forests, Poor People: Resource Control and Resistance in Java*. Berkeley: University of California Press.

Perlman, Janice. 1976. *The Myth of Marginality: Urban Poverty and Politics in Rio de Janeiro*. Berkeley: University of California Press.

Pezzoli, Keith. 1995. "Mexico's Urban Housing Environments: Economic and Ecological Challenges of the 1990s." In *Housing the Urban Poor: Policy and Practice in Developing Countries*. Ed. B. C. Aldrich and R. Singh Sandhu, 140–67. London: Sage Publications.

———. 1998. *Human Settlements and Planning for Ecological Sustainability: The Case of Mexico City*. Cambridge: MIT Press.

Phantumvanit, D., and Panayotou, T. 1990. "Industrialization and Environmental Quality: Paying the Price." Paper presented at the 1990 TDRI Year-End Conference, December 8–9, Chon Buri, Thailand.

Piccolomini, Michele. 1996. "Sustainable Development, Collective Action, and New Social Movements." *Research in Social Movements, Conflict, and Change* 19:183–208.

Pickvance, Chris. 1996. "Environmental and Housing Movements in Cities after Socialism: The Cases of Budapest and Moscow." In *Cities after Socialism*. Ed. G. Andrusz, M. Harloe, and I. Szelenyi. Cambridge: Blackwell.

Polanyi, Karl. [1944] 1957. *The Great Transformation*. With a foreword by Robert M. MacIver. Boston: Beacon Press.

Political Committee of the Ninth District Organization of the Hungarian Socialist Workers' Party. 1960. Hungarian National Archives. MDP-MSZMP Archives. No document number. April 28. Fonds M-Bp-14/1960. Group 1. Preservation Unit 6, 15–16.

Pornchokchai, Sophon. 1992. *Bangkok Slums: Review and Recommendations.* Bangkok: School of Urban Community Research and Actions.

Portes, Alejandro, ed. 1995. *The Economic Sociology of Immigration: Essays on Networks, Ethnicity, and Entrepreneurship.* New York: Russell Sage Foundation.

Postel, Sandra. 1991. "Emerging Water Scarcities." In *The World Watch Reader on Global Environmental Issues.* Ed. Lester R. Brown, 127–46. New York: Norton.

Princen, Thomas. 1997. "The Shading and Distancing of Commerce: When Internalization Is Not Enough." *Ecological Economics* 20 (3): 235–53.

Putnam, Robert. 1993. *Making Democracy Work.* Princeton: Princeton University Press.

———. 1995. "Bowling Alone: America's Declining Social Capital." *Journal of Democracy* 6 (1): 65–78.

———. 2000. *Bowling Alone: The Collapse and Revival of American Community.* New York: Simon and Schuster.

Quadri de la Torre, Gabriel. 1991. "Una Breve Crónica del Ecologismo en México." In *Servicios Urbanos, Gestion Local, y Medio Ambiente.* Ed. Martha Schteingart and Luciano d'Andrea, 337–53. México D.F.: El Colegio de México and CE.R.FE.

———. 1993. "Agua: Economía y Sustentabilidad en la Ciudad de México." *Examen* Año 4 (2): 37–40.

Rapoport, Eduardo H., and Ismael R. López-Moreno, eds. 1987. *Aprotes a la Ecología Urbana de la Ciudad de México.* Sponsored by the Instituto de Ecología, the Museo de Historia Natural de la Ciudad de México, and the Program on Man and the Biosphere (MAB, UNESCO). México D.F.: Noriega editores and Editorial Limusa.

Reich, Teréz. 1990. "Community Action for Environment and Health: A Case Study from Hungary." In *Environment and Health in Eastern Europe: Proceedings of the Symposium on "Occupational Health during Societal Transition in Eastern Europe,"* June 22–27 in Pécs, Hungary. Ed. B. Levy and C. Levenstein, 57–62. Boston: The United States–Eastern Europe Exchange for Occupational and Environmental Health, Management Sciences for Health.

Revista dos Tribunais 548 (June 1981): 57–89.

Robinson, Nicolas A., ed. 1993. *Agenda 21: Earth's Action Plan.* IUCN Environmental Policy and Law Paper no. 27. New York: Oceana Publications, Inc.

Rojpriwong, S. 1992. *The Slum People's Power and the Struggle for Shelter.* Bangkok: NGO Coordinating Committee on Rural Development.

Rolnik, Raquel. 1994. "São Paulo in the Early Days of Industrialization: Space and Politics." In *Social Struggles and the City: The Case of São Paulo.* Ed. Lúcio Kowarick, 77–93. New York: Monthly Review Press.

Rueschemeyer, Dietrich, and Peter B. Evans. 1985. "The State and Economic Transformation: Toward an Analysis of the Conditions Underlying Effective Intervention." In *Bringing the State Back In.* Ed. P. B. Evans, D. Rueschemeyer, and T. Skocpol, 44–77. New York: Cambridge University Press.

Ruggie, John. 1994. "At Home Abroad, Abroad at Home: International Liberalisation and Domestic Stability in the New World Economy." *Millennium: Journal of International Studies* 24 (3): 507–26.

Santos, Boaventura de Sousa. 1997. "Participatory Budgeting in Porto Alegre: Toward a Redistributive Democracy." Paper presented at the Conference on Global Futures, Institute of Social Studies, October 8–10 in The Hague.

São Paulo (Estado). Conselho Estadual de Recursos Hídricos. 1990. *Plano Estadual de Recursos Hídricos: primeiro plano do Estado de São Paulo—Síntese.* São Paulo: DAEE.

———. Conselho Estadual do Meio Ambiente. 1984. *Ata da 7ª Reunião,* May 3–4.

———. Coordenadoria de Planejamento Ambiental, Secretaria do Meio Ambiente. 1995. *Recursos Hídricos: Histórico, Gestão, e Planejamento.* São Paulo: Secretaria do Meio Ambiente.

———. Secretaria do Meio Ambiente. 1990. *Legislação Estadual, Controle de Poluição Ambiental Estado de São Paulo.* São Paulo: CETESB.

———. 1993. *CONSEMA: Dez Anos de Atividades.* São Paulo: A Secretaria.

———. Secretaria do Meio Ambiente e Secretaria de Recursos Hídricos, Saneamento, e Obras. 1997. *Gestão das Aguas: 6 Anos de Percurso.* São Paulo: Secretaria do Meio Ambiente.

São Paulo (Município). 1992. Secretaria de Negócios Jurídicos da Prefeitura do Município de São Paulo. Procuradoria Geral do Município. Centro de Estudos Jurídicos. *Aguas Públicas da Grande São Paulo.* São Paulo: Gráfica Municipal.

Sassen, Saskia. 1988. *The Mobility of Capital and Labor: A Study in International Investment and Labor Flow.* New York: Cambridge University Press.

———. 1991. *The Global City: New York, London, Tokyo.* Princeton: Princeton University Press.

———. 1997. "Cities in the Global Economy." *International Journal of Urban Sciences* 1 (1): 11–31.

Schmidheiny, Stepan. 1992. *Changing Course: A Global Business Perspective on Development and the Environment.* Cambridge: MIT Press.

Schnaiberg, Allan. 1980. *The Environment.* New York: Oxford University Press.

Schnaiberg, Allan, and Kenneth A. Gould. 1994. *Environment and Society: The Enduring Conflict.* New York: St. Martin's.

Schneider, Ben Ross. 1991. *Politics within the State: Elite Bureaucrats and Industrial Policy in Authoritarian Brazil.* Pittsburgh: University of Pittsburgh Press.

Schöpflin, George. 1995. "Post-Communism: A Profile." *The Public* 2 (1): 63–72.

Schteingart, Martha. 1986. "Movimientos Urbano-Ecológicos en la Ciudad de México: El Caso del Ajusco." *Estudios Politicos* 5 (1): 17–23.

———. 1987. "Expansión Urbana, Conflictos Sociales, y Deterio Ambiental en la Ciudad de México. El Caso del Ajusco." *Estudios Demograficos y Urbanos* 2 (3): 449–77.

———. 1989. "The Environmental Problems Associated with Urban Development in Mexico City." *Environment and Urbanization* 1 (1).

———. 1994. *Urban Research in Mexico, Colombia, and Central America: An*

Agenda for the 1990s. Vol. 3 of *Urban Research in the Developing World.* Ed. Richard Stren. Toronto: Centre for Urban and Community Studies, University of Toronto.

——, ed. 1997. *Probreza, Condiciones de Vida y Salud en la Ciudad de México.* México D.F.: El Colegio de México.

Schteingart, Martha, and Luciano d'Andrea, eds. 1991. *Servicios Urbanos, Gestion Local, y Medio Ambiente.* México D.F.: El Colegio de México and CE.R.FE.

Schwartz, Peter, and Peter Leyden. 1997. "The Long Boom: A History of the Future 1980–2020." *Wired,* July.

Selby, H. A., A. D. Murphy, and S. A. Lorenzen (with I. Cabrera, A. Castaneda, and I. Ruiz Love). 1990. *The Mexican Urban Household: Organizing for Self-Defense.* Austin: University of Texas Press.

Selznick, Philip. [1949] 1966. *TVA and the Grass Roots: A Study in the Sociology of Formal Organization.* New York: Harper and Row.

Sengupta, Chandan. 1994. "Empowerment of Urban Poor for Environmental Management: The Case of Bombay." *Asian Journal of Environmental Management* 2 (1): 17–26.

Setchell, Charles A. 1995. "The Growing Environmental Crisis in the World's Mega-Cities: The Case of Bangkok." *Third World Planning Review* 17 (1): 1–18.

Shaw, Randy. 1999. *Reclaiming America: Nike, Clean Air, and the New National Activism.* Berkeley: University of California Press.

Shen, Yao-pin. 1994. *Community Mobilization and the Transformation of Urban Meaning: The Case Analysis of Taipei's Ching-Cheng Community* (in Chinese). Master's thesis, the Graduate School of Architecture and Urban-Rural Studies, Nation of Taiwan University, Taipei.

Sikkink, Kathryn. 1991. *Ideas and Institutions: Developmentalism in Argentina and Brazil.* Ithaca, N.Y.: Cornell University Press.

Simmel, Georg. 1971. *On Individuality and Social Forms.* Chicago: University of Chicago Press.

Soberón, Jorge. 1990. "Restauración Ecológica en el Ajusco Medio." *Oikos* 5 (4). A publication of the Centro de Ecología, UNAM, México D.F.

Steering Committee of Taiwan 2000 Study, ed. 1989. *Taiwan 2000: Balancing Economic Growth and Environmental Protection.* Taipei: Institute of Ethnology, Academia Sinica.

Stepan, Alfred, ed. 1989. *Democratizing Brazil.* Oxford: Oxford University Press.

Stone, Deborah A. 1989. "Causal Stories and the Formation of Policy Agendas." *Political Science Quarterly* 104 (2): 281–300.

Strange, Susan. 1995. "The Defective State." *Daedalus* 24 (2): 55–74.

Sun, Hsiu-huei. 1997. "They Didn't Know the Buildings Were Dangerous, They Only Saw Them Collapse" (in Chinese). *Global Views Monthly* 135:76–77.

Szasz, Andrew. 1994. *Ecopopulism: Toxic Waste and the Movement for Environmental Justice.* Minneapolis: University of Minnesota Press.

Szirmai, Viktória. 1993. "The Structural Mechanisms of the Organization of Ecological-Social Movements in Hungary." In *Environment and Democratic*

Transition: Policy and Politics in Central and Eastern Europe. Ed. A. Vári and P. Tamás, 146–56. Boston: Kluwer Academic Publishers.

Szlávik, János. 1991. "Piacosítható-e a környezetvédelem?" (Is environmental protection marketizable?) *Valóság* 34 (4): 20–27.

Taga, Leonore Shever. 1976. "Externalities in a Command Society." In *Environmental Misuse in the Soviet Union.* Ed. Fred Singleton. New York: Praeger.

Tarrow, Sidney. 1994. *Power in Movement: Social Movements, Collective Action, and Politics.* New York: Cambridge University Press.

Taylor, Bron Raymond, ed. 1995. *Ecological Resistance Movements: The Global Emergence of Radical and Popular Environmentalism.* Albany: State University of New York Press.

TEI (Thailand Environment Institute). 1995. "Environmental Movement in Thailand." Paper presented at the First Workshop on Asia's Environmental Movements in Comparative Perspective, November 29–December 1, Honolulu.

Telles, Vera da Silva. 1994. "The 1970s: Political Experiences, Practices, and Spaces." In *Social Struggles and the City: The Case of São Paulo.* Ed. Lúcio Kowarick, 174–201. New York: Monthly Review Press.

Tendler, Judith. 1997. *Good Government in the Tropics.* Baltimore: Johns Hopkins University Press.

Tseng, Hsu-Cheng. 1993. "The Formation of the Taipei ren [person]" (in Chinese). In *Research on the Immigration into Taipei County.* Ed. Hsin-Huang Michael Hsiao et al., 79–121. Taipei: Taipei County Culture Center.

Tung, Mong-Lung. 1998. "90 Percent of People Interviewed Consider that Hillsides Have Been Overdeveloped" (in Chinese). *China Times,* July 22.

UNESCAP. 1993. *State of Urbanization in Asia and the Pacific.* Bangkok: United Nations Economic and Social Commission for Asia and the Pacific.

United Nations. 1994. *World Urbanization Prospects: The 1994 Revision.* New York: United Nations Population Division.

———. 1997a. *Report of the United Nations Conference on Human Settlements* (Habitat II), Istanbul, June 3–14, 1996. New York: United Nations.

———. 1997b. *World Urbanization Prospects: The 1996 Revision.* New York: United Nations Population Division.

United Nations, Department of Technical Co-operation for Development. 1989. *Legal and Institutional Factors Affecting the Implementation of the International Drinking Water Supply and Sanitation Decade.* Natural Resources / Water Series no. 23. New York: United Nations.

United Nations Development Programme (UNDP). *A Study on Aid to the Environment Sector,* report submitted to the government of Vietnam, Hanoi. Hanoi: UNDP.

United Nations, Economic Commission on Latin America. 1979. *Water Management and Environment in Latin America.* Oxford: Pergamon Press.

United Nations, Food and Agriculture Organization. 1983. "Water Legislation in South America." Legislative Study no. 19. New York: United Nations.

Vági, Gábor. 1982. *Versengés a fejlesztési forrásokért: Területi elosztás—társadalmi egyenlötlenségek* (Rivalry for development funds: Spatial allocation,
social inequalities). Budapest: Közgazdasági és Jogi Könyvkiadó.
———. 1991. *Magunk, Uraim: Válogatott írások településekröl, tanácsokról,
önkormányzatokról* (Ourselves, my sirs: Selected writings on settlements,
councils, and self-governments). Budapest: Gondolat.
Veress, József. 1982. "A környezetvédelmi szabályozásról—vállalatgazdasági
nézöpontból" (On environmental regulation—from a microeconomic angle).
Iparpolitikai Tájékoztató 19 (11): 46.
Villas-Boas, Renata. 1995. "Morar ou Presarvar? Conflitos e negociações na
preservação das áreas de mananciais na gestão municipal de Luiza Erundina.
1989–1992." *Pólis* 23:43–74.
Viola, Eduardo. 1987. "O Movimento Ecológico no Brasil (1974–1986): Do
Ambientalismo à Ecopolítica." In *Ecologia e Política no Brasil,* ed. José Au-
gusto Pádua. Rio de Janeiro: Espaço e Tempo / IUPERJ.
Wan, Zen-Quai. 1998. "No Hope for Monetary Compensation and Resettle-
ment: The Victims of Mudslide Are Trapped" (in Chinese). *China Times,*
August 19.
Watson, Gabrielle. 1992. "Water and Sanitation in São Paulo, Brazil: Successful
Strategies for Service Provision in Low-Income Communities." Thesis sub-
mitted to the Department of Urban Studies and Planning in partial fulfillment
of the requirements for the degree of Master in City Planning, Massachusetts
Institute of Technology, Cambridge.
———. 1995. *Good Sewers Cheap: Agency Customer Interactions in Low-Cost
Urban Sanitation in Brazil.* Washington, D.C.: World Bank, Water and San-
itation Division.
Watson, Gabrielle, and N. Vijay Jagannathan. 1995. "Participation in Water
and Sanitation." Environment Department Papers: Toward Environmentally
and Socially Sustainable Development, Participation Series paper no. 002.
Washington, D.C.: World Bank.
Watts, Michael. 1999. "Contested Communities, Malignant Markets, and
Gilded Governance: Justice, Resource Extraction, and Conservation in the
Tropics." In *People, Plants, and Justice.* Ed. Charles Zerner. New York:
Columbia University Press.
Weaver, James H., Michael T. Rock, and Kenneth Kusterer. 1997. *Achieving
Broad-Based Sustainable Development: Governance, Environment, and
Growth with Equity.* West Hartford, Conn.: Kumarian Press.
Weller, Robert P., and Hsin-Huang Michael Hsiao. 1998. "Culture, Gender,
and Community in Taiwan's Environmental Movement." In *Environmental
Movements in Asia.* Ed. Arne Kalland and Gerard Persoon, 83–109. Ho-
nolulu: University of Hawaii Press.
Wignaraja, Ponna. 1990. *Women, Poverty, and Resources.* New Delhi: Sage.
Wilk, David. 1991. "Controles de Uso de Suelo y Contención del Crecimiento
en Areas Conurbadas: Estudios de Caso de Tlalpan y Chalco en el Area
Metropolitana de la Ciudad de México." Report prepared for the Conference
Controles de Crecimeinto en Areas Metropolitanas de México y Estados

Unidos: Políticas, Instrumentos y Técnicas de Análisis, June 17–19 in Mexico City.

Woolcock, Michael. 1997–98. "Social Capital and Economic Development: Towards a Theoretical Synthesis and Policy Framework." Parts 1 and 2. *Theory and Society* 27 (1): 1–57; 27 (2): 151–208.

World Bank, Agriculture and Environment Operations Division. 1997. *Vietnam — Economic Sector Report on Industrial Pollution Prevention*. Washington, D.C.: World Bank.

World Commission on Environment and Development. 1987. *Our Common Future*. Oxford: Oxford University Press.

Yang, Chin-yen. 1997. "Chungshan No. 1 Park—Completed a Year Ahead of Schedule" (in Chinese). *United Daily*, October 23.

———. 1998. "Two Parks Developed as Cultural Area, Details to Be Finalized within a Year" (in Chinese). *United Daily*, March 4.

Yap, K. S., ed. 1992. *Low Income Housing in Bangkok: A Review of Some Housing Sub-Markets*. Bangkok: Division of Human Settlements, AIT.

Yeung, Yue-man. 1996. "An Asian Perspective on the Global City." *International Social Science Journal* 48 (1): 25–31.

Yu, Tao-ling. 1994. *A Research on the Process of Mobilization of Community Protest: Three Cases of Taipei* (in Chinese). Master's thesis, the Graduate School of Architecture and Urban-Rural Studies, National Taiwan University, Taipei.

INTERVIEWS CITED

Ancona, Ana Lúcia, Municipal Secretary of Planning, 1990–93. São Paulo, July 1, 1991.

Anonymous engineer, Hungary. Summer 1997.

Barth, Flávio, former head of planning department, DAEE (Departamento de Águas e Energia Elétrica). São Paulo, May 13, 1999.

Bezzaril, Paulo, Superintendent of DAEE, 1987–1990. São Paulo, May 26, 1999.

Costa, Hermínio Gerônimo, SATS (Servico Aero-Terrestre de Salvamento). São Bernardo, July 11, 1991.

Costa e Silva, Rodolfo, former director, Fundação SESP (Serviço Especial de Saúde Pública), and a consultant to CETESB (Companhia de Tecnologia de Saneamento Ambiental). São Paulo, August 6–7, 1992.

Farias, Virgílio Alcides de, MDV (Movimento de Defesa da Vida). Diadema, July 18, 1991; May 23, 1998.

Kassai, Miklos, METESZ (Alliance of Technical and Scientific Associations, Hungary). Spring 1996.

Mantovani, Mario, SOS–Mata Atlantica. São Paulo, June 1996.

Nucci, Nelson, formerly of SABESP (Cia. de Saneamento Básico do Estado de São Paulo), now head of a private engineering firm. São Paulo, May 26, 1999.

Rocha, Gerôncio Albuquerque, DAEE, first executive secretary of the Alto Tietê

basin committee, head of FEHIDRO (the São Paulo state water fund). São
  Paulo, May 28 and 29, 1998.
Valovits, Emil, head of Hungaropec. Hungary, fall 1997 (phone interview).
Vitor, Fernando (Fernando Vitor de Araujo Alves), Comité de Defesa da Represa
  Billings. Diadema, July 12, 1991.
Zulauf, Werner, former director, CETESB. São Paulo, April 22, 1991.

List of Contributors

ORATHAI ARD-AM is professor in the Institute of Population and Social Rescarch at Mahidol University, Bangkok. She is now working as a research fellow at the Research Center on Development and International Relations, Department of Development and Planning, Aalborg University, Denmark, and is writing a Ph.D. dissertation tentatively titled "Democracy, Civil Society, and Socioeconomic Development in Thailand." Her publications include "The Province of Nan: On Its Path towards Civil Society in Thailand" (1998), "Strengths and Weaknesses of Donwan Sub-district in Upgrading to the Community of Good Governance" (1999), "AIDS Care Volunteer Network Building" (1997), and "What Factors Are Important to Make Strong Community: Experiences and Lessons Learned from Nan and Mahasarakam" (1999).

MIKE DOUGLASS is a professor in the Department of Urban and Regional Planning at the University of Hawaii. A specialist in planning in Asia, his current research includes globalization and urbanization on the Pacific Rim, urban poverty and the environment, foreign workers in Japan, rural-urban linkages in national development, and managing mega-urban regions in Pacific Asia. He has been a Shorenstein Distinguished Lecturer at the Institute for International Studies at Stanford University, Perloff Chair in Urban Planning at UCLA, a visiting fellow at the University of Hong Kong, a senior research fellow at the Program on Environment East-West Center, and a visiting scholar in the Faculty of Economics at Tokyo University. His most recent books are *Cities for Citizens: Planning and the Rise of Civil Society in a Global Age* (1998, coedited with John Friedmann) and *Culture and the City in East Asia* (1997, coedited with Won Bae Kim).

PETER EVANS is professor of sociology at the University of California, Berkeley. He is also director of the Working Group on Social Capital and Economic Development of the Project on Social Capital and Public Affairs, a project of the American Academy of Arts and Sciences. His recent books include *Embedded Autonomy: States and Industrial Transformation* (1995) and an edited collection entitled *State-Society Synergy: Government and Social Capital in Development* (1997). His current research interests include environmental politics in the metropolitan region of Curitiba, Brazil, which is known as Brazil's "ecological capital," and in the northern suburbs of Rio de Janeiro, which are sometimes considered ecological disasters.

ZSUZSA GILLE was a participant in the peace and environmental movements in Hungary during the 1980s. She is assistant professor of sociology at the University of Illinois at Urbana-Champaign. Her main interests are environmental sociology, state socialism and postsocialism, globalization, economic sociology, and the sociology of knowledge. Her publications include "Cognitive Cartography in a European Wasteland: Multinationals and Greens Vie for Village Allegiance," in *Global Ethnographies* (2000); "Legacy of Waste or Wasted Legacy? The End of Industrial Ecology in Hungary," in *Environmental Politics* (2000); and "Conceptions of Waste and the Production of Wastelands: Hungary since 1984," in *Environmental Issues and World-System Analysis* (forthcoming).

HSIN-HUANG MICHAEL HSIAO is a research fellow at the Institute of Sociology, Academia Sinica, and professor of sociology at National Taiwan University, in Taipei. He is one of Taiwan's leading sociologists and has written widely since the 1980s on the transformation of Taiwanese social structure, particularly the position of the middle classes. His work has also focused on environmental protest movements and the dynamics of civil society during the course of Taiwan's democratization. His recent publications include *East Asian Middle Classes in Comparative Perspective* (editor, 1999), *Taiwan's Social Welfare Movements* (editor, 2000), *Changes in Southeast Asia* (editor, 2000), and *Chinese Business in Southeast Asia* (coeditor, 2001).

MARGARET E. KECK is professor of political science at the Johns Hopkins University. Her most recent book, *Activists beyond Borders: Advocacy Networks in International Politics* (1998, with Kathryn Sikkink), looks at the interaction of local and transnational environmental politics. Her many years of research on Brazilian politics is reflected in *The Workers' Party and Democratization in Brazil* (1992). She is currently working on a book on environmental politics in Brazil, tentatively titled *Politicizing the Environment: Activist Networks in Brazil,* from which her chapter in this volume is drawn.

IK KI KIM is professor of sociology at the Dongguk University, in Seoul. His recent publications include "Environmental Management of the Urban Poor: A Case Study of Wolgoksa-dong, Seoul, Korea," in *International Journal of Urban Sciences;* "The Effects of Population Growth on Environment and Sustainable Development in Korea" (1995); and "The Environmental Problems in Urban Communities and the Protection of the Environment in Korea" (1994) in the *Korea Journal of Population and Development.*

HWA-JEN LIU is a Ph.D. student in sociology at the University of California, Berkeley. She coauthored and published several pieces on Taiwan's anti-pollution protests and urban development in *Asia's Environmental Movements* (1999) and *Chinese Sociology and Anthropology* (1997). Her main interest is Third World social movements, and she is now writing a working paper on the environmental protests among Taiwanese peasants and fishermen during the repressive 1970s as a new form of anti-industrialism.

DARA O'ROURKE is an assistant professor in the Department of Urban Studies and Planning at the Massachusetts Institute of Technology. He has worked extensively with NGOs and international agencies to analyze the impacts of industrial pollution on communities and workers, to advance alternative production practices that prevent environmental and health hazards, and to develop systems for monitoring multinational supply chains. He conducted one of the first independent assessments of Nike's manufacturing practices in Asia, documenting the occupational and environmental health hazards faced by Nike workers. Recent publications include "Reinventing Environmental Regulation from the Grassroots Up," in *Environmental Management;* "Industrial Ecology: A Critical Review," in the *International Journal of Environment and Pollution;* and "Ratcheting Labor Standards," in the *Boston Review.* He received his Ph.D. from the University of California, Berkeley.

KEITH PEZZOLI conducted field research on urban communities and environmental issues in Mexico City over a period of almost fifteen years. His book *Human Settlements and Planning for Ecological Sustainability: The Case of Mexico City* (1998) chronicles the results of this research. He received his Ph.D. in planning from UCLA. Currently, Pezzoli is the director of field research and a lecturer in the Urban Studies and Planning Program at the University of California, San Diego. He is the principal investigator of U.C. San Diego's Regional Workbench Program, a collaborative network of researchers and community-based partners dedicated to linking knowledge to action for sustainable urban and regional development (http://regionalworkbench.org). Pezzoli is currently working on a book project titled *Frontiers of Ecological Regionalism: Theory, Methods, and Practice.*

Index

Text: 10/13 Sabon
Display: Sabon
Cartographer: Bill Nelson
Compositor: Binghamton Valley Composition
Printer and Binder: Maple-Vail Manufacturing Group